Exploring Japanese University English Teachers' Professional Identity

NEW PERSPECTIVES ON LANGUAGE AND EDUCATION

Series Editor: Professor Viv Edwards, *University of Reading, Reading, Great Britain*

Series Advisor: Professor Allan Luke, *Queensland University of Technology, Brisbane, Australia*

Two decades of research and development in language and literacy education have yielded a broad, multidisciplinary focus. Yet education systems face constant economic and technological change, with attendant issues of identity and power, community and culture. This series will feature critical and interpretive, disciplinary and multidisciplinary perspectives on teaching and learning, language and literacy in new times.

Full details of all the books in this series and of all our other publications can be found on http://www.multilingual-matters.com, or by writing to Multilingual Matters, St Nicholas House, 31-34 High Street, Bristol BS1 2AW, UK.

Exploring Japanese University English Teachers' Professional Identity

Diane Hawley Nagatomo

MULTILINGUAL MATTERS
Bristol • Buffalo • Toronto

Library of Congress Cataloging in Publication Data
A catalog record for this book is available from the Library of Congress.
Nagatomo, Diane Hawley.
Exploring Japanese University English Teachers' Professional Identity/Diane Hawley Nagatomo.
New Perspectives on Language and Education: 23
Includes bibliographical references and index.
1. English language–Study and teaching–Japan. 2. English language–Study and teaching–Japanese speakers. 3. English teachers–In-service training–Japan.
4. English teachers–Training of–Japan. 5. English teachers–Japan.
I. Title.
PE1068.J3N25 2012
428.0071'152–dc23 2011048969

British Library Cataloguing in Publication Data
A catalogue entry for this book is available from the British Library.

ISBN-13: 978-1-84769-647-2 (hbk)
ISBN-13: 978-1-84769-646-5 (pbk)

Multilingual Matters
UK: St Nicholas House, 31-34 High Street, Bristol BS1 2AW, UK.
USA: UTP, 2250 Military Road, Tonawanda, NY 14150, USA.
Canada: UTP, 5201 Dufferin Street, North York, Ontario M3H 5T8, Canada.

Copyright © 2012 Diane Hawley Nagatomo.

All rights reserved. No part of this work may be reproduced in any form or by any means without permission in writing from the publisher.

The policy of Multilingual Matters/Channel View Publications is to use papers that are natural, renewable and recyclable products, made from wood grown in sustainable forests. In the manufacturing process of our books, and to further support our policy, preference is given to printers that have FSC and PEFC Chain of Custody certification. The FSC and/or PEFC logos will appear on those books where full certification has been granted to the printer concerned.

Typeset by Datapage International Ltd.
Printed and bound in Great Britain by Short Run Press Ltd.

Contents

Acknowledgements ix
Foreword. xi

1 Introduction. 1
   Rationale for the Study. 1
   English Classes at the Tertiary Level 2
   Model Teachers and Teacher Education 2
   University Entrance Examinations. 4
   Motivation for the Study 6
   Overview of the Book. 6

2 The Japanese Context 9
   Introduction. 9
   The Historical Context of English Language
   Teaching in Japan. 10
   Explanations for Poor English Skills in Japanese People 15
   The Connection between Education and
   Industry in Japan. 18
   Japanese Women: Education and Employment. 25
   Japanese Women and Education. 27
   Gendered Aspects of English in Japan 31
   The Japanese Professor 34
   Female Professors in Universities 42
   Summary of Chapter 2 47

3 Knowledge, Beliefs and Identity 49
   Introduction. 49
   Teacher Cognition. 49
   Teacher Identity 54
   Importance of the Social Context in Teaching 59

  The Japanese Context 61
  Summary of Chapter 3 66

4 The Participants and the Data Collection 68
  Introduction 68
  Narrative as a Research Method 68
  The Participant Teachers 70
  Interviews 70
  Transcription Method for Interviews 74
  Process of Analysis 76
  Classroom Observations 77
  My Position within the Studies 77
  Summary of Chapter 4 78

5 Developing Professional Identity 79
  Introduction 79
  Identity 81
  Participants and Data Collection 84
  Analysis and Interpretation 86
  Conclusion of Chapter 5 111

6 It's a Man's World 116
  Introduction 116
  Analytical Framework: Gee's (2000) Perspective on Identity 118
  The Participants 120
  Analysis and Interpretation 121
  Conclusion of Chapter 6 146

7 Teaching Is What I 'Do', Not Who I Am 152
  Introduction 152
  The Participant 153
  Data Collection 153
  Analysis and Interpretation 157
  Conclusion of Chapter 7 177

8 Conclusion 181
  Summary of Overall Findings 182
  Pedagogical Implications of the Studies 186
  Concluding Remarks 188

References 190

Name Index 207
Subject Index 211

Acknowledgments

First and foremost, my heartfelt gratitude goes to the Japanese university English teachers who kindly agreed to participate in my research. This book could not have been written without their honest and insightful comments provided during the interviews. I am especially appreciative of 'Miwa', who not only spent many hours being interviewed, but also allowed me to observe her English classes.

Words simply cannot express the gratitude that I feel toward Dr Stephen Moore for his guidance and wisdom from the earliest stages of my research. Without Dr Moore's critical eye, this project would never have been able to leave the ground. I am also extremely grateful for the ongoing encouragement and friendship of Dr Melodie Cook, which began at the onset of our doctoral study and will, I hope, continue for many years. A very special thank you goes to Professor Chris Candlin for providing the forward to this book.

I would also like to thank my excellent and supportive colleagues in the English Department of Ochanomizu University, from whom I have learned a great deal. In particular, I would like to thank Professor Emeritus Michiko Nishio for being such a wonderful mentor.

I'd also like to say thanks to my 'Identity Study Group' members, Dr Alison Stewart, Dr Ellen Motohashi, Dr Masuko Miyahara and Dr Patrick Kiernan, for giving me a great deal of insight into identity issues and narrative research during our discussions, and to Dr Andrew King for his comments and advice on an earlier version of Chapter 6. Thanks must also go to Dr Tamah Nakamura, who was a tremendous source of inspiration to me throughout my research, and to my friend and neighbor, Catherine Oshima, who proofread an earlier manuscript.

Earlier versions of certain sections of the book have appeared in the following articles: 'The impact of 'imagination of students' in the development of the professional identity of four Japanese teachers of English in Japanese higher education' (2011) *Asian TEFL Journal Professional Teaching Articles* 51, 2011, 63–71 (with kind permission of The Asian EFL Journal) and 'A case study of how beliefs toward language learning and language teaching influence the teaching practices of a teacher of English in Japanese higher education' (2011) *The Language Teacher* (35) 6, 25–29 (with kind permission of JALT, the Japan Association for Language Teaching).

I am grateful to Professor Daizen and Professor Yamanoi for permission to reprint Tables 2.9, 2.10 and 2.11, which originally appeared in their article, 'The Changing academic profession in the era of university reforms in Japan' (2008).

This project could have never evolved into book form without the support of the staff of Multilingual Matters. A big thank you to Professor Viv Edwards, the series editor, and to the editorial staff, Anna Roderick and Sarah Williams, for making the publication process so smooth.

To my husband Shin, my son Eric and my daughter Alicia – thank you for your love, encouragement and support. Finally, I would also like to acknowledge my family on the other side of the Pacific Ocean, who have been my most enthusiastic and lifelong cheerleaders: my mother Ruth Hawley and my brother Doug Hawley.

Foreword

This is an exciting and important book. It is so, principally, because it works to demolish myth and to offer as an alternative evidence-based exploration grounded in the study of participant belief and the conduct of interaction. Further, in that it accomplishes this reformulation through the critical presentation of a set of related ethnographic and discursively-based studies directed at a reappraisal of the identities of individual teachers seen through the lens of their narratives of their pedagogic practice. That it does so not only synchronically, through a study of contemporary action, but also diachronically as seen through the history of the pedagogic trajectories of its chosen actors, contributes to its innovative and revelatory character.

At each point in this remarkable account, Diane Nagatomo makes plain her personal sense of *motivational relevancy* – what drives her to her study – but marries that with an exposition of the relevancies of her co-participants, those teachers whose sense of their complex and institutionally-bounded, yet still individual identities, forms the narrative of voices of this book. What we have here comes close to Cicourel's construct of *ecological validity* (Cicourel, 1992), how a discussion of the institutional order governing the behaviours and thinking of participants is continually in play with the interaction order of their practices, each affording and constraining their and our construction of identity. It is this central focus on *practices* within a loose *community of practice* which for me marks out the distinctiveness of this book. What it is saying is that look to what people *do*, and how they *describe, interpret, explain* and *value* what they and their fellow members *do*, if we want to find keys to understanding their beliefs and their sense of identity as complex professionals.

What then are its principal strengths?

Firstly, that it shows the power of close attention to a principle- and theory-based analysis of authentic data – here in the form of narrative accounts of experience, accounts which do not simply tell stories but which reveal preferred meanings and explanations of events. Such meanings are not nonce happenings; as Diane Nagatomo shows in her thorough and focused analysis of the pervasiveness of gendered experience to her women teachers, they construct a history of pervasive and discriminatory experience across professional sites and professional lives. Such processes of meaning-making always embody the negotiation of various forms of capital, often presented in the forms of metaphors that teachers in their narratives of experience construct about themselves, their learners and their teaching. Such metaphorically-laden narratives in community settings of teaching offer, as here, powerful semiotic evidence of these processes. For her teachers, despite the warmth of her analysis and the sympathy of her reckoning, teaching is a site of struggle among competing identities. Classrooms, we might remember, are always challenging, risky, and at times personally confrontative places.

Secondly, and now drawing on Goodwin's construct of *'professional vision'* (Goodwin, 1994), we draw from this book the importance of emphasising the co-responsibility of researcher and participant to effect an understanding of what Stevick (1980) calls *'a world of meaningful action'* where the interpersonal judgements of teacher and researcher, teacher and student, cohere to provide shared insights into the reasons for action and non-action. This is not just a matter of reflection *on* and reflection *in*, in Schon's phrase (Schon, 1987), it is also the basis and grounds for *reflexive* action, that action which leads to local and systemic change. In this, the book is much more than a rich archive of experience; it constitutes a powerful argument for a new direction, one driven by a recognition of the 'professionality' of teaching.

Finally, this book exemplifies a pattern of research practice which commends itself to other and more diverse settings than the one highlighted here. Diane Nagatomo makes applied linguistics matter in this book, she makes her methodology matter, and she identifies relationships as the core of applied linguistic research. Empirically warranted, authenticated by reference to a wide scope of existing and relevant research, and, above all, inspired by personal engagement, this book stands as a document to the potential of carefully constructed and exercised applied linguistic research to make a difference.

References

Cicourel, A. (1992) The interpenetration of communicative contexts: Examples from medical encounters. In A. Duranti and C. Goodwin (eds) *Rethinking Context: Language as an Interactive Phenomenon*. Cambridge: Cambridge University Press.
Goodwin, C. (1994) Professional vision. *American Anthropologist* 96 (3), 606–633.
Schön, D. (1987) Changing patterns in inquiry in work and living. *Journal of the Royal Society of Arts Proceedings* 135 (5367), 225–231.
Stevick, E. (1980) *Teaching Languages: A Way and Ways*. Rowley, MA: Newbury House.

Professor Christopher N. Candlin
Macquarie University, Sydney, Australia
November 2011

Enter the apocryphal Hiroshi Yamato. It bewilders you that although this colleague is an associate professor of English and expert on Charles Dickens, he can hardly speak English. However, this seems less amazing once you observe his teaching methods. He lectures blithely away on discrete anomalies of syntax, pronunciation, and sentence-level translation, despite the fact that few of his students are listening. One gets the impression that he knows nothing of life outside the university, especially since his social world is restricted to exactly three other teachers the same age and one elder professor. You wonder why they are so subservient to this older professor, who seems to dominate them. He not only dictates their opinions, but also exploits them as unpaid research assistants, and yet, Hiroshi 'yes man's' this elder professor's every suggestion and seems unable to undertake even the smallest of academic tasks on his own.

Kelly & Adachi, 1992

I was not trained to be an English language teacher but to be a researcher. It is not only I, but all graduate students of ex-imperial universities in Japan who major in literature. We have been encouraged to study, but never to improve teaching skills! I think this doesn't hold true for English language majors and education majors. As a literature major, I have been baffled at the gap between my graduate school days and now.

Japanese university English teacher's response to an email interview question

1 Introduction

Rationale for the Study

The purpose of this book is to draw attention to an under-researched and yet extremely powerful group of teachers that has a wide-reaching influence on English language education in Japan: Japanese teachers of English in Japanese universities. The studies presented in this book hope to move the discourse concerning these teachers away from the stereotypical and negative portrayal of the apocryphal Professor Hiroshi Suzuki described in the epigraph on the previous page. Such an image is widely held (see also McVeigh, 2002, who calls Japanese higher education a 'myth'), but if perpetuated, it can limit the exploration of an important dimension of English language education in Japan. Instead, it is more constructive to investigate the specific teaching beliefs, identity and actual teaching practices of these teachers who wield a great deal of power over English language education, which influences the ultimate outcome of Japanese people's English abilities.

It is often lamented that many Japanese people are unable to speak even simple English, even though most people have learned English for a minimum of six years if they have completed secondary school, and even more if they go to university. University graduates' lack of English ability has brought forth a great deal of criticism from the business community, who need to invest time and money in improving the communicative skills of their newly hired recruits. To address this problem, the Federation of Economics Organizations in Japan demanded an English education that would result in students attaining better communicative skills (Aspinall, 2006).

In attempts to improve Japanese students' English ability, the Ministry of Education revised its course of studies in 1989/1990 and 1998/1999 and again in 2002/2003. Under its new name, the Ministry of Education, Health, Science and Welfare (hereafter referred to by its commonly known acronym, MEXT) directed an emphasis on spoken communication and the study of culture (Neustupny & Tanaka, 2004). The last revisions in 2002/2003, known as the 'Action Plan', had concrete goals to improve English language education in Japan, such as improving secondary schools' English classes; improving secondary school teachers' English communicative and pedagogical skills; increasing student motivation; creating alternative types of university entrance examinations; introducing English language education in elementary schools and improving students' Japanese language abilities (MEXT, 2003).

What is notably absent from the Action Plan is any attention paid toward *university* English classes or *university* English teachers. The only mention of English at the tertiary level concerns the improvement of university entrance exams and the call for more university classes to be taught in English. No mention at all was made of improving university teachers' communicative or pedagogical skills or raising the quality of teacher education programs. Failing to bring tertiary English education into the official discourse of reforming English education in Japan may thwart the overall goals of the Action Plan to create a nation of English speakers because such top-down educational initiatives are, for three reasons that will be discussed in the following sections, unlikely to bring results.

English Classes at the Tertiary Level

First, half of all 18-year-olds in Japan advance to higher education where English is nearly always a required subject and where many of these English classes are taught by Japanese professors. Because secondary school students have completed six years of English instruction prior to university entrance, it is assumed that students should have already learned all of the basic structures and vocabulary of English. Accordingly, English language instruction at the tertiary level is limited and students learn *about* English-related subjects such as literature or linguistics *in* Japanese (Aspinall, 2006; Neustupny & Tanaka, 2004). Nagasawa's (2004) survey of Japanese English teachers' practices in 19 universities (national and private) echoes this common understanding. He found that academic English classes, such as literature or linguistics, are taught in Japanese 95% of the time, and that non-academic classes, such as conversation, cross-cultural understanding and teaching methodology are taught in Japanese 65% of the time. The English language instruction of hundreds of thousands of students—nearly half of the 18-year-old population—seems to be ignored by official policy because of the Action Plan's lack of attention to tertiary level English language instruction. Considering that there is generally a four-year gap between secondary school graduation and entrance into the workforce, university teachers must accept some responsibility for the ultimate outcome of students' English language abilities.

Model Teachers and Teacher Education

Japanese teachers not only teach English language classes, regardless of their academic backgrounds, they are also often responsible for teaching required courses for obtaining an English teaching license. Their language teaching methodology plays an important role in influencing the teaching practices of secondary school teachers, for teachers tend to model their own teaching practices on the years of practicing what Lortie (1975: 61) calls an 'apprenticeship of observation'. This means that the thousands of hours spent as a student – as a silent observer in the classroom – ultimately shapes the practices of a future teacher.

The process of obtaining this license in Japan is as follows: students are required to take 24 academic credits in English, in addition to required credits for their major, but the actual number and the types of courses students take is determined by individual universities, many of which do not have an education faculty. Only *one* class must be in English linguistics, British/American culture or English communication, and *two* classes must be in cross-cultural understanding, ELT methodology or integrated English. The teachers conducting these classes, however, often do not have teaching licenses themselves and are often left to their own devices as to how to go about teaching them (Nagasawa, 2004).

Kizuka (1999) argues that a major problem with teacher education is that many university teachers have 'little actual interest in teacher preparation' (cited in Gorsuch, 2001: paragraph 12). Furthermore, as Neustupny and Tanaka (2004: 24) point out, teacher education in Japan has 'ignored and continues to ignore the results of applied linguistics research over the last 30 years, including research about social issues in language acquisition'. With little interest in acquiring knowledge about language pedagogy and an outdated understanding of how people actually learn languages, it is likely that university teachers continue to draw upon their own language learning experiences and perpetuate the long-criticized Japanese version of the grammar-translation method, known as *yakudoku* (Hino, 1988), where the academic focus is often on turning English into Japanese, at the expense of teaching students how to read widely or to express one's opinion in writing – real communicative skills.

Gorsuch (2001: paragraph 20) notes the impact that tertiary teachers have over secondary school teachers' pedagogical practices, and attributes the difficulty of diffusing MEXT's goals of communicative language teaching into secondary schools to the pre-service teacher education system which 'is inadequate to the task of supporting the development of fundamental changes in instruction implied by policies'. Since English language and English education classes at the tertiary level are said to be concerned with talking *about* English *in* Japanese (Nagasawa, 2004), it is not surprising that many secondary school teachers feel unprepared for English language teaching after graduating from university (Browne & Wada, 1998; Lamie, 1998, 2000, 2002), and indeed unprepared to implement

MEXT's new goals for more classroom communication (Butler & Iino, 2005; Nishino, 2008).

University Entrance Examinations

University English teachers are also responsible for constructing the English component of university entrance examinations, which is recognized to be one of utmost importance in shaping secondary school teaching practices in Japan (e.g. Browne & Wada, 1998; Gorsuch, 2001; Guest, 2000; Nishino, 2008; Sakui, 2004; Smith & Imura, 2004). Although university English teachers make these examination questions, many have no specialized knowledge in language testing (Brown & Yamashita, 1995). Kimura and Visgatis (1996) found questions on these exams to be more difficult than MEXT's officially approved English language textbooks, suggesting that university teachers are not aware of, or perhaps are not paying enough attention to, the official guidelines for secondary schools. Pressure is thus placed upon secondary school teachers, who need to 'second guess' what may be asked of their students on these exams.

Preparing students to successfully pass high-stakes university entrance exams is one of the most important concerns of students, parents and teachers (e.g. Smith & Imura, 2004) and success or failure in these exams has a profound impact on the outcome of students' lives (e.g. Beauchamp, 1987; Ishida, 1993; Ono, 2001). Classes identified as communication-based classes often focus on 'teacher-fronted grammatical explanations, chorus reading and vocabulary presentations' (Sakui, 2004: 157) because accumulating such knowledge to pass an entrance examination is a more important and immediate goal than developing communicative competence in English.

In sum, the English goals of MEXT may not be in harmony with the realities of English language education in Japan, and there is a clear need to include the teaching practices and beliefs of tertiary English teachers in the discourse of discussing English language education and its reform in Japan. This is necessary to create reforms that can take root from the bottom up – which may result in greater success in diffusing curricular change in Japan – than from top-down directives that are 'perceived to be inappropriate at a grass-roots level' (Smith & Imura, 2004: 38). Aspinall (2006) argues that although the steps taken toward the improvement of Japanese people's English ability has received approval and encouragement from governmental agencies and from the business community, the failure for English communicative improvement in Japanese lies in the myriad of 'small cultures' (Holliday, 1999), which are more responsible for shaping teaching and learning behavior when teachers and students come together than the larger cultural context in which people live. Aspinall calls for more investigations into the small cultures of teachers in Japan, because they can provide insight into reasons for language education policy failure.

To date, there have been a number of publications critical of English language teaching in Japan, particularly at the tertiary level (e.g. Bueno & Caesar, 2003; Hall, 1997; McVeigh, 2002, 2004; Wordell, 1992). However, Poole (2010: 13) is rightfully critical of much of the existing discourse surrounding Japanese higher education, and says, 'unfortunately much of the comparative educational debate on Japanese education in the U.S. and Europe is sometimes fueled by journalistic, and occasionally overblown polemic reports on Japanese education that are not often substantiated with qualitative data'. Indeed, an examination of the reference section in McVeigh's (2002) book entitled *Japanese Higher Education as Myth* shows that nearly half of the references are newspaper articles. Yet, as of May 2011, Google Scholar shows that McVeigh's (2002) book had been cited in 139 research articles, indicating a strong interest in Japanese tertiary education. Clearly there is a need, as Poole (2010) asserts, for more qualitative research focusing on Japanese higher education in general, and on English language education at the Japanese tertiary level in particular.

In addition to much of the previous research concerning English language Japanese higher education being negative in tone, the few qualitative studies to date that focus on the beliefs, practices and identity of teachers in Japanese higher education have tended to examine both Japanese and non-Japanese teachers (e.g. Simon-Maeda, 2004a; Stewart, 2005, 2006). The aim of this book is to explore the teaching practices, beliefs and identities of only *Japanese* English teachers. Although the differences in Japanese and foreign teachers are interesting, Japanese teachers constitute 97% of tertiary educators in Japan (MEXT, 2006). More light may be shed upon their beliefs, teaching practices and identity when not comparing them to their foreign counterparts. The teachers in my study are also employed by different types of tertiary institutions throughout Japan, unlike the teachers in Stewart's (2005) study, who are affiliated with prestigious national research institutions where they teach their academic specialties, as well as English language, to highly motivated students. However, the majority of colleges and universities in Japan are private liberal arts institutions of varying academic quality (Kinmouth, 2005) and students in these various universities have significantly different English abilities and significantly different projected career outcomes (Ono, 2001, 2004). An exploration of teachers in a variety of universities is essential to gain a wider perspective of Japanese teacher identity in higher education settings.

Motivation for the Study

The motivation for my study stems from the nearly 30 years of experience I have had teaching English at several Japanese universities. During this time I have also taught teacher education classes, and many of my students have become secondary school English teachers. Occasionally, some students, especially those who continue to the PhD program, become university English teachers. Seven or eight years ago I ran into one such student who was working toward her PhD in linguistics. She had begun teaching English part-time at a university in Tokyo, and when I asked her how her classes were going, she rolled her eyes, sighed and spoke of the difficulty she was having in motivating her students. She said that she could not understand them well because they behaved so differently from what she was accustomed to: they read comic books, put on cosmetics and slept during class.

That conversation remained with me for many months and I became curious about how Japanese university teachers, with academic degrees in English-related areas such as literature or linguistics gained at prestigious universities, come to terms with teaching English language skills, which is an important obligation of being a university English teacher in Japan. Furthermore, I wondered how university teachers, who are products of an elite education, deal with students whose academic backgrounds may be significantly different from their own. Because there is a wide range of academic quality in the nearly 1200 colleges and universities in Japan, the academic abilities and interests of the students in these institutions also varies. This difference may be one explanation for why my former student mentioned above had difficulty in relating to her students. There are, of course, other possible factors contributing to a conflicting student-teacher relationship, such as individual personality differences, personal inclinations toward study, gender and family background. I became interested in exploring these issues and the seed for the three studies presented in this book was planted. My investigation into the teaching practices, beliefs and professional identity of Japanese teachers of English in higher education began.

Overview of the Book

This book is comprised of eight chapters, of which the first four provide background to the study and the data collection. The next three chapters present the data from three separate studies, which taken together offer a glimpse into tertiary English education in Japan from three separate perspectives. The final chapter summarizes the main findings of the three studies and discusses the pedagogical implications that these studies have brought forth.

Chapter 2 (The Japanese Context) locates the study within the sociocultural context of Japan. It focuses on a range of issues that influence English language education in Japan. First I provide a brief historical overview of English language education in Japan, followed by several explanations for why English language education in Japan has not resulted in widespread English proficiency. Next I show the complex relationship between educational backgrounds and positions in industry, but then go on to point out that such a relationship is generally reserved for men. The number of female students in higher education has reached parity with male students, but a stratified educational system, together with gendered sociopolitical attitudes toward women, has limited women's professional opportunities. Then I examine the gendered role of English, which as a subject area is one of the most popular areas of study for Japanese women. Next the profession of the Japanese professor is discussed, followed by a description of how female professors are situated within the Japanese academy.

Chapter 3 (Knowledge, Beliefs and Identity) discusses the literature that pertains to the unobservable dimension of teaching and introduces several key studies that deal with the professional identity development of non-native English-speaking teachers in EFL contexts and in the Japanese context.

Chapter 4 (The Participants and the Data Collection) introduces the teachers who took part in this study and lays out the methods used for data collection and the process of analysis.

The data analysis and the significant findings from the analyses addressing the central questions are discussed in Chapters 5–7.

Chapter 5, Developing Professional Identity, investigates how four relatively new teachers develop their professional identity as teachers, researchers, and members of the wider academic community. The aim of this study was to determine the principal work-related activities these teachers engage in and how they construct their identity as they become accustomed to the demands of their jobs. Narrative data drawn from interviews were analyzed using Wenger's (1998) theory of identity as a theoretical framework. The research questions that guided this study are the following:

(1) What are the principal activities that Japanese teachers of English in higher education engage in as a part of their work practices?

(2) How do Japanese teachers of English in higher education construct their professional identity as they become members of the community of practice of English teachers?

Chapter 6, It's a Man's World, also a narrative study, investigated the impact of gender upon the professional identity of seven female teachers ranging in age from their early 30s to their early 60s, using Gee's (2000) theoretical framework. The research questions that guided this study are the following:

(1) What, if any, is the impact of gender in the professional identity of female teachers of English in Japanese higher education?
(2) What, if any, are the main similarities and main differences in the professional identity development among female university teachers of various age groups?
(3) How do female teachers in Japanese universities appropriate and negotiate their professional identity in a social context that is predominantly male oriented?

Chapter 7, Teaching Is What I 'Do', Not Who I Am, presents an in-depth case study of Miwa, one of the female participants who is also featured in Chapters 5 and 6. The aim of this study was to uncover how classroom-teaching practices reflect personal and professional identity. The research questions that guided this study are the following:

(1) What beliefs does Miwa hold about language teaching and language learning?
(2) How are these beliefs manifested in Miwa's teaching?
(3) What is the strength of the relationship between Miwa's beliefs, professional identity and her classroom practices?

Chapter 8 concludes the book by re-examining the findings of each of the studies presented in Chapters 5–7 and with thoughts for future direction and with some concrete pedagogical suggestions for English language education in the Japanese tertiary context.

2 The Japanese Context

Introduction

In the previous chapter, I described the power that university English teachers have over English language education in Japan and established the need to research the identity, beliefs and practices of this group of educators. The purpose of this chapter is to introduce the sociopolitical context of Japan, which has shaped its English language learning and language teaching. My rational for doing so in this chapter supports Wolcott's (2001) position that the writing and analyzing of qualitative research often needs to be situated within a broader context rather than simply follow a traditional linking of previous studies. When we analyze the teachers' narratives in Chapters 5–7, it is important to recognize that their stories are more than factual statements concerning their lives; these narratives are permeated by sociocultural, sociohistorical and social influences as well. Thus, the aim of this chapter is to introduce the underlying issues that underpin my participants' multiple identities as Japanese, as English language learners, as English language teachers and as professionals in their field.

I begin the chapter with a brief summary of the history of English language education in Japan. This section will show the essential role that English had in the modernization of Japan, because it (as well as other languages) was the primary vehicle that imported Western knowledge and technology. Once this knowledge became transmittable in *Japanese,* communicative proficiency in English was no longer necessary and the purpose of English language education moved away from gaining knowledge to *use* English to gaining liberal arts knowledge *about* English (e.g. Ike, 1995; Ota, 1994). The historical backdrop of foreign language education sets the stage for the following section, which summarizes oft-cited explanations for why English language education in Japan has been relatively unsuccessful to date even though a great amount of time and money has been invested in learning and teaching it.

In the subsequent section, I discuss the complex relationship between education and industry, which directly and indirectly influences language education policies in Japan. Tertiary education has become widely available in Japan during the past 50 years, but several educational tracks have been established in order to produce a competent and yet stratified workforce. This section looks at the sociopolitical context that determines who has access to the type of education that will culminate in a prestigious and well-paying career and who does not.

In the next section, I examine the relationship between Japanese *women* and industry, because the path toward a prestigious career through an elite education mainly applies to Japanese *men*. Sociopolitical attitudes toward Japanese women guide the type of education they generally receive, which results in limited career opportunities (e.g. Amano, 1997; Brinton, 1988; Fujimura-Fanselow, 1995; Ono, 2004). Related to the type of education that Japanese women tend to receive is the gendered attitude toward English, which is generally perceived as a 'feminized' subject for women to study as well as a subject that can open career doors for women (e.g. Bailey, 2006; Kobayashi, 2002; Koike, 2000).

Finally I discuss the profession of university teachers in Japan by looking at the work that they do and by using Poole's (2010) ethnography of a Japanese university to guide the discussion. Returning to the issue of gender, I examine how female university professors fare in Japanese academia in relation to male university professors.

The Historical Context of English Language Teaching in Japan

Due to the isolationist policies established by the Japanese government that kept its borders closed to the outside world, English language education in Japan has a relatively short history of approximately 140 years. The Meiji era (1868–1912) marked the end of Japan's isolation from world trade and the beginning of Japan's modernization. The Meiji oligarchs understood that the key to avoiding colonialization by Western countries lay in creating a competent Japanese workforce that was knowledgeable about Western thought and technology. Although Japan's literacy rate was similar to that of advanced Western countries because of the *terakoya* (temple schools) that had been established by feudal lords in the mid 1800s (Reischauer, 1974), gaining and disseminating foreign knowledge became a top priority, and one third of the total government educational budget was allocated for both hiring foreign experts to teach in Japan and sending Japanese students to study abroad. The University of Tokyo, the first imperial university, was established in 1877, followed by four more imperial universities—Kyoto, Tohoku, Kyushu and Hokkaido. These imperial universities were to produce bureaucrats and government officials, as well as to train knowledgeable and competent teachers to disseminate knowledge to the masses through lower-order institutions throughout Japan (Poole, 2010). Thus, two tracks of education were established: one was to provide an education for the elite, and the other was to provide an education for everyone else. Compulsory primary education was instituted and middle schools and technical schools were widely established, so that by 1905, most young Japanese had at least five years of schooling (Goodman, 2009).

Because of its late entry into the world trade market, there was much 'catching up' for Japan to do in order to become modernized. Thus, foreign language instruction at that time had practical aims – namely to understand the foreign experts who taught their subjects in Japan in their various languages, and to understand texts written in foreign languages. In other words, students were simultaneously acquiring content knowledge and foreign languages. Koike and Tanaka (1995: 16) explain, 'The purposes of teaching foreign languages in those earlier days were practical and cultural. Understanding advanced cultures and technology was the first and foremost requisite to the island people of Japan'.

In its race to catch up with the rest of the world, there was a prevailing attitude that considered all things Western to be advanced, and things traditionally Japanese to be backward. Arinori Mori, the Minister of Education in 1885, for example, strongly advocated English to be taught at all levels, and encouraged the adoption of English as Japan's national language because he felt Japanese to be a 'meager language', which would be of no use outside Japan (Ota, 1994). Because the majority of classes at The University of Tokyo (even those offered by Japanese professors) were taught in English or other languages,[1] some Japanese students came to feel more at home in English than they did in Japanese (Koike & Tanaka, 1995; Ota, 1994). Inazo Nitobe, the author of *Bushido*, whose picture is featured on the 5000-yen banknote, had this to say about his educational background:

> When I entered Tokyo English school..., we studied every single subject in English. Mathematics, geography, history, etc. – all subjects were taught in English. Because of such education, it is very easy for me to read books written in English. It is somewhat different nowadays, but in my twenties I read English books with much greater facility than Japanese books. (Cited in Ota, 1994: 201)

However, there were those that believed that English was having a detrimental effect on mother tongue proficiency. For example, Kato Hiroyuki, who was the head of the Faculties of Law, Science and Arts at The University of Tokyo, raised concern in his memo to the Ministry of Education in 1877 by saying, 'Those who boast themselves to be graduates of the University of Japan may be proficient only in English and incompetent in Japanese' (Miyake, 1946, cited in Ota, 1994: 202).

Thus, by the 1880s, there was some fear that Japanese people could lose their sense of national and cultural identity, and steps were taken to bring about a sense of nationalism. Shiga Shigetaka, who had visited the Pacific islands and had seen firsthand the negative impact that colonialism had had on the local people, wrote about the dangers of colonialism and of the importance of establishing a sense of national identity in his 1881 book *Nihon Jin* (*The Japanese*), and the adoration for 'all things Western' thus became counterbalanced with the subsequent publication of numerous books attempting to foster a national sense of pride in 'all things Japanese' (Ike, 1995: 5).

When widespread Westernization in Japan slowed down, newly qualified Japanese professors and specialists replaced foreigners, whose salaries had been considerably greater than those of their Japanese counterparts. The official language of instruction at The University of Tokyo became Japanese in 1883, and from that point onward university lectures were conducted in Japanese.

Oral proficiency in English (or other languages) was no longer essential for university students. Elite preparatory schools, whose students aspired to enter prestigious universities, also replaced their expensive foreign teaching staff with Japanese teachers. By 1881, for example, all content-based classes taught at the preparatory school to the university were taught by Japanese teachers – including five of the seven English classes (Ota, 1994).

Instruction *in* Japanese *by* Japanese teachers thus resulted in a rapid decline in the English oral proficiency of the educated elite, but because textbooks continued to be written in various languages, students' reading comprehension skills remained high. One reason for this was the extraordinary amount of time devoted to foreign language study. For example, a student (who later became president of The University of Tokyo) at the Number One Higher School wrote in his 1911 diary that out of 32 class hours per week, he and his classmates studied English for nine hours and a second foreign language for another nine hours (Ota, 1994).

However, when the Ministry of Education phased out foreign textbooks in 1911 and replaced them with Japanese ones, the overall academic skills in foreign languages declined. The purpose of English language education shifted, and the question of whether or not English should be abolished as a compulsory subject was even debated (Ike, 1995). However, Rinshiro Ishikawa (cited in Ike, 1995) argued in *The Theory and Problems of English Education* that language learning should be encouraged because it facilitates a better understanding of one's own language, can be a mental stimulation and can broaden one's view of the world. English study thus came to be seen as a lens from which to view and understand Japanese culture. Whereas the initial purpose was to develop practical and necessary skills in students, English came to be taught as a liberal arts subject, and in particular, as an intellectual exercise for screening students to enter higher education, a situation that continues to this day (Ike, 1995; Kitao & Kitao, 1995; Ota, 1994).

During World War II, due to nationalistic policies, English was abolished entirely in the middle school curriculum for girls, and the number of classes was greatly reduced in the middle school curriculum for boys (Koike & Tanaka, 1995). English became an important subject once again during the postwar years, but far fewer hours were devoted to language study in comparison to prewar education. One reason for this may have been to increase the number of class hours devoted to general academic subjects. In the early 1900s, Number One Higher School, for example, had only 10 hours per week allotted for general academic classes after 18 hours of foreign language, three hours for physical education and one hour for moral education (Ota, 1994).

Thus, the postwar aim of English education was not to produce proficient speakers of English, but to develop intellect and to foster a deeper understanding of Japanese language and culture through awareness of linguistic and cultural differences (Ike, 1995). This attitude still exists today. In fact, the sixth of the seven goals listed in MEXT's (2003) report entitled 'Regarding the establishment of an action plan to cultivate "Japanese with English abilities"' explicitly states:

> In order to cultivate communication abilities in English, the ability to express appropriately and understand accurately the Japanese language, which is the basis of all intellectual activities, will be fostered.
>
> The acquisition of English is greatly related to students' abilities in their mother tongue, Japanese. It is necessary to foster in students the ability to express appropriately and understand accurately the Japanese language and to enhance communication abilities in Japanese in order to cultivate communication in English.
>
> Also, in order to foster Japanese people rich in humanity with an awareness of society, who will live as members of an international society, it is important to enhance students' thinking ability, foster students' strength of expression and sense of language, deepen their interest in the Japanese language, and nurture an attitude of respect for the Japanese language.

MEXT (2003) then outlines concrete methods through which the Japanese language will be utilized in promoting English learning. They include placing more focus on increasing Japanese literacy, improving Japanese verbal communication, providing opportunities for Japanese children to interact more with members of the community, introduce daily Japanese reading activities into classrooms and raising the pedagogical skills of Japanese teachers (as well as other subjects).

The notion that English study is an important means of understanding the outside world from the perspective as *Japanese* people has had a strong and prevailing impact over English language education in Japan. Books written by scholars such as Nakane's (1970) *Japanese Society* or Doi's (1971) *The Anatomy of Dependence* that describe Japanese people and Japanese culture as unique, have contributed to an image that because Japanese are so 'different', acquiring a foreign language may be too 'difficult' for them. Until fairly recently, Japanese who were proficient at English were actually viewed with suspicion because they were not considered to be 'pure' Japanese (Hayes, 1979). Reischauer and Jansen (1988: 392) went so far as to say, 'Ridiculous though this may seen, there appears to be a genuine reluctance to have English very well known by many Japanese. Knowing a foreign language too well, it is feared, would erode the uniqueness of the Japanese people'.

These attitudes concerning Japanese 'uniqueness' are reflected in the following factors that Koike and Tanaka (1995) have identified that have guided foreign language policy:

(1) Japan's geographical isolation.
(2) Japanese people's tendency for group consciousness.
(3) Japanese people's outward communication is not necessarily consistent with their inner feelings.
(4) Japan's hierarchical structure.
(5) Japan's unique and different language, which means a great deal of effort is necessary to acquire a foreign language.
(6) The grammar-translation method, although heavily criticized, has nevertheless been used as the main method for communicating with foreigners.

English language education in Japan underwent another ideological shift in the late 1980s in an attempt to improve Japanese people's English communicative abilities. This shift was mainly fueled by industry, which demanded better English skills in university graduates (Aspinall, 2006). Reforms included the introduction of oral communication classes in secondary schools and bringing in native English speakers to assist Japanese teachers in these classes with the establishment of the Japan Exchange and Teaching Program (JET) in 1985. As discussed earlier, in 2003, MEXT created a five-year 'Action Plan' with concrete steps aimed at developing students' English communicative abilities. These steps included improving secondary school English classes, upgrading teachers' skills, increasing motivation, developing different criteria for university entrance examinations, introducing English language education in elementary schools and, as discussed above, improving students' Japanese skills as well (MEXT, 2003). In spite of such curricular reforms, however, few are optimistic about their ultimate success in actually improving Japanese students' English abilities. Studies investigating secondary school teaching practices show a great deal of resistance in and barriers to implementing communicative activities in the classroom by the Japanese teachers of English (e.g. Browne & Wada, 1998; Cook, 2010; Sakui, 2004). Furthermore, there is even debate concerning the definition of and the interpretation of the term 'communicative' and how such teaching should be carried out (e.g. Lo Castro, 1996; Seargeant, 2008).

The next section will explore other reasons why English language education in Japan has to date been unsuccessful in creating widespread English proficiency.

Explanations for Poor English Skills in Japanese People

It is commonly lamented that few Japanese are proficient in English, even though it is a compulsory subject in most secondary and tertiary institutions. Millions of dollars are spent annually on employing native English speakers in schools, on private English lessons with native and non-native English-speaking teachers, on supplementary English language materials and on studying abroad. There is no dearth of theories explicating the lack of success among Japanese in mastering English even though much time and money is invested in studying it. Such theories include Japan's isolated history and geographical location, which resulted in limited opportunities for interaction with foreigners (Koike & Tanaka, 1995); an adherence to a Japanese version of the grammar-translation method (called *yakudoku*) that was originally used to convert Chinese and then Dutch documents into Japanese (Hino, 1988); educational policies that emphasize examination outcomes rather than productive English skills and poor linguistic role models – teachers who may know *about* the English language but not necessarily know how to *speak* it, and a lack of confidence in how to teach speaking (McConnell, 1996, 2000). Japanese cultural traits, such as shyness, nervousness, embarrassment and adherence to a group mentality that inhibit language learners, as well as a large linguistic gap between English and Japanese, have also been attributed to the lack of linguistic success among English language learners in Japan (Hughes, 1999). Some have even gone so far as to suggest that the culprit for poor language learning may lie in physiological differences in the Japanese brain, which results in an innate inability to master English (Clark, 1998).

One of the most commonly cited reasons for Japanese people's poor English skills is the pedagogical method utilized for teaching English. Because university entrance examinations are at the forefront of secondary school teachers' minds, there is a tendency to overemphasize grammatical details at the expense of communicative and sociolinguistic competence (e.g. Guest, 2000; Neustupny & Tanaka, 2004; Seargeant, 2008). Even though secondary school teachers are now required to teach English for communication, most continue to teach using *yakudoku* because many teachers are poor at communicating in English themselves and because they are unclear what communicative language teaching is (e.g. Browne & Wada, 1998; Butler & Iino, 2006; Lo Castro, 1996; Nagasawa, 2004; Reesor, 2003; Sato & Kleinsasser, 2004).

The English component of university entrance examinations is recognized to be of utmost importance in shaping secondary school teaching practices in Japan (e.g. Browne & Wada, 1998; Gorsuch, 2001; Guest, 2000; Nishino, 2006; Sakui, 2004; Smith & Imura, 2004). However, these examinations have been widely criticized for their lack of validity and reliability, stemming from the fact that many university teachers have no specialized knowledge in language testing (Brown & Yamashita, 1995) who often create questions that are more difficult than MEXT's officially approved English language textbooks (Kimura & Visgatis, 1996).

Secondary school teachers thus need to 'second guess' what may be asked of their students on these exams and teach accordingly, because preparing students to successfully pass high-stakes university entrance exams is one of the most important concerns of students, parents and teachers (e.g. Smith & Imura, 2004), and success or failure in these exams has a profound impact on the outcome of students' lives (e.g. Beauchamp, 1987; Ishida, 1993; Ono, 2001). Accumulating the knowledge to pass an entrance examination is a more important and immediate goal than developing students' communicative competence in English.

Second, English language instruction in universities may also contribute to poor communicative skills because many Japanese English teachers have backgrounds in literature or linguistics and little or no knowledge in language pedagogy (Nagasawa, 2004). When English is seen as an 'academic pursuit', it is likely that teaching will be concerned more *about* English, and university teachers may look back to how they were taught English in teaching their own classes. Native English speakers often teach university English classes, which are communication-based; however, an attitude exists that such classes are not quite as 'academic' as those taught by Japanese (Law, 1995), and such classes are accorded less value within the curriculum. Such attitudes may lead teachers (as well as students) to believe that learning English communicatively is not as serious an undertaking as learning 'academic' English (e.g. Law, 1995; Simon-Maeda, 2004a; Stewart, 2005).

A third explanation for the poor outcome of English language education in Japan lies with the students. It is understandable that many secondary school students wish to focus on acquiring English grammatical and lexical knowledge perceived essential for gaining access to higher education because successful entry to a good university ensures a prosperous career (e.g. Becker, 1990; Beauchamp, 1987; Ishida, 1993; Ono, 2001; Rohlen, 1977). However, university students without the pressure of entrance examinations are also seen to be passive and reluctant to participate in classes that are communication-based (e.g. Kwan, 2002; Matsumoto, 1994; McVeigh, 2004). Anxiety is listed as one of the main causes for such reluctance (e.g. Brown *et al.*, 2001; Williams & Andrade, 2008; Yamashiro & McLaughlin, 2001).

There is also a prevailing notion that the socialization process that occurs during Japanese students' university years, through part-time jobs and club activities, is more important than academic study (Warrington, 2006). Because *entrance into* high-level universities was, and still is, used by industry to determine students' abilities rather than educational achievement *during* university, Japanese people have often viewed the university years to be a 'four-year vacation' for young people—a time of enjoyment between 'examination hell' and joining the workforce as a *shakaijin* (official member of society) (Eades *et al.*, 2005; Newby *et al.*, 2009). Although university reforms during recent years are aimed at correcting such an image by placing more emphasis on teaching and learning (Goodman, 2005, 2009), students may be reluctant to continue to study once they have overcome the hurdles of university entrance examinations. Furthermore, as Newby *et al.* (2009) note, as most Japanese university students (approximately 75%) do not believe that the knowledge they accumulate in university will be applicable to their future careers in industry, initiatives to improve tertiary students' motivation to study hard during university may not take hold.

The Connection between Education and Industry in Japan

I mentioned earlier in this chapter that two educational tracks had been established in Japan during the Meiji era. One was to provide a higher education to prepare the elite for bureaucratic positions, and the other was to provide a general and a technical education for the masses to create a competent workforce. This section examines in greater detail the connection between education and industry in Japan. Although Japanese universities were originally modeled after private German universities, which were said to follow principles of *Lehrfreiheit* (freedom to teach) and *Lernfreiheit* (freedom to learn), the primary purpose of Japanese universities was to serve the economic interests of Japan (Goodman, 2009). Graduates from Imperial universities, and from elite private universities, such as Keio, Doshisha and Waseda, which were also established during the Meiji Era, were ensured leadership positions in government and in industry. It wasn't until the thriving economy of the postwar years that secondary and higher education in Japan became widely attainable. At the end of the war, there were only 48 universities with approximately 100,000 students. Due to public demand for educational reform, however, many prewar private and public higher schools were converted into universities and the government relaxed restrictions, allowing the establishment of new, mostly private, universities and junior colleges. An academic 'pecking order' was established on the basis of the age of the university and the type of university: the oldest research universities stand at the top of the hierarchy, and the newer, liberal arts universities at the bottom (Daizen & Yamanoi, 2008). Soichi Oya, a prominent nonfiction writer and critic, even coined the term *ekiben*[2] *daigaku* ('tinpot university' or 'Mickey Mouse university') to criticize the vast number of minor local liberal arts colleges of questionable academic standards that were established mainly along express stop routes on train lines. Many of these universities began as, and continue to operate as, conservative family-run businesses, which according to Kemper and Makino (1993) serve to further the social prestige of the families.

The increase in the numbers of two- and four-year institutions is shown in Tables 2.1 and 2.2,[3] and the increase in the number of students attending high school and university is shown in Table 2.3.

Although the proportion of 18-year-olds in higher education institutes is currently at a high, due to a decline in the birthrate, the total number of tertiary students has actually decreased by nearly 200,000 during the past 10 years. This decrease is reflected in Tables 2.4 and 2.5 that show student

Table 2.1 Numbers and types of four-year universities

	1955	1965	1975	1985	1995	2005	2009
National	72	72	81	95	98	87	86
Local	35	33	34	34	52	86	92
Private	122	209	305	331	415	552	595
Total	229	317	420	460	565	726	773

(MEXT, n.d.)

Table 2.2 Numbers and types of two-year junior colleges

	1955	1965	1975	1985	1995	2005	2009
National	17	27	31	37	36	10	2
Local	43	40	48	51	60	42	26
Private	204	301	434	455	500	436	378
Total	264	369	513	543	596	488	406

(MEXT, n.d.)

Table 2.3 Percentage of students going to high schools and universities

	High school	University
1950s	50%	19%
1970s	90–95%	35%
1990s	97%	37%
2000s	96%	49%

(MEXT, n.d.)

enrollment figures in universities and junior colleges during the past five decades. The conversion of many junior colleges into universities during the past 10 years partially accounts for the decrease in students at junior colleges and the increase in private universities.

The population decline of students with the increase in the numbers of universities has led to the current situation where there is a surplus of universities and an insufficient number of students to populate them, putting many of the *ekiben daigaku* at risk of closure. Not only do Japanese

Table 2.4 Total numbers of students entering universities

	1955	1965	1975	1985	1995	2005	2009
National	46,155	54,681	75,479	88,103	108,599	104,130	101,847
Local	5,494	9,130	10,848	11,364	18,835	26,050	28,414
Private	80,647	186,106	337,790	312,526	473,023	493,580	478,470
Total	132,296	349,917	423,942	411,993	568,576	603,760	608,731

(MEXT, n.d.)

Table 2.5 Total numbers of women entering junior colleges

	1955	1965	1975	1985	1995	2005	2009
National	1,409	2,502	4,371	5,601	3,807	300	0
Local	5,397	6,495	8,189	9,244	10,620	5,541	4,185
Private	30,739	71,566	162,857	158,658	218,314	93,680	68,978
Total	37,544	80,563	174,930	173,503	232,741	99,431	73,163

(MEXT, n.d.)

universities lose a significant portion of their income through a decrease in enrollment (student tuition accounts for 60% of a private university's budget), they also stand to lose government subsidies (which are approximately 166,000 yen, or $2000 per student) if they cannot maintain 50% of their student quota (Ishikida, 2005). To encourage high school students to apply, many private universities, particularly those that are academically lower ranked, have relaxed admission requirements (Poole, 2010). As a result, many students are ill prepared for college study, and in 1997, nearly half of all colleges offered remedial high school level courses for incoming university students (Kuroki, 1999, cited in Ishikida, 2005).

Although demography has resulted in a situation where anyone who desires a university education can obtain one, as mentioned earlier, in Japan *where* one goes to university has traditionally been considered to be more important than *if* one goes to university. Admission into the best universities is still fiercely competitive. Statistical data provided by the University of Tokyo's website shows only 3167 successful applicants out of 14,274 candidates in 2005. To qualify to sit for this exam, these applicants had already received a necessary accumulative qualifying score of 91% on the National Center University Exams (World Education News and Reviews, 2006), a standardized test given to more than 500,000 applicants annually (Otsu, n.d.).

Universities considered to be high-ranking are those with more advanced levels of teaching by professors with more advanced degrees, as well as those with graduate and research facilities (e.g. Benjamin & James, 1989; Eades, 2005). Graduates from these universities have more job offers upon graduation, and eventually have significantly higher earnings and greater opportunities for promotion in corporations and government bureaucracies (e.g. Beauchamp, 1987; Ishida, 1993; Ono, 2001). This type of educational credentialism is closely calibrated with cultural capital (Bourdieu, 1991; Bourdieu & Wacquant, 1992), and is not only viewed by business and government as 'an effective system for training and selecting able manpower' (Amano, 1989: 115), but is also widely considered a measure of character and ability (Rohlen, 1977), which can even affect one's marital status (Becker, 1990).

The tale of the boy from a poor family gaining admission to The University of Tokyo after a period of hard work, suffering and endurance is a beloved theme in Japanese novels, comic books and television dramas. Such stories perpetuate the popular belief that educational success in Japan is available to anyone with determination and ability, but there are numerous other factors that play gatekeeping roles in restricting access to the most prestigious universities. These factors include family backgrounds (e.g. LeTendre et al., 1998; Ono, 2001; Rohlen, 1977; Stevenson & Baker, 1992), relationships with teachers (e.g. Fukuzawa, 1994; LeTendre, 1994), places of domicile (e.g. Benjamin & James, 1989; Gordon, 2005; Rohlen, 1977) and, not least, gender (e.g. Amano, 1997; Fujimura-Fanselow, 1989, 1995).

The high school from which one graduates is nearly as important as one's university; they are ranked hierarchically from highly academic ones that prepare students for prestigious universities to non-academic vocational schools that prepare students to enter the workforce. High schools are generally considered 'an official verdict about one's capabilities and future opportunities' (Kariya & Rosenbaum, 1987: 172). For example, the graduates of the top 20 private junior and senior high schools in Japan made up 41% of students entering The University of Tokyo in 1975 (Rohlen, 1977) and this trend continues today (e.g. Beauchamp, 1987; Okano & Tsuchiya, 1999).

Admission into a prestigious high school, however, is not an automatic guarantee of a successful future, because subsequent university entrance and employment entrance involves more competition. Rosenbaum (1978: 252) has likened this selection process to a tournament where the rules are simply, *'when you win, you only win the right to go on to the next round; when you lose, you lose forever'*. Shimizu and Tokuda (1991, in Ono, 2001) expand on the tournament metaphor and argue that a 'reverse tournament' takes place because winners and losers are simultaneously selected. That Japanese education is a selection process aimed at preparing students for future workforce participation as members of the major or minor elites, white-collar workers or blue-collar workers (Cutts, 1997) is highlighted in Table 2.6, which shows a predicted lifetime trajectory of students who graduate from various types of Japanese schools.

Table 2.7 shows the distribution of students across the three types of educational institutions: national, public and private. Public education is available through junior high school. Public schools follow a nationally standardized curriculum with the same expenditure per child. The majority of Japanese children attend local public elementary schools, but some parents, particularly in urban areas, choose to send their children to private schools from junior high in order to get an academic edge later on. Private schools provide supplementary lessons (such as English conversation[4]), extra hours for academic subjects and opportunities to study abroad. This does not come cheaply, however. In addition to the cost of tuition, other expenses incurred by parents when sending their children to private schools include significant entrance fees, school uniforms, school trips and transportation costs to and from school.

Students must take an entrance exam to enter high school. The most selective schools admit a very small fraction of the applicants through

Table 2.6 Academic and life paths started at the time of high school

	Elite academic	Medium academic to non-academic	Vocational
High schools	Public and private	Mostly private	Public
Universities	Prestigious public and private (Such as Tokyo, Kyoto, Waseda and Keio)	Somewhat selective to non-selective (mid-level universities and less well-known universities, technical colleges and junior colleges)	None
Employment	Large corporations, national civil servants	Less prestigious jobs, service industry and small companies	Lower mass strata of workforce

(Adapted from Okano, 2000)

Table 2.7 Distribution of percentages of student enrollment

	National[5]	Public	Private
Kindergarten	.04%	20.3%	79.3%
Elementary	.07%	98.4%	1.0%
Junior high	.09%	92.6%	6.4%
Senior high	.2%	70.3%	29.5%
University	22.2%	4.4%	73.4%
Technical college	.1%	3.7%	96.2%

(MEXT, n.d.)

highly competitive examinations. Acceptance is based on a relative scale rather than an absolute scale, and many children attend *juku* (cram schools) to gain an academic advantage. National high schools are at the top of the hierarchy, followed by academically high-level public and private schools. At the bottom of the hierarchy are those that are academically low-level or commercial high schools that prepare students to enter the workforce.

Families with sufficient financial resources can afford to send their children to private schools, where the curriculum may be more accelerated than that at public schools, which parents believe would give their children an edge when it comes time to sit for university entrance examinations. These families can also afford private teachers and *juku* or *yobiko* (preparatory schools for students who failed a university entrance exam) fees. According to Roesgaard (2006: 65), a representative from a top *juku* in Tokyo that prepares students for an elite educational track admits that families who send their children to study at this *juku* are financially well off. Not only are the *juku* fees high, parents must be prepared to pay high private school fees at the schools they hope their children will enter. Roesgaard, in citing the prospective educational costs in a manual designed to aid parents in selecting an appropriate school for their children, says that the yearly *juku* fees for a sixth grader hoping to gain admission into an elite private junior high are approximately 1.24 million yen (approximately $15,000), and the fees for the first year of a private junior high could be as high as 1.959 million yen (approximately $24,000). With three years of junior high school and three years of high school to be completed *before* university entrance, the costs incurred to unsure a 'good' education can be quite significant.

In the 1970s, Rohlen (1977) found that students in lower-ranking public schools often came from families where income levels were low and thus were unable to afford the type of private schooling described above, and this trend still exists today (Newby et al., 2009).

Teachers in junior high schools consider students' financial backgrounds when advising them which high school exams to sit for (Fukuzawa, 1994). As discussed earlier, the high school that one attends plays a significant role in determining the course of a person's life, and therefore, to improve one's chances at entering the highest ranking school possible, it is common for students to aim at both public and private high schools. They can take as many private high school exams as they wish, but the fee for each exam may be several hundred dollars, which could be a burden for low-income families. Because all public school exams are offered on the same day, teachers' advise students on which one they should aim for. Fukuzawa (1994) says that teachers not only take into account students' academic abilities, but also their family's financial ability to send their child to a private school in the event of failing the public school exam. She found that teachers advise students to aim for a lower-level school rather than take a chance of not being accepted into any high school at all when they believe students' families cannot afford a backup plan of a private school.

On the other hand, parents with sufficient financial resources generally prefer to send their children to academically low-ranking private secondary schools than to low-ranking public ones, especially if the only option available is a vocational school. This trend is motivated by employment statistics: in 1992, 1.28 million high school graduates found employment, but in 2002, only 240,000 did (Honda, 2004). Parents believe that their children would have greater career opportunities if they go to university than if they learn a vocation in high school.

Many private schools are known as escalator schools, providing schooling from as early as kindergarten to university, and others from junior or senior high school to university. Entering highly selective escalator schools is extremely tough at any stage of entry, but lower-ranking escalator schools, which may also have attached universities, are often selected by parents because of the belief that such institutions can help their children, particularly daughters, bypass examination hell. But once enrolled in such schools, students may be unable to aim for more competitive universities because the curriculum may not effectively prepare them, or even qualify them, to do so. Even though students who graduate from non-elite academic high schools may not be able to attend prestigious universities at the top of the academic hierarchy, they may be able to, however, enter lower-ranked two-year colleges and four-year universities. Many of these lower-ranking universities have established relationships with local businesses, and graduates from these universities provide the workforce for mid-level and smaller companies (Walker, 2006).

In sum, students' economic and social backgrounds control access to services that influence performance in schooling selection processes. Okano and Tsuchiya (1999: 93) say that 'the privileged's relationship with schooling differs from that experienced by the poor', and as Rohlen (1977: 56) explains, 'families are not equal in their capacities to compete in the "private sphere", that extensive part of education over which public schools and public policy have little or no influence'. Schools play a gatekeeping role in streaming students into a multi-stratum society, and parental finances influence students' access to these schools.

Japanese Women: Education and Employment

It is important to state that the foregoing description of career pathways in relation to education pertains mainly to *men*. Career opportunities for Japanese women have been, and still are, extremely limited due primarily to sociopolitical ideologies that keep women as peripheral members of the workforce by promoting an idealized image of women as housewives and mothers (e.g. Amano, 1997; Brinton, 1988; Fujimura-Fanselow, 1995; Liddle & Nakajima, 2000). In fact, the 2010 World Economic Forum Global Gender Gap Index, which takes into account economic participation and opportunity, educational attainment, health and survival and political empowerment, ranks Japan 94 out of 134 countries (Hausman *et al.*, 2010). That Japanese women have the longest life expectancy in the world and that they have attained high levels of education, their low ranking on the Gender Gap Index indicates women's participation in political and economic spheres to be extremely under-represented. Liddle and Nakajima (2000: 18) sum up the situation as follows:

> The view of women currently promoted by the state in Japan is one which accepts their working lives and recognizes their changing identities, but is attempting to hold back or reverse the changes that have come about. The idea is that women should continue to give first priority to marriage and the family; they should bear as many children as the state thinks is desirable; they should regard their paid work as marginal to the economy, and take up jobs only to fill in the empty spaces in their lives when they are not servicing the family.

Although women comprise 50% of the workforce, they are mainly in low-status and low-wage 'feminine' jobs related to childcare, teaching, nursing, or in clerical positions in companies.

Women are seen as temporary, peripheral, and replaceable workers because they tend to exit the workforce in their late 20s and early 30s because of societal expectations of them to place priorities on family and home. In other words, even though educational opportunities have improved considerably in the postwar era for Japanese women, as they have for Japanese men, employment opportunities have not (e.g. Amano, 1997; Brinton, 1988; Dilatush, 1976; Fujimoto, 2005; Fujimura-Fanselow, 1995; Habu, 2000).

In 1985, more than 40% of companies admitted that female employees had no opportunity for promotion, citing the low number of expected working years as the reason: 43% of women quit within one year of getting married (Brinton, 1988). After the Employment Opportunity Act was passed in 1986, a dual employment track was introduced by many companies, comprising a 'comprehensive track' in which promising women (from prestigious universities) could choose to be employed under equal terms with men; and a 'general track' that included support jobs for those on the comprehensive track. Although many women joined the comprehensive track, 45.6% quit within three years (Amano, 1997). Likely reasons for this are the lack of available childcare and lack of institutional support, as well as unchanging Japanese values concerning marriage and motherhood, which make it difficult for women to balance work and careers (Fujita, 2006). Lebra's (1984: 247) comment of more than 25 years ago still holds true: a career woman 'must work like a male peer, that is, as if she had no domestic burdens'.

Another reason Japanese women quit the workforce may lie in widespread beliefs concerning the importance of engaging in self-fulfilling activities rather than in career-oriented ones (e.g. Bonney et al., 1994; Kobayashi, 2007a; Matsui, 1995). Habu (2000) explains that since Japanese women are considered peripheral and temporary workers, they have more flexibility in leaving jobs and making midcareer changes than Japanese men have, as men are expected to find lifetime employment upon graduation and to build professional careers (e.g. Burton, 2004; Kobayashi, 2007b; Ono & Piper, 2004).

Another explanation for limited opportunities for Japanese women lies in the perceived purpose of higher education for women. Tertiary education has been considered more important for raising women's social status to enhance marital chances rather than for providing employment opportunities (e.g. Amano, 1997; Matsui, 1995). As discussed earlier, an elite education is paramount to obtaining a prestigious job. However, parental aspirations for their sons' educational attainments have generally been higher than those for their daughters (Amano, 1997). This discrepancy in the quality of education between male and female students provides another explanation why Japanese women have difficulty in entering the workforce in career positions and will be discussed further in the next section.

Japanese Women and Education

Even though the number of female students has achieved parity with the number of male students, two gendered educational paths with two different functions have been created (e.g. Amano, 1997; Brinton, 1988; Fujimura-Fanselow, 1995). One function is to provide a professional education, which is aimed mainly at male students for 'entry to professions and jobs with high income and social status' (Amano, 1997: 217). This notion is reflected in male students' stated purpose for going to university, which is to obtain financial security after graduation (Fujimura-Fanselow, 1995). The other function is to provide a general education for female students to signify 'the social class and culture to which they belong' (Amano, 1997: 217). This notion is reflected in the types of universities female students generally attend, the 'feminine' subjects they study and their low career aspirations (e.g. Amano, 1997; Brinton, 1988; Fujimoto, 2004, 2005; Fujimura-Fanselow, 1995).

Parental attitudes play an influential role in the educational contexts of their children, affecting entry into the labor market (Brinton, 1988). As mentioned earlier, a prestigious education is an essential step toward a prestigious career, and many parents see putting their sons through 'examination hell' as an investment toward the future. Because of this, they are more likely to endure the financial hardship of the cost of expensive tuition or the costs of supporting a son living alone to attend university (e.g. Amano, 1997; Brinton, 1988; Fujimura-Fanselow, 1995; Ono, 2004).

In contrast, due to societal expectations for women to marry and raise a family, many parents may decide to 'spare' their daughters from 'examination hell' by sending them to less-competitive academic institutions at the secondary and tertiary level, which are usually private, and often all-female (Amano, 1997). Parents may wish to 'protect' their daughters rather than to hold them back, but such attitudes toward educating women, especially in women's-only institutions,[6] have contributed to gender stratification in the workforce for several reasons.

First, the type of education offered by most women's-only tertiary institutions does not prepare women for a profession (Amano, 1997). Students traditionally study 'feminine' subjects such as education, home economics, liberal arts or child care (Amano, 1997; Fujimoto, 2005). This is particularly true of women attending junior colleges, which was the main tertiary track for women until the 1990s. Even though a junior college education has been noted to be one of the strongest causes for the gendered wage gap in industry (e.g. Brinton, 1988; Okano & Tsuchiya, 1999), many parents during the 1970s and 1980s felt that two years of higher education was sufficient for their daughters. Not only was the reduced cost in tuition attractive, job prospects for junior college graduates were actually better than for those from four-year institutions. Graduates could enter the workforce at the age of 20, and therefore work several years longer than graduates from four-year universities entering the workforce at age 22. This made junior college graduates a more cost-effective human resource investment, especially considering there was no significant difference in the type of work female graduates did, whatever their tertiary degree's duration or whatever they majored in (e.g. Amano, 1997; Fujimoto, 2004, 2005).

Social attitudes toward women's tertiary education shifted during the 1990s. Many junior colleges converted into four-year universities, and in order to attract more students and to appear to be keeping abreast of the times, they began offering more career-oriented subjects such as business and law. Amano (1997) asserts that in order for women's universities to survive, it is important to make them an advantage for women to attend rather than a disadvantage. This seems to be the stance that many women's universities have now taken,[7] for in a recent symposium of women's university presidents, it was stated that the goals of women's universities should be to empower women and to promote a more gender-equal society (Ishikawa, 2008).

Nevertheless, Fujimoto (2004, 2005) argues that a major role of women's only universities is to supply an obedient and docile workforce to support the work that men do and to provide prospective marriage partners for their employees. These women should be willing to quit working after marriage to enable their husbands to work even harder on the company's behalf. Many women's universities and junior colleges have linkages with businesses in order to supply such a workforce through a recommendation system. In other words, Fujimoto (2005: 656) asserts that a major role of women's universities is to supply the 'OL [office lady] market', one of the main career choices for women, which 'move[s] women from school into suitable marriages'. Although Brinton's (1988) comment that education for a woman is 'good *to a point*' is more than 20 years old, this attitude holds true today. In Japan, it is still commonly believed that women should marry men with greater academic credentials, and therefore, if a woman becomes too educated, the pool from which to select eligible husbands is reduced (Ono & Piper, 2004).

A second area where parental attitudes influence the type of university their daughters attend lies in enduring social attitudes that girls should live with their parents until marriage. Daughters are often sent to universities to which they can commute from home, which means that for girls living in the countryside, the more prestigious universities located in Tokyo are often literally out of their reach (e.g. Amano, 1997; Brinton, 1988; Fujimura-Fanselow, 1995; Ono, 2004). The attitude that girls should live with their parents is also reflected in the hiring practices of many companies, who *only* hire graduates who live with their parents, because such women are said to be docile and dependent upon authority, feminine characteristics thought to be ideal for supporting a male workforce (Fujimoto, 2005). Thus, parental and corporate attitudes toward what is appropriate for women play a strong role in regulating which universities women are able to attend.

In spite of the limitations Japanese women face in education mentioned above, it is necessary to point out that many women do go to good universities and aspire to and attain careers (e.g. Dilatush, 1976; Lebra, 1984; Liddle & Nakajima, 2000; Strober & Chan, 2001). Such educational success is linked to parental educational backgrounds. Fathers (and sometimes mothers) served as role models to encourage their daughters (Lebra, 1984), and women in top universities often come from families with educated mothers and with fathers working in elite corporations or as professionals (Amano, 1997). Amano cautions that these women also tend to come from Tokyo: in 1990, 74.4% of the female students at the most prestigious University of Tokyo commuted from home, compared with only 53.8% of the male students, supporting the notion that the universities that female students are able to attend are those that are usually close to home.

Although some women do attend prestigious universities, current statistical data provided by the websites of top prestigious national and private universities in Japan indicate that the percentage of female students is still lower than that of males, and that women still specialize in 'feminine' subjects. Keio University (n.d.) reports that 32% of its undergraduate students are female, and 28.3% of its graduate students and 36.44% of its doctoral students are female. The University of Tokyo has an even smaller percentage of female undergraduate students, only 18.3%, with slightly more graduate students at 26.3% (University of Tokyo, n.d.). Furthermore, female students at both universities are more likely to study liberal arts and human sciences than courses that are career based such as natural sciences, economics or engineering.

Despite these tendencies, some universities are seeking to promote greater gender equity. Because the percentage of female students at The University of Tokyo increased to only 17.5% in 2001 from 7% in 1982, the university is now taking concrete measures to raise the numbers of female researchers to 30% in the short term and to 50% in the long term by improving the working environment for women. It also hopes to encourage more women to enter sciences and engineering by providing a sexual harassment-free environment (University of Tokyo, n.d.).

Although women have often been disadvantaged in the workplace and in education, it is important to point out that in the postwar years, there have been a number of professional working women in Japan, albeit admittedly few. Liddle and Nakajima's (2000: 306) longitudinal study of 120 professional women (professors, doctors, top-grade civil servants and managers in private companies) spanned 20 years. They found that these women relied upon the cultural capital obtained from their elite educations in order to separate themselves from the majority of women who worked in short-term positions. This was particularly important in gaining respect in their fields as professionals, as one of their respondents below describes:

> My having a PhD influenced people's treatment of me as an equal to men. Without it, like most women, I wouldn't have been someone noticeable.... The fact that I got a PhD from the USA influenced my friends – they gave me more respect. I knew I would become a professional so society would treat me as someone. Being a girl isn't someone. I used to work for a publishing company; clients would say: Aren't I important enough that they send me a woman editor? I was mad at men outside the company; I felt angry towards the clients. It was a shock to me how clients treated me. But if I were a professional, people would treat me as independent and a proper person. I became a professional for independence and respect.

This woman's comment reflects an overall discriminatory attitude held by many Japanese male workers toward female workers. Her male clients complained when she was assigned to them as their editor, which made her determined to gain respect, power, and prestige through education, particularly through a PhD from an American university. It was only through increasing her educational capital that she was able to command equal treatment by her colleagues. Otherwise, she would have continued to be treated as just a 'girl'.

In sum, this section has described in some detail women's education in the Japanese context, and has shown that the purpose of women's education in Japan differs from that of men. Parental support of their children's education differs as well: sons may have more access to better universities because such an education is perceived to be a career investment. On the other hand, parents may wish to 'spare' their daughters the rigors of examination hell because women, who are generally considered peripheral members of the workforce, are not seen to need a prestigious education as the foundation for a career. Instead, the purpose of education for women is to raise their cultural capital in order to enhance their marital prospects. Therefore, some parents (and companies) believe that too much education for women does more harm than good when it comes to marriage and employment.

In spite of such attitudes, many women, particularly those with educated parents, do attend prestigious universities. These graduates have a greater chance of being hired at a prestigious company than those from low- and mid-ranking universities. Although some may have the option to join a company on a career track, the difficulties of combining a career and a family have made many women abandon their careers (Amano, 1997). The Japanese Ministry of Labor has itself addressed the necessity of incorporating more university-educated women into the workforce in its 1998 *White Paper on Working Women* to deal with the decrease in the working population that will occur in the mid-21st century. If endorsed and accepted by Japanese society, women's education and their subsequent employment could undergo a great transformation in the coming years.

Gendered Aspects of English in Japan

The previous section established the context of Japanese women and tertiary education. This section now turns to the role that English language education plays in the education of Japanese women. The question of whether male or female students are better at language learning has been a main focus of research on the influence of gender in second language learning (e.g. Ellis, 1994; Ehrlich, 1997; Sunderland, 2000), and has generally 'explained' female students' higher success rate as owing to 'feminine' characteristics such as a willingness to communicate and cooperate with others and a better ability to interact with people. Schmenk (2004) argues, however, that such explanations ascribe stereotypical gendered attributes to men and women, and fail to take into account the role of the sociopolitical contexts in which the language learners live.

In Japan, English education is important for nearly all secondary school students because of its critical role in university entrance examinations (Lo Castro, 1996). However, English is given a feminized status, which renders it more popular as an area of study among female students (Kobayashi, 2002) because many believe that English ability will enable them to obtain good jobs (Bailey, 2006; Kelskey, 2001). Kobayashi (2007b: 567) argues, however, that the rhetoric behind an image that English ability will be an important asset for a career plan masks underlying ideologies that situate Japanese women in gender-stratified positions, and that unequal access to educational facilities due to individual gendered and socioeconomic backgrounds prevent people from obtaining the right sort of educational credentials. Therefore, English education itself may not empower women because the existing corporate culture engages in gendered discriminatory practices which 'attaches paramount importance to men with certain backgrounds as the legitimate labor force' at the expense of women. In other words, women may not be able to convert the English they learn in the type of educational institutions they attend into remunerated work.

Nevertheless, English is still perceived to be the key to financial security for many women in Japan. Although some may see English as a means of gaining more career opportunities, the real appeal of attaining English skills may be that it allows women to earn an income while simultaneously raising a family (e.g. Burton, 2004; Kan, 2009).

The Desire to Study Abroad

Many women also view education attained overseas as a way to break through the gendered career market in Japan. Unlike men who are often financially supported by companies, women tend to quit their jobs and, using their own financial resources, go overseas to not only improve their English language skills, but to also attain advanced degrees such as MAs and MBAs (Matsui, 1995; Ono & Piper, 2004). However, it is difficult for Japanese women to obtain career positions in Japanese companies after completing their overseas degrees, especially once they have exited the workforce (Liddle & Nakajima, 2000). Thus, many Japanese women opt to remain abroad or work for foreign companies. Matsui (1995) says the brain drain that this is causing (for example, there are more Japanese women working on Wall Street than there are in Japan's financial center) is not recognized by Japanese industry because Japanese women are not seen as a vital part of the economy. Therefore, common beliefs about English as a tool of empowerment and the realities of future employment may not reconcile neatly.

Japanese women often go abroad to improve their English proficiency, but many believe that their overseas language learning experiences will not necessarily result in concrete professional benefits. Therefore, the main rationale behind such study for women in their 20s and 30s is the 'opportunity for psychological liberation' (Matsui, 1995: 376). This is seen as a once-in-a-lifetime opportunity to achieve 'cosmopolitan' status before conforming to social norms of marriage and motherhood in Japan (Burton, 2004; Habu, 2000; Kobayashi, 2007a; Matsui, 1995; Ono & Piper, 2004; Piller & Takahashi, 2006; Raymo, 2003).

Marketing English for Women

The private *eikaiwa* (English conversation) industry, in Japan is a multibillion yen business that spends a great deal of time and energy recruiting Japanese women who are seen to have a significant amount of disposable income to spend on English lessons. Advertisements from such schools promote the image that English study will lead to a better job, a more fulfilled self, internationalization and even beauty or a boyfriend (Bailey, 2006; Habu, 2000; Kelskey, 2001; Takahashi, 2006) and companies that arrange study-abroad programs entice women through catchy slogans such as 'You can be who you want to be', 'Change your life through studying in Australia' and 'Let's start a new life' (Piller & Takahashi, 2006).

It has been argued that one reason for the success of the *eikaiwa* industry lies in a pervasive yearning, or desire, called *akogare* for all things foreign. English is thus not only seen as an essential component to provide more career opportunities, it is also seen as a way for women to adopt a new persona from the cultural and linguistic constraints of Japanese, to promote one's sexuality and to obtain sexual freedom (Bailey, 2006; Kelskey, 2001; Kobayashi, 2002; Koike, 2000; Piller & Takahashi, 2006; Takahashi, 2006). Bailey (2006) found that *eikaiwa* schools with a large female client base rely on advertising images that include a nice-looking Western male teacher hinting at the possibility of romance with the Japanese student pictured in the advertisement. In contrast, schools with a large male client base that consider themselves 'businessmen's schools' do not resort to such eroticized advertising as a way to recruit students.

English Empowers Women

The notion that women can become free of Japanese cultural norms through English is also evident in the way that some language teachers incorporate feminist ideals into their lessons as a way to empower women (Norton & Pavlenko, 2004). In the Japanese context, Simon-Maeda's

(2004b) university students studied controversial gender-based topics from a linguistic perspective in order to question societal views toward women. The adult women in McMahill's (2001) class, which has been continuing for 20 years, combine English language skill development with increasing knowledge about feminism through attending conferences or translating feminist materials.

In sum, the previous sections have shown that the educational opportunities for women in Japan are regulated by gendered familial and societal ideals. Although Japanese women have access to secondary and tertiary education, the educational paths that they are encouraged to take may not provide them with the knowledge or training to gain access to a profession. Education for women traditionally has been, and still is, a means for enhancing cultural capital in order to make a good marriage. English as a subject is seen as a type of cultural collateral as well. However, while it used to be seen as a subject akin to a 'finishing school' cultural subject to prepare women for marriage, it is now seen as, and promoted as, a key to open the door to a career.

The Japanese Professor

This chapter has thus far examined English education in Japan from its historical and sociopolitical context. It has also examined the relationship between education and industry and discussed the impact that gender has on students gaining access to the type of education that would enable them to obtain careers. We have seen how female students may not enjoy the same sort of benefits that their male counterparts may have access to. Now we turn specifically to the profession of teachers in Japanese higher education. The purpose of this section is to provide an overview of the profession of the Japanese professor.

Before I examine in greater detail the work that Japanese professors are currently engaged in, let us look at the numerical distribution of the four types of university teachers in Japan as highlighted in Table 2.8.

Tenure is generally offered when a person in their 20s or 30s is hired as an assistant professor, and promotion to associate professor and professor occurs fairly automatically over time (e.g. Evanoff, 1993; MEXT, 2006; Poole, 2010).

The category of part-time teachers constitutes the greatest number of university teachers, and they are heavily relied upon in Japanese tertiary education because they reduce personnel costs and they provide specialist lectures for students (Kinmouth, 2005; Poole, 2010). Part-time faculty are of mainly two types: those who only teach part time, and those who teach

Table 2.8 Distribution of Japanese[8] university teachers in Japan in 2005

	Total
Part-time	162,393
Assistant professor	20,451
Associate professor	38,076
Professor	64,940

(MEXT, 2006)

part time in addition to holding a full-time tenured position at another university. Part-time teachers may ultimately teach more classes than full-time teachers do, but they have no administrative responsibilities at the institutions where they teach, nor do they have long-term job security. At the onset of an academic career, part-time teaching provides experience and is a good source of income, but the opportunity to obtain tenure decreases with age, and therefore many teachers remain part-time teachers.

Although it is not mentioned in the table above, it is important to point out that another type of a full-time academic position was introduced into Japanese universities by the Ministry of Education in 1997: a contract position (*ninkisei*). Under this position, a teacher is hired as an instructor to teach a full-time load of classes, but like part-time teachers, has no administrative responsibilities or job security. It is likely that many of those listed above as assistant professors fall under this category.

When universities were first established in Japan, professors enjoyed positions of great prestige. According to Shimbori (1981), those first professors were graduates from The University of Tokyo, the only school with a graduate program, and as such they were entitled to mingle with politicians and even the imperial family. Later generations of professors emerged from their own universities' graduate schools, where a system of 'academic inbreeding' (MEXT, 2006) became established. In general, graduates could find work at academic institutions that were lower in rank, but not at those that were higher in rank from where they received their degrees (Shimbori, 1981).

Because of the increase in the number of students seeking higher education and the increase in the number of universities established in Japan during the postwar years, there was also an increase in the number of positions for professors. When many higher schools were converted into universities, those who were previously teachers then became professors. Shimbori (1981: 80) argues that this created an unproductive situation:

> Although many of them [the new professors] had appropriate training and potential ability as scholars they had neither a commitment to nor an interest in undertaking scientific research. Because of the Japanese tradition of permanent employment tinged with paternalism and *gakubatsu* [a form of patronage for graduates of a particular university], it is common for a faculty member, once appointed to a university position, to retain it until retirement age. Consequently, the universities have been forced to retain these unproductive faculty.

Shimbori (1981) distinguishes the tenure system for Japanese academics from that of the West. Unlike the West, where tenure 'is a safeguard to ensure freedom and autonomy of research' (p. 84), in Japan it is seen as lifetime employment and is offered immediately upon being hired and not after an academic probation period. Many universities originally operated under a chair system, which originated in Germany, where a department is comprised of a professor, an associate professor and an assistant professor. Promotion occurred when the senior professor retired and the others moved up in rank and a new underling was hired. Shimbori says the advantage of the chair system is that it 'cultivates intimate and personal relationships among faculty in one chair, often leading to fruitful scholarly cooperation'. The disadvantages of the chair system, however, are that it can 'foster isolationism, exclusiveness, favoritism, *gakubatsu*, and feudalistic relationships, gerontocracy and the like' (p. 85). Currently, research output (the publication of a minimum of three papers in international journals or sole authorship of a book), teaching performance and contribution to society are the criteria for promotion to professor at some universities, particularly research-oriented ones, although the years of experience may play a greater role in others (MEXT, 2006).

Daizen and Yamanoi (2008) examined the changing profession of the Japanese professor by comparing the results of their 2007 Changing Academic Profession (CAP) Survey of 1408 professors in three national research, one private research, four national non-research and 11 private non-research universities with the results of the Carnegie Academic Profession Survey carried out in 1992 to see if differences exist among the professors in these four different categories of schools. Several areas of their study are worth noting. First, the number of professors holding PhDs has increased. Compared with the Carnegie study in 1992, where 57.8% of university professors had doctorate degrees, the CAP Survey in 2007 found a significant jump, with 78.5% of professors holding doctorates. As a result, those with only masters' degrees and bachelors' degrees decreased. The distribution of those with PhDs in the various academic institutions differs, however; more faculty at national institutions hold PhDs than faculty at private institutions. There are two reasons for this increase in doctorate degrees among professors. First, the number of academics who have received degrees from abroad has increased, and whereas it had previously been nearly impossible to obtain a PhD from a Japanese university, governmental reforms have made Japanese PhDs more attainable (Hada, 2005). Furthermore, it is now practically impossible to obtain a tenured position without holding a doctorate (MEXT, 2006). Table 2.9 shows the academic credentials held by members in different universities.

Another area of interest is the professors' time allotment with their workload. Professors in Japanese universities enjoy a great deal of autonomy in deciding how to spend their time, but Daizen and Yamanoi (2008) found they generally engage in five types of professional activities: teaching, research, service, administration and 'other'. When classes are in session, they work 55.5 hours per week, and when classes are not in session, they work 47.6 hours per week. The decrease in time devoted to teaching leads to an increase in time devoted to research. Table 2.10 below shows how this time is distributed among the various types of universities in 1992 and in 2007. Hours spent in teaching, service, administration and other have increased since the 1992 survey, but hours devoted to research have decreased.

Table 2.9 Academic credentials of faculty by type of university

		Doctorates	Masters' degrees	Bachelors' degrees
National research	2007	92.2%	7.8%	0.0%
	1992	88.5%	9.8%	1.8%
National non-research	2007	78.7%	18.7%	2.6%
	1992	62.6%	27.9%	9.5%
Private research	2007	81.5%	16.9%	1.5%
	1992	72.4%	23.6%	3.8%
Private non-research	2007	72.0%	22.4%	5.6%
	1992	41.6%	29.5%	28.9%

(Daizen & Yamanoi, 2008: 303)

Table 2.10 Time spent per week on professional activities by type of university

	2007	1992
Teaching		
National research	17.2	14.3
National non-research	20.4	17.4
Private research	19.5	16.2
Private non-research	25.5	23.8
Research		
National research	21.7	24.6
National non-research	17.2	23.6
Private research	18.3	24.2
Private non-research	16.2	18.9
Service		
National research	3.3	3.5
National non-research	5.6	3.9
Private research	6.5	3.9
Private non-research	3.9	3.0
Administration		
National research	8.1	7.4
National non-research	8.4	6.1
Private research	6.5	6.8
Private non-research	7.4	5.2
Other		
National research	4.1	3.9
National non-research	3.2	2.9
Private research	4.2	3.2
Private non-research	2.9	.3

(Daizen & Yamanoi, 2008: 305)

In spite of the decrease in the hours devoted to research, Japanese professors are quite productive. Daizen and Yamanoi (2008: 310) state that although there are differences among professors depending upon their academic disciplines, 'On average, over a three-year period, in 2007, a Japanese faculty member writes 1.9 academic books, edits 0.7 books, publishes 9.8 papers in academic journals, publishes 1.5 monographs and presents papers 6.7 times at academic conferences'. This productivity was also noted by Enders and Teichler (1997), who analyzed the International Survey of the Academic Profession from an international perspective. They found that Japan placed second out of eight countries in indicating a preference toward research over teaching. In comparison to professors in other countries, Japanese professors were the only ones who devote a significant amount of time to research even when classes are in session. However, it is important to point out that there might be a discrepancy in the quantitative output of research as reported to Daizen and Yamanoi (2008) in their survey and the quality of the research. Although many Japanese professors do publish research that is critically acclaimed in international journals, many Japanese universities have in-house journals (*daigaku kiyo*), which publish unreviewed articles written by the professors from those universities. Cummings and Amano (1979) criticize this system and say that such in-house publishing has interfered with the sharing of professional ideas and professional standards with other scholars. They also note that many professors prefer to write for commercial publishers. Such articles and books are often unreviewed by academic peers, but they reach a wider audience and professors are financially remunerated for them.

Table 2.11 shows that the teachers in all four types of universities tend to prefer research over teaching, which may account for the time they devote to research even when classes are in session. Nevertheless, as Table 2.10 showed, time devoted to teaching increased as well as a slight increase in a preference to teaching. This trend, according to Daizen and Yamanoi (2008), may be due to higher expectations of the professors to educate a population of students that is declining in number as well as declining in academic ability.

An Ethnography of a Japanese University

Now I would like to turn to a study that provides an in-depth analysis of a Japanese university. Poole's (2010) ethnography of professors in a private university in the greater Tokyo area during a time of sweeping tertiary reform throughout Japan is a particularly useful study for framing the studies in this book. As a participant-observer in his research context, a small private university in Tokyo he called 'Edo University of Commerce',

Table 2.11 Preference for teaching or research by type of university

		Primarily teaching	In both, but leaning toward teaching	In both, but leaning toward research	Primarily research
National research	2007	1.7%	8.7%	68.6%	21.1%
	1992	0.0%	7.4%	55.8%	35.0%
National non-research	2007	4.6%	21.6%	50.7%	15.1%
	1992	1.9%	17.8%	63.0%	17.2%
Private research	2007	1.5%	20.0%	58.5%	20.0%
	1992	0.0%	15.3%	65.3%	19.1%
Private non-research	2007	8.5%	30.6%	50.7%	10.1%
	1992	5.7%	34.7%	49.5%	10.0%

(Daizen & Yamanoi, 2008: 309)

he engaged in all activities that are assigned to the Japanese professoriate: he taught classes, was a member of the *kyojyukai* (professors' council), participated in committee work and interacted with professors both on and off campus in both formal and informal gatherings. He investigated how the university professors and the university administrators interacted to build their social world and to construct values that create their identities as 'good' professors. He identified two competing discourses that reflect two contrasting ideologies that are likely prevalent in other universities as well. The first, *uchimuki* (facing inward), is based on the ideology that reflects a discourse of tradition. The other, *sotomuki* (facing outward), is based on management practices within the business world and reflects a discourse of reform. These two areas of discourse are briefly summarized below in Tables 2.12 and 2.13.

Membership in either of the discourses means that a professor is an *insider* in the university and enjoys the rights and privileges that a part-time teacher or a contract teacher cannot. Poole says these two ideologies operate along a continuum with professors 'straddling' the ideologies and moving back and forth when the situation warranted it. Nevertheless, he found the *uchimuki* ideology to be the more dominant of the two at his university. Furthermore, *uchimuki* professors were not only members of the inner circle; they also were what the university considered to be 'good professors'. 'Good professors' were those who gave a highly visible appearance of working hard on behalf of the university, built relationships with administrative staff and professors and spent hours advising and socializing with students. Most

Table 2.12 Uchimuki
Uchimuki Characteristics

Role of university	University is a tight-knit family
Ideologies	Values tradition, consensus, harmony Long-term commitment to the university Social obligation (*giri*) and personal compulsion (*ninjou*) Collegiality among colleagues is important Freedom/autonomy (to teach as seen fit, according to individual pedagogical philosophies) Conflicts are solved on the micro level Time used on behalf of the school is not wasted time Committed to lifelong employment Promotion based on longevity Power is gained through administrative work
Symbolic capital	Authority is legitimized by the university Intimacy with fellow colleagues, committee chair/offices/status titles/membership in 'inner circles'/respect for position

Poole (2010)

importantly, a 'good professor', Poole argues, was a person who would put the affairs of the university ahead of personal concerns, even one's own research, which was not highly evaluated nor criteria for promotion.

Poole points out that the *uchimuki* discourse may not be as prevalent at research-oriented universities, which do place high value on *sotomuki* capital in the form of PhDs and refereed journal articles. In large national universities, professors are expected to conduct research, publish results and gain international recognition – in other words, to build up their *sotomuki* capital. In spite of such expectations, however, excessive committee work often prevents national university professors from having sufficient time to do so (private conversation with national university professor).

Poole's book provides useful insight into the workings of a Japanese university, which I believe to be representative of other similar small, private liberal arts universities in Japan – especially those that are operated as family-run businesses. How university teachers see themselves positioned in their universities and how they believe others see them is going to play an important role in their professional identities as teachers. In the next section, I would like to examine how *female* university professors are situated within the context of Japanese universities.

Table 2.13 Sotomuki

	Sotomuki Characteristics
Role of university	University is a place of employment and operated like a business
Ideologies	Values reform Short-term (if necessary) commitment to the school Restriction/standardization (to teach a standardized syllabi/curriculum) Accountability (to students) Conflicts are solved on the macro level Time used on behalf of the school is an inefficient waste of time Career oriented, possibility of moving out and upward Promotion based on research and ability
Symbolic capital	Authority is legitimized by outside sources PhD/refereed journal articles/outside positions of power (e.g. MEXT)/teaching awards/invitations to speak/grants/positive student feedback

Poole (2010)

Female Professors in Universities

Earlier I described how career opportunities for Japanese women working in companies are limited due to sociopolitical gendered attitudes about work, women and marriage. The differences in education that male and female students receive were also shown to contribute to the limitations placed on women's opportunities in the workforce. As with other occupations, women are a minority in academia as well. The purpose of this section is to examine how Japanese women fare in Japanese academia. First let us look at the actual numbers of female academics as shown in Table 2.14.

A breakdown of the academic positions held by men and women is shown in Table 2.15. How many of those who occupy *ninkisei* (contract) positions is unclear, but it is reasonable to assume that a number of those who are assistant professors fall under this category.

Table 2.16 shows an analysis of the areas that female academics specialize in. It is interesting to note that even in fields that have traditionally been considered women's areas, such as home economics, male professors are still in the majority. Not surprisingly, in areas of study

Table 2.14 Distribution of Japanese tenured university teachers in 2005

Male full-time faculty members	Female full-time faculty members	Total number of full-time faculty
114,718 (85.5%)	16,659 (14.5%)	131,377

(MEXT, 2006)

Table 2.15 Distribution of Japanese university teachers in Japan in 2005

	Total	Female	Percentage of women faculty
Part-time	162,393	40,028	24.6%
Assistant professor	20,451	4,927	17 %
Associate professor	38,076	6,446	24.1%
Professor	64,940	6,559	10.1%
Total	285,860	57,960	20.3%

(MEXT, 2006)

Table 2.16 Percentage of female researchers in Japanese universities

Area of study	Percentage
Home economics	31.2%
Humanities	16.5%
Education	12.7%
Social sciences	7.7%
Science	3.7%
Agriculture	1.6%

(Adapted from Fujita, 2006)

considered to be 'masculine', female researchers are practically nonexistent. MEXT (2006) attributes this bias in specialization to the socially constructed beliefs that some areas of study are better suited for men and some are better suited for women, as well as suggesting that female students' interest in science declines while in secondary school.

Considering that women researchers are severely underrepresented in higher education, it is not surprising that reports of the difficulties they face have emerged. Sodei's (2005) study of Japanese scientists found that female academics are about five years behind men in terms of promotion: they were promoted at a slower rate and they filled more part-time positions than men. She attributes this lag to women having less opportunity to study abroad on sabbaticals or attend international conferences, and to having fewer mentoring opportunities from bosses and senior professors than male academics do.

Many women also report having been victims of sexual (*sekuhara*) and academic (*akahara*) harassment[9] in Japanese universities: 21.4% of staff in junior colleges, 34.3% of staff in universities and 26.7% of undergraduate students (Sodei, 2005). Such harassment includes the withholding of research funds, not having the cooperation of a supervising male professor, being denied first authorship on papers they had written and being gossiped about in a sexually inappropriate manner (McNeill, 2007; Normile, 2001; Sodei, 2005).

The greatest difficulty for female academics (as well as for women in other professions) in Japan may be the balancing of family and professional life. Kubo (2006), former director of the Gender Equality Promotion Division in the prime minister's Cabinet Office, said in a workshop on 'Women in Science, Engineering and Technology' given in Ottawa that one of the greatest issues that holds women back professionally in Japan is the burden of housework and child care, calling Japanese husbands in duel-income families 'lazybones', (p. 3) citing statistics that they put in less than 30 minutes per day on household tasks while their working wives put in more than four hours.

In spite of the difficulties currently encountered by female academics, we may see a different trend in the future. In its review of higher education in Japan, MEXT (2006: 72) optimistically writes this about the sexual harassment and sexual discrimination problems that female students face:

> Various institutions of higher learning have established councils and consultation offices on sexual harassment, and efforts are being made to prevent inappropriate treatment based on differences in sex. As a result of the increased awareness and environment improvements it is expected that equity in connection with sexual discrimination in tertiary education is ensured more effectively.

The University of Tokyo, in order to promote gender equality for female researchers, has established the Todai Model Support Plan '10 Years to

Establish a Career', stating that the current situation for its female population is inappropriate for a university of its world standing. The plan proposes to investigate the gendered barriers that exist for female graduate students and attempt to remove them. This includes providing day care facilities that can also accommodate sick children, improving safety features in laboratories and offices for pregnant women and improving child-care leave and maternity benefits (University of Tokyo, n.d.). Furthermore, a concrete step was taken to close the career gap experienced by female scientists who find it nearly impossible to reenter academia after taking child-care leave. A two-year postdoctoral reentry fellowship was created to begin in 2006 and 2007 to assist female scientists to reenter research. Applicants for the 60 places (30 each year) this fellowship offered exceeded 350, indicating a strong desire by women to return to full-time research (Japan Society for the Promotion of Science, 2006).

Another issue that may change women's access to positions in higher education is related to the widespread phenomenon of large numbers of Japanese women quitting their jobs in their twenties and thirties to study overseas and who return with advanced degrees. Women may pursue advanced degrees even though the chances of later obtaining a permanent tenured position in academia are slim. Unlike men who may be pressured to hold onto a career once they are established, women are often not seen as, nor do they see themselves as, a part of the permanent workforce. One of the English professors interviewed by Stewart (2005: 147–148) explains why it may be easier for women, particularly in languages, to pursue a path toward academia:

> Maybe it's easier for a woman actually…in Japan where men are expected to get married and support the family, whereas the woman isn't really expected to support, and many women say they don't want a full-time job they just want part-time teaching. So I suppose it's a little bit easier for women. 'Cos their families, their parents, they don't expect the daughter to support them. So if the daughter has to go to graduate school for extra years and can't find a job and has to do part-time teaching, the parents don't really mind, whereas if their son was doing that, well, I don't really know (laughs) … In other fields like science it's very difficult for women to become. In languages there tend to be more women … though not as many as there should be.

This professor's statement is interesting for several reasons. First, she says that parents may be more willing to support daughters than sons to go to graduate school because of the uncertainty of obtaining a tenured position upon completion. Then she qualifies this statement by suggesting that this trend may be more applicable for women in languages (or other traditionally feminine fields) rather than for women in male-dominated fields such as science. Even though she stated that it may be easier for women in languages to become academics than for women in other fields, she acknowledges, almost as an afterthought, that women are nevertheless still underrepresented, and goes on to explain the situation at her university:

> For instance, at my university, when I was a student there used to be only just one or maybe two full-time female teachers out of say 120 or 130, just one or two. Then when I was hired, by the time I was hired there were more than ten. Still, it's only 10, right? We still have a group, we used to have a women teachers' group and we'd meet once a year at the beginning when a new woman teacher came, and then we'd say one of these days there's going to be more women than men and the men'll have to have these gatherings instead (laughs). But still it's not half; over 70% of the students are girls. There's still only 20% of the teaching staff. Which isn't very many.

It is important to acknowledge that Japanese women are not alone in their gendered isolation in academia. Although the percentage of female academics in Japan may be lower than that of other countries, they are nonetheless underrepresented throughout the world: female professors constitute only 22% in Finland, 18% in the United States and 16% in Sweden (Newby et al., 2009). Furthermore, O'Leary and Mitchell (1990) found issues facing female academics in the United States to be similar to those of women in Japan. These issues included a lack of mentors to help facilitate women's career advancement and gatekeeping measures run by an old-boy network that controlled access to research funds and to the dissemination of new research ideas. Poole et al. (1997), in their analysis of the Carnegie Foundation's International Survey of the Academic Profession from a gendered perspective, found that among eight countries, women academics were more positively oriented toward teaching than their male counterparts, who were more oriented toward research. They point out that this may be due in part to women being employed more often in part-time or adjunct positions, and because women are underrepresented in the fields of science and engineering. They also say that this may be because men might be savvier in knowing how to navigate the academic system to obtain and maintain positions of power within their institutions. It is clear that some of the issues facing female academics around the world are similar to those facing Japanese academics, but Japanese women are still fighting a deep-rooted societal bias that expects women to place emphasis on the family and the home at the same time.

Summary of Chapter 2

This chapter has provided a brief overview of the Japanese historical and sociopolitical context of English language education in order to set the scene for the three studies that will be presented in Chapters 5, 6 and 7 that focus on the beliefs, practices and identities of Japanese teachers of English in Japanese higher education. The beliefs that these teachers carry with them into their classrooms are not only an accumulation of their own language learning and language teaching experiences, but are also the result of the sociopolitical context in which they live and work.

I summarized the brief history of English language education in Japan and common explanations for the low English communication skills among Japanese in spite of having many years of English schooling. I showed that the goals concerning English language education in Japan had undergone several paradigm shifts in the past 150 years and that these shifts were politically motivated and guided by the perception of how language education was to best serve the economic interests of the country. In its early days, the aim of foreign language education was to provide a linguistic tool for the educated elite to acquire Western knowledge and technology as future leaders of the country, but then the aim shifted to become a measurement tool for predicting intellectual performance in secondary and higher education institutions. What came to matter was not if a student *knew* English, but if a student *knew about* English.

Then the connection between education and industry was discussed. Because of the economic success during the postwar years, the rate of those completing secondary schools and entering tertiary institutions increased from 19% in the 1950s to 49% in the 2000s, resulting in the establishment of numerous private liberal arts universities and creating a situation where anyone who is desirous of a university education can attain one. However, the prestige of the university ultimately determines the career outcome of its graduates, and access to the right sort of university depends on numerous factors, such as students' socioeconomic backgrounds, place of domicile, parental educational backgrounds and gender. The impact of sociopolitical attitudes toward women's access to careers was also discussed. Women are not gaining access to the type of education that culminates in a profession, but instead they tend to go to less competitive universities that are located within commuting distance, and they tend to study 'feminine' subjects that are of interest to them rather than those that are career-oriented.

In this chapter, I also briefly discussed the profession of Japanese professors in Japanese higher education and showed that female professors are underrepresented in all areas of academic specialization and that they tend to lag behind male professors in terms of promotion because of gender-related bias in the workplace and because of the difficulty of balancing family and career. Poole (2010), in his ethnography of a private university in Tokyo, found two competing discourses, *uchimuki* and *sotomuki*, which provide a useful analytical tool in considering the degree of identification those who work for Japanese universities have and how they are considered as 'good professors' by the university, and which will be used in considering the narratives of the teachers presented later in this book.

In the next chapter, I provide further background for Chapters 5, 6 and 7 by reviewing studies that deal with teacher knowledge, beliefs and identity. I first introduce studies that emerged from general education, which influenced subsequent studies of EFL/ESL teacher identity. The chapter will look in detail at the identity development of non-native English-speaking teachers and review several studies that have taken place in the Japanese context.

Notes

(1) In 1877, 75% of the full professors at The University of Tokyo were foreigners, but by 1883, this number dropped to 36% (Ota, 1994).
(2) The term *ekiben* means station (*eki*) lunch (*bento*), and refers to Japanese boxed lunches that contain a little bit of everything of the local cuisine served up in one meal.
(3) These figures do not include correspondence courses, schools for special needs or colleges of technology.
(4) English conversation was officially introduced into pubic elementary schools in 2010, but private schools have long held such classes.
(5) National kindergartens, elementary schools and junior high schools are attached to national universities with education departments. They often act as escalator schools up to junior high, but students need to compete for entrance to the attached high school and to the attached university.
(6) There are a handful of highly competitive and academically excellent women's universities in Japan, which do prepare women for careers, but most of these are located in major cities.
(7) A recent conversation with a teacher from a well-known private girls' high school in the Kanto area revealed that the school's educational philosophy had changed dramatically after the former president retired. Previously, the aim of that that school had been to educate girls to be good wives and mothers, but it has now shifted to provide the type of education that would enable women to achieve financial independence.
(8) Within this group, there are 5,652 non-Japanese university teachers, 1,347 (23.8%) of whom are female.
(9) For highly publicized incidents of sexual and academic harassment in Japanese universities, see Normile (2001).

3 Knowledge, Beliefs and Identity

Introduction

In the previous chapter, I discussed a number of issues that surround the sociopolitical context that has shaped English language education in Japan. Now I would like to turn to the literature that deals with the unobservable dimensions of teaching, namely teacher knowledge, beliefs and identity. Then I will look at the importance of the social context when evaluating and considering methodological practices of English language teaching. Here, two different educational philosophies concerning second and foreign language learning that have evolved from two different educational contexts will be discussed. The first evolved from Western countries such as Britain, Australasia and North America (BANA), and the second evolved from tertiary, secondary and primary educational institutions throughout the world that teach English as a foreign language (TESEP) (Holliday, 1994). The chapter will conclude with a review of three studies that focus on the Japanese context.

Teacher Cognition

Studies of teacher behavior conducted in the latter half of the 20th century found that the role of the teacher is much more complex than had previously been thought. In one of the first review articles of teacher cognition, Shavelson and Stern (1981: 456–457) noted a shift in the beliefs that teachers are merely transmitters of knowledge to students, to the view that teachers are unique and rational beings who 'make judgments, and carry out decisions in an uncertain, complex environment' and that teachers' behavior is 'guided by their thoughts, judgments and decisions'. In a subsequent review of research on teacher cognition, Clark and Peterson (1986) found that teaching involves two domains: the act of teaching, which is observable, and the unobservable thinking that underlies teacher behavior. The latter includes teacher planning, teachers' interactive thoughts and decisions and teachers' theories and beliefs. The notion that the act of teaching is dependent upon individual teachers' thoughts and beliefs has led to numerous in-depth studies to determine what these thoughts and beliefs are and how they influence classroom teaching (e.g. Clandinin, 1985, 1986; Elbaz, 1983; Shulman, 1986, 1987).

Two interrelated areas of research that fall under the domain of unobservable teacher behavior are the study of teachers' knowledge and the study of teachers' beliefs, and they will be considered in the next section with a brief summary of the major findings concerning teacher knowledge in general education. The seminal studies described below (Clandinin, 1985, 1986; Clandinin & Connelly, 1987; Elbaz, 1983; Shulman, 1987), which were influential in identifying the characteristics of teacher knowledge, lay the foundation for subsequent studies of the knowledge and beliefs held by second and foreign language teachers.

Teacher Knowledge

Elbaz's (1983) case study of a high school English teacher in the United States identified five areas of knowledge that teachers draw upon when making instructional decisions. These areas are: *situational*, which is knowledge oriented to context, *theoretical*, which is knowledge that is acquired by theory, *personal*, which is knowledge that demonstrates an understanding of the balance of the teachers' goals and outcome of students learning, *social*, which is knowledge of the context outside of the classroom and *experiential*, which is knowledge which evolves through classroom experiences.

Clandinin (1985, 1986) and Clandinin and Connelly (1987) expanded on Elbaz's (1983) framework of personal knowledge with their construct of 'personal practical knowledge', which they say is deep-rooted, moral, personal and evolves from individual personal and professional experiences. This, they argue, leads teachers to create personal philosophies toward teaching that can explain their teaching practices.

Shulman's (1986) identification of teachers' interrelated knowledge domains demonstrates the breadth and width of the knowledge that teachers hold. These domains include content knowledge, general pedagogical knowledge, curriculum knowledge, pedagogical content knowledge, knowledge of learners and their characteristics, knowledge of educational contexts and knowledge of educational ends, purposes and values. Later, Shulman (1987) expanded these areas to account for the individual characteristics of teachers and proposed a conceptual framework of knowledge to include personal propositional knowledge (principles), case knowledge (maxims) and strategic knowledge (norms).

These studies of teacher knowledge in general education have shown that teachers utilize more than their knowledge of the content matter to be taught; they also draw upon the knowledge they have gained through their wide-ranging personal experiences and their personal backgrounds, and they utilize this knowledge to manage all aspects of their classroom teaching.

In second and foreign language education, interest in teachers' knowledge followed the lead set by research in general education. Whereas earlier studies viewed language teaching as the application of an appropriate methodology or an approach (e.g. Fries, 1947; Krashen, 1981), or placed attention on the language learners themselves (e.g. Corder, 1967; Krashen & Terrell, 1983), researchers in the field of foreign language education became interested in the relationship between teacher knowledge and classroom practices (e.g. Freeman, 1993, 1996a, 1996b, 2002; Freeman & Richards, 1996; Freeman & Johnson, 1998). Studies of ESL and EFL teachers have shown that their personal practical knowledge influences the majority of their instructional decisions (e.g. Gatbonton, 1999; Golembek, 1998; Tsang, 2004).

Golembek (1998) identified four overlapping categories of personal practical knowledge in language teachers that are shaped and reshaped through the teachers' experiences both inside and outside of the classroom and that inform their teaching practices. These categories are: *knowledge of self, knowledge of subject matter, knowledge of instruction* and *knowledge of content*. *Knowledge of self* involves the overlapping identities of the teacher, such as language learner, teacher and spouse. *Knowledge of subject matter* is a result of the culmination of knowledge gained from the teachers' academic discipline. *Knowledge of instruction* covers general and specific knowledge that teachers employ for their own teaching situation. *Knowledge of context* refers to the broader settings of the institutional and sociopolitical settings in which the teachers work.

Golembek (1998), as well as Gatbonton (1999) and Tsang (2004), suggest that one source of teachers' knowledge comes from pedagogical theories that are taught in school, but much of their knowledge evolves through their own personal experiences. They propose that pre-service teacher education programs should help teachers become aware of the knowledge they bring with them into teaching in order to help them incorporate their theories into philosophies of teaching.

Teacher Beliefs

Closely related to teacher knowledge is the concept of teacher beliefs. Pajares (1992) argues that attempts to differentiate these two concepts – that knowledge concerns the *knowing of something*, but beliefs concern the *feelings about something*, are problematic because these terms are not dichotomous but are interwoven and influence each other. He calls beliefs 'a messy construct' because they are hard to define and because they range in flexibility. People's 'core beliefs', which are closely connected to a person's identity, are hard to change, but those that are a matters of 'preference' are easier to change. Pajares argues that teachers hold intersecting beliefs about every aspect of themselves as teachers, about their students, about the subject matter and about their pedagogical practices that guide every aspect of their teaching practices.

In foreign language education, Horwitz (1985, 1988) was among the first to examine the beliefs concerning language learning held by pre-service teachers. Through a questionnaire she had constructed entitled Beliefs About Language Learning Inventory (BALLI), she found that many of her students' beliefs ran counter to established second language acquisition (SLA) theories. Subsequent studies of foreign language teacher beliefs supported Horowitz's initial findings, and found that such incorrect beliefs in language teachers may be detrimental to language students' motivation and may lead to student dissatisfaction in language classes (e.g. Kern, 1995; Peacock, 1999).

Other studies of pre-service teachers' beliefs have suggested that teacher education classes accommodate and incorporate teachers' beliefs into training programs in order to bridge the gap between the theoretical knowledge prospective teachers are taught and the personal knowledge they hold (e.g. Almarza, 1996; Breen et al., 2001; Brown & McGannon, 1988; MacDonald et al., 2001). Breen (1991) suggested, more concretely, that teacher-training programs use actual classroom events to encourage prospective teachers to verbalize and reflect upon these events to construct and examine their own beliefs and theories.

The personal beliefs of experienced language teachers have also been found to strongly impact classroom practices. Burns' (1996) case study of six experienced ESL teachers in an Australian Migrant English Program (AMEP) found that the teachers' beliefs toward the school program, language learning and language teaching and educational materials were at the heart of their teaching practices. Because these beliefs were found to be so important, she argued that prospective teachers should be encouraged to develop their personalized theories about language teaching and language learning in collaboration with established theories taught in pre-service training programs.

However, even if foreign/second language teacher education programs collaborate with pre-service teachers to help them merge their beliefs with theory, it is important to note that some studies have found that teacher beliefs, even those in teacher education programs, may be resistant to change (e.g. Bramald et al., 1995; Holt-Reynolds, 1992). Almarza (1996) found that although *some* beliefs may change because of what is learned during teacher education programs, she suggested that such changes might be more connected to students' prior knowledge than to what was taught in the programs. Resistance to changing a personal philosophy toward learning may be related to the depth of core beliefs, which, Pajares (1992) argues, are more difficult to change.

Peacock (2001), in one of the few empirical studies of teacher beliefs, found in his longitudinal study of 146 student-teachers in Hong Kong that beliefs concerning language learning are extremely stable and are unlikely to change. He nevertheless argued that it is essential to eliminate 'detrimental' beliefs that prospective teachers hold because these beliefs could hinder their future students' language learning. What is particularly relevant about Peacock's study in relation to the current study is that it took place in an Asian context where the prospective teachers had been English language learners themselves. He found that the teachers' deep-rooted beliefs, especially toward teaching and learning grammar and vocabulary, did not shift over time as a result of their teacher training program, but they remained stable and reflected the ways they managed to learn language themselves.

However, it is necessary to point out that some problems may arise when theories presented in teacher education programs attempt to correct 'detrimental' beliefs, especially when such beliefs may be widespread within the educational contexts in which the participants will eventually teach. This will be discussed more fully when we address the importance of the social context in language teaching, but a brief example of such a conflict is evident in Farrell's (2003, 2005) study of Wee Jin, a first-year Singaporean high school teacher. Wee Jin's first year of teaching was complicated and full of tensions because his beliefs toward second language learning, which were acquired in his pre-service teacher education program, ran counter to those held by the other teachers in his school.

Another issue to consider is that teachers' stated beliefs and actual teaching practices are often not in synchrony. Basturkmen *et al.* (2004) found that teachers' beliefs, which may have been obtained through teacher education programs, are often inconsistent with their actual teaching practices, especially when teachers have to make unplanned decisions. They explain that this discrepancy may be due to two types of knowledge involved in classroom decision-making: *abstract knowledge*, which reflects a technical understanding of theory, and *personal practical knowledge*, which may be deeper and reflects their true beliefs. Teachers may rely on abstract knowledge when planning what to do, but fall back on personal practical knowledge when spontaneous classroom decisions need to be made. Interestingly, Phan Le Ha (2008: 90) found that even native-speaking

TESOL teachers, who espoused CLT methodology in their teacher education classes, failed to teach in a communicative manner in actual practice. This gap between stated beliefs and actual practice was confusing for the Vietnamese TESOL students, who were wondering why their Australian lecturers in the courses on methodology, which were teaching them 'how' to teach, were teacher fronted and so boring because all the teachers did were to read lecture notes from beginning to end while students listened and took notes.

Summary of Teacher Cognition

Although the previous two sections examined the literature concerning teacher knowledge and teacher beliefs separately, it is necessary to reiterate that these two terms, as Pajares (1992) argues, are difficult to tease apart in order to establish clear definitions. Woods (1996), in his comprehensive study of teacher cognition, also noted the difficulty in separating the notions of knowledge and beliefs because they are part of the same mental processes. Therefore, he conflated these terms under one label to include beliefs, assumptions and knowledge (BAK). *Knowledge* includes commonly accepted facts, *assumptions* recognize acceptance of these facts and *beliefs* indicate a personal acceptance of a notion to be true. These processes, he argues, join together in influencing teachers' perceptions of teaching.

Borg (2003: 81) also uses the term 'teacher cognition' to describe the 'unobservable cognitive dimension of teaching – what teachers know, believe and think'. In addition to teacher knowledge and beliefs, he includes teachers' theories, attitudes, images, assumptions, metaphors, conceptions and perspectives *about* teaching, teachers, learning, students, subject matter, curricula, materials, instructional activities and the self. In his review of 64 studies that occurred between the 1970s and 2003, he found that all of these studies 'highlight[ed] the personal nature of teacher cognition, the role of experience in the development of these cognitions and the way in which instructional practice and cognition are mutually informing' (p. 83) and demonstrate the 'complexity of teachers' lives' (p. 86).

Teacher Identity

Now I would like to turn to the issue of teacher identity. In the past 25 years, numerous studies of teachers' professional identity in general education have been conducted. Beijaard *et al.* (2004) found in their review article that these studies have mainly followed three threads. The first is concerned with the process of identity formation, the second with clarifying the identity characteristics of teachers and the third involves an examination of professional identity through teachers' stories. Studies under the first category have shown that the process of identity formation involves constant movement between the personal and the professional, and that teachers' self-conceptions constantly evolve, often with some struggle (e.g. Coldron & Smith, 1999). Studies under the second category have dealt with specific issues that may influence professional identity, such as dealing with educational changes (e.g. Beijaard et al., 2000). Studies under the third category have relied on the teachers' storytelling to uncover instances of professional identity. In particular, under this category, the work of Connelly and Clandinin (1985, 1990, 1995, 1999) (see also Clandinin & Connelly, 1987, 1996, 2000) has been influential in showing that through stories, or narratives, teachers are able to create and recreate their professional identity through reference to the 'landscapes' in which they live and work.

The study of the professional identity of language teachers has followed the lead set in general education, especially in terms of classroom-based research, which has indicated that language teaching and language learning involved more than the application of an appropriate teaching methodology (e.g. Nunan, 1988), and what teachers think, believe, and know influence every aspect of classroom teaching (e.g. Borg, 2003; Burns, 1992; Golembek, 1998; Richards, 1998; Woods, 1996).

Varghese et al. (2005: 35) in their review of studies of language teacher identity note four prominent areas of research: (1) marginalization; (2) the position of non-native speaker teachers; (3) the status of language teaching as a profession and (4) the teacher-student relationship. The second of these, non-native speaker teachers, is particularly relevant for this book. Canagarajah (1999), for example, argues the commonly held notion that the linguistic abilities of native English speakers are superior to non-native English speakers[1] is a remnant of the political and economic power imperialist countries had over former colonies. This notion is perpetuated because native English-speaking teachers and researchers, especially from the 'Inner Circle' countries[2] (Canagarajah, 1999; Kachru, 1989, 1992), have had more opportunity to obtain advanced degrees in linguistics and applied linguistics from those countries, and thus have had a greater platform for disseminating Western ideas concerning pedagogy and language to other parts of the world (Canagarajah, 1999; Kubota, 1999; Pennycook, 1994, 1998). Liu (1998: 4) argues that these teaching methodologies, especially CLT endorsed by the Inner Circle countries, are politically loaded with a 'methodological dogmatism'.

The issue of the language identity of non-native English-speaking teachers has been found to influence hiring practices of English-teaching institutions' ESL contexts (e.g. Braine, 1999a, 1999b; Kamhi-Stein, 2004; Rampton, 1990; Tang, 1997), student attitudes toward teachers (e.g. Mahboob, 2004; Mahboob et al., 2004) and teachers' perceptions of themselves (e.g. Amin, 1997; Liu, 1999; Reves & Medgyes, 1994; Samimy & Brutt-Griffler, 1999).

Language identity is also an important issue for professional identity in contexts where non-native English-speaking teachers generally share a common language with their students. Reves and Medgyes (1994) found in their survey of 216 EFL/ESL teachers (of which only 10% claimed to be native English speakers) in 10 countries that although non-native English-speaking teachers generally feel that they are better 'qualified' than native English-speaking teachers, the teachers' language proficiency guides their teaching behavior. Feelings of linguistic limitations, Reves and Medgyes (1994) argue, can create a poor self-image and lead to feelings of inferiority when compared to native speakers. This may be especially true when non-native English-speaking teachers feel inadequate in adopting pedagogical methods from the West that may not be appropriate for their individual teaching contexts (Holliday, 1994).

Next I would like to consider in some detail two studies that explore the professional identities of foreign language teachers in second language contexts. First, Tsui (2007) looks at how her participant Minfang dealt with tensions between his own language learning and language teaching beliefs and the CLT practices that were imposed upon him as a language learner and as a language teacher in a Chinese tertiary context. Second, Phan Le Ha (2008) shows how Vietnamese-English language teachers construct their multiple identities after obtaining advanced degrees from Western TESOL institutions.

Tsui (2007)

Tsui's (2007) narrative study of the professional identity development of a Chinese English teacher found that the professional identity development of her participant, Minfang, was wrought with tension between his personal beliefs concerning language learning and the Western-influenced pedagogical philosophy at the Chinese university where he studied and subsequently became a teacher. As a poor boy from a minority region in China, he gained admission to the English department of a prestigious university through hard study. There he felt like a 'country bumpkin' because he not only needed to learn English from communicative language teaching (CLT), with which he was unfamiliar, but in addition, standard Cantonese as well. Because of his own language learning experiences using what was denigrated as 'traditional methods', he could not identify with CLT. He felt it was 'soft' because it did not explicitly teach language; it was 'unrealistic' because neither teachers nor students ever had the opportunity to use English in real communicative situations and it was 'cruel language teaching' because it ignored students' need to learn structure. Drawing upon his previously successful method of study, he 'secretly' studied on his own, focusing on structure and vocabulary to prepare for exams, but then was reprimanded by his teachers for not completing the CLT assignments. When he ultimately passed his exams, however, his teachers attributed his success to their CLT teaching, and not to the effort that he made studying.

Upon graduation, Minfang began teaching at his alma mater. He was required to teach using the CLT method even though he felt that 'hard' study was essential for students to pass the stringent exams. After an unannounced visit from an inspector found him teaching a grammar-based class, he was warned that the department would be ruined if he failed to teach CLT properly. Afraid for his career, he subsequently taught using only CLT methods, but he felt a conflict between his desires to do what he felt was best for his students and his allegiance to his institution. In spite of his reservations about CLT teaching, Minfang became recognized as an authority in CLT: he trained new teachers at the university in CLT pedagogy, and he presented model classes to observers. Engagement in these activities enabled him to strongly identify as a member of his department. However, even though he aligned his practices with his university, his beliefs toward language learning did not fundamentally change.

It was not until Minfang learned the theoretical underpinnings of CLT in graduate school that he found that fluency and accuracy in language education were not dichotomous approaches to language learning. His graduate study enabled him to reconcile the tensions that he had in teaching and enabled him to 'theorize his personal practical knowledge, which empowered him to reclaim the meaning of EFL teaching' (p. 673). Up to that point, he felt like he was a 'faked CLT practitioner' to deal with a teaching approach that has been idolized as 'a religion' in his university (p. 673), and it wasn't until Minfang explored his own deeply rooted beliefs about language learning in conjunction with Western applied linguistics that he was able to appropriate an identity as a language teacher that was comfortable for him.

What is particularly tantalizing about Tsui's study is its clear illustration of Minfang's tensions in his professional identity development through the process of situated learning (Lave & Wenger, 1991; Wenger, 1998) in his struggle to come to terms with the linguistic imperialism (Phillipson, 1992) that shaped the Western pedagogical practices (CLT) that were enforced at his university. Minfang's prior experiences of language learning were ignored and trivialized, making him feel marginalized as a language learner and as a language teacher. Such marginalization in language teaching has been criticized as a product of colonialism (Pennycook, 1994, 1998), where the powerful inner circle of English-speaking countries from the West, known as the 'Center', are said to aggressively and systematically linguistically 'colonize' the countries located in the 'Periphery' through imposing the notion that English is a superior language and that Western ELT practices – namely CLT – are the superior method to spread it (Phillipson, 1992).

Minfang's university's assumption that CLT was superior to the more traditional forms of learning that he was accustomed to seems to be the result of the Western positivist view of teaching that Western teachers brought with them to China during the 1980s. Sampson (1984: 29) argued a prevailing attitude among applied linguists at that time considered the pedagogical methods they brought with them to China to be modern and correct, and the traditional pedagogical methodologies employed by the Chinese to be 'old-fashioned' and incorrect. This led the Western teachers to consider methods of memorization with 'derision and scorn'. That this attitude still exists today is reflected in Bax's (2003: 279) observation that a 'country without CLT is somehow backward'.

Phan Le Ha (2008)

Phan Le Ha (2008: 87), in her study of Vietnamese EFL teachers' identity, also explored reasons why CLT, which she calls 'a colonizing force' in Western TESOL classrooms, may not be entirely applicable for the Vietnamese context, explaining that cultural expectations of teachers and students may result in ethical and moral conflicts, especially when examining the traditional role of the teacher in Vietnam. English language learning is considered to be serious business to be carried out in order for students to attain their serious goals. The CLT notion that teachers are merely facilitators who enable students to direct their own learning through inductive and 'entertaining' communicative activities goes against the cultural grain that sees teachers as moral leaders who are the holders of knowledge. As a person who initially learned English in a TESEP (Holliday, 1994) context and who subsequently obtained advanced degrees from abroad, Phan Le Ha was in a similar position to that of her participants, and she poignantly writes about how the teachers (and how she herself) took their multiple identities and claimed an identity as a Vietnamese teacher of English:

> The Western-trained EIL Vietnamese teachers experienced changes in their identities as a result of their exposure to new context with different cultural and pedagogical practices, but they seemed to negotiate their identities on the basis of 'dominant' identities. These consisted of Vietnamese national/cultural identity, Vietnamese teacher and Vietnamese student. These are the very identities that provided them with strong foundations and commitments, on which they asserted all their identities.
>
> These teachers negotiated their Vietnamese identities alongside their multiple identities. They identified themselves with different groups, such as Australian lecturers, Vietnamese students, Vietnamese teachers of English, Vietnamese teachers and Western-trained teachers, and acknowledged changes in their identities. However, they insisted on holding on to their 'existing' and persisting Vietnamese values. (p. 182)

Phan Le Ha's (2008) study is an important addition to the literature investigating NNESTs because it clearly gives a voice to teachers from the Periphery in Circle research. In writing about her own language learning experiences, Phan Le Ha (2008) says she sees harmonization and complementation of her two identities – her inbred Vietnamese identity and her acquired Western identity. These two identities, she asserts, have enabled her to maintain her cultural identity as a Vietnamese teacher and as a scholar and academic in the Western arena who can introduce Vietnamese philosophies into a previously Western-dominated discourse of TESOL. She recommends that TESOL students from Peripheral countries explore their multiple and emerging hybrid identities through explicit and systematic ways in teacher education programs to enable them to develop complimentary and professional identities that will enable them to gain the linguistic and professional power from the West and to maintain and promote their own unique cultural identities to add to the body of knowledge of Western applied linguistics.

Importance of the Social Context in Teaching

Both of the studies discussed in the previous section draw attention to the relationship between the teachers' sociopolitical and cultural context of where they have learned English, and where they teach English and to their professional identities. This section turns its focus toward the wider social context. In particular, it focuses on Holliday's (1994) distinction of two academic cultures that shape foreign language teaching throughout the world. These two academic cultures, which shape the beliefs and practices among teachers within their schools' communities of practice (Lave & Wenger, 1991) may account for having what Peacock (2001) has called 'detrimental' beliefs concerning language learning and will be considered in some depth.

Holliday (1994) describes two methodological cultures that have emerged in English language teaching, each with different aims and purposes, and argues that the social context of where language teaching takes place is an essential factor to consider when developing materials and encouraging pedagogical practices. The first one is 'BANA', which reflects the methodology that developed from second language acquisition research in Britain, Australasia and North America. Published research from BANA countries generally considers the best methodologies of language learning and language teaching to be learner-centered, and the focus is on communicative language teaching. These methodologies follow an integrationist paradigm that uses skills-based and discovery approaches toward learning (Bernstein, 1971, in Holliday, 1994). The second is called 'TESEP'. The methodology under this culture evolved from teaching that occurred in tertiary, secondary and primary academic institutions throughout the world that teach English as a foreign language. Teaching methodologies under the TESEP category tend to follow a transmission style of teaching and often employ the grammar-translation method. TESEP teachers are usually (but not always) native speakers of the language of the culture in which they live, and the way that they learned English is usually (but not always) from the traditional methodologies employed in their culture. Education in TESEP-oriented cultures is collectionist[3] in nature where there is often a strong allegiance toward specialized subject knowledge such as literature or linguistics (Holliday, 1994).

In spite of there being two distinct methodological cultures concerning second language education, they have not enjoyed the same degree of power in their global influence. The impact and influence of BANA methodologies is evident in second language teacher education programs, language teaching conferences and academic journals and books (Holliday, 2005). Western scholars often disapprove of traditional methods used by TESEP teachers. Richards and Rogers (2001), for example, hold the view that grammar translation 'is a method for which there is no theory' (p. 5), and yet this method is widely employed throughout the world where many language learners can and do gain proficiency. Widespread beliefs that Western methodologies are the 'best' and 'correct' way to teach and learn foreign languages may not be well received by the teachers or students, as demonstrated in Tsui's (2007) and Phan Le Ha's (2008) studies. Another example is provided by Canagarajah (1993), who found that his Tamil students resisted the content and methodologies in an imported EFL textbook because they did not want to acquire the culture or the discourse of British English. Instead, his students were willing to study the *grammar* and *vocabulary* of British English to pass exams in order to further their educational goals. The students' attitudes in shunning communicative language learning on the one hand but embracing grammar-based product-oriented learning on the other hand may seem contradictory, but Canagarajah argues that such attitudes enable students to give priority to learning the language while at the same time retaining their own sense of identity.

Prabhu's (1990) argument that different teaching methods are best for different contexts, and less attention should be paid to what would be the 'best' method, and more to what is the most plausible method for a teacher to employ to result in productive teaching is a notion that is being examined by more non-native English-speaking TESEP teachers (e.g. Brutt-Griffler & Samimy, 2001; Liu, 1999; Pham, 2005; Phan Le Ha, 2008; Tsui, 2007).

The Japanese Context

Now I would like to turn our attention to examine teacher beliefs, knowledge and identity within the Japanese context. As discussed in the previous chapter, English language education in Japan has undergone several shifts in pedagogical ideologies that are related to the perceived needs of English education for Japanese in Japan. Whereas the purpose of foreign language learning was initially to gain access to Western knowledge, fears of losing a sense of national Japanese identity led to the notion that English education in Japan was to provide a window to view oneself as a Japanese (Ike, 1995; MEXT, 2003), and also as a gatekeeping method for gaining access to higher education (Kitao & Kitao, 1995; Ota, 1994). In spite of a number of educational reforms by MEXT that aim to improve the English communicative abilities of Japanese for them to take their place in an international world, Hashimoto (2000: 39) argues 'the commitment of the Japanese government to internationalization in education actually means the 'Japanization' of Japanese learners of English'. Considering the discussion in the previous section that called CLT a 'colonizing force' (Phan Le Ha, 2008), Japanese institutional resistance to adopting communicative methods may be somewhat understandable. Nevertheless, the official discourse is confusing – particularly for secondary school teachers who are required to teach 'communicatively' on one hand, but on the other hand, have a duty to their students to ensure their successful climb up the academic ladder. The 2003 Action Plan has laid out a number of concrete steps to be taken in order to raise the communicative abilities of Japanese in response to the demands of industry to improve the English skills of those who are joining the workforce. But as discussed in the introduction to this book, unless some focus is on *university* English teachers and on university English classes, the Action Plan, with its top-down directive, is unlikely to be successful. To date, there has been a considerable amount of research conducted on the teaching practices, beliefs and identity of secondary school English teachers in the Japanese context (e.g. Browne & Wada, 1998; Gorsuch, 1999, 2000, 2001; Nishino, 2008; Sakui, 2004; Sato, 2002; Sato & Kleinsasser, 2004), but relatively few that have focused on tertiary teachers. A selection of these studies is highlighted in Table 3.1, followed by a more in-depth discussion of three of the studies that are explicitly concerned with professional identity and that are particularly pertinent to my own studies: Duff and Uchida, 1997; Simon-Maeda, 2004a; and Stewart, 2005, 2006.

The context of Duff and Uchida's (1997) study was actually a post-secondary institution, an established language school and not a university. But this study is important because it was among the first to investigate professional identity in relation to the EFL environment in Japan. The participants, two Americans (one male and one female) and two Japanese (both female), were interviewed and observed to see how sociocultural identity transforms over time and how culture is transmitted through teaching. This language school required its teachers to incorporate culture into their classes and to create an 'entertaining, mind-broadening, nurturing and exciting classroom environment' (p. 469), but the teachers' individual interpretations of this philosophy resulted in practices not entirely congruent with the school's philosophy. In other words, the school's planned curriculum and what was actually taught differed because of the impact the teachers' personal experiences of education, work, language learning and travel had on their teaching beliefs and teaching practices.

Various conflicts arose in some of the teachers because they were unable to identify with the espoused philosophy of the school. For example, one of the Japanese teachers, Miki, resented the institute's requirement to teach culture. She considered herself a specialist in teaching *language* and an expert role model for students to emulate, and she believed that the entertaining aspects of language learning should be left up to the native English-speaking teachers. The proposed curriculum of the school differs from the lived curriculum because the school's philosophy is reinterpreted

Table 3.1 Studies of English teacher identity in the Japanese context

Reference	Participants	Method	Theoretical model	Focus
Duff and Uchida (1997)	2 FJTE 1 MNTE 1 FNTE	Ethnographic study (six months)	Sociocultural identity: Hall (1995)	Professional identity
Matsuura et al. (2001)	41?NTE college teachers 41?JTE 300?JSE	Questionnaire	None	Beliefs about learning and teaching
Bueno and Caesar (2003)	3 FNTE 11 MNTE	Autobiographical narratives of teaching experiences	None	Professional identity
Sakui and Gaies (2003)	1 JFTE	Narrative self-study	None	Teacher beliefs
Simon-Maeda (2004)	7 FNTE 2 FJTE	Life-history interviews	Narrative analysis: Polking-horne (1988) Ochs and Capps (2001)	Professional identity
Stewart (2005, 2006)	3 FJTE 1 MJTE 2 FNTE 2 MNTE	Three-stage interviews	Positioning theory (Harre and van Langenhove, 1999)	Professional identity
Kiernan (2010)	15 MNTE 7 FNTE 9 FJTE 11 MJTE	Interviews	Discourse analysis: Fairclough (2003)	Professional identity

FJTE = Female Japanese teacher of English
MJTE = Male Japanese teacher of English
FNTE = Female native teacher of English
MNTE = Male native teacher of English
JSE = Japanese students of English
? = Gender is undetermined

and filtered through the teachers' lived experiences that shape what they do in the classroom. Duff and Uchida (1997) found that as students, none of the teachers in their study had been socialized into the type of teaching or the type of learning that the institute promoted. This was one reason why the teachers needed to negotiate and renegotiate their professional identities in order to carry out the duties of their jobs. Self-image and beliefs were found to be in a state of flux and identity shifted through constant negotiations between themselves, their students and the context of the language school.

Although Duff and Uchida (1997) provide important insight into the process of teacher identity development, the context of their study is a language school where the overall goals of the institution are focused on language learning and where the philosophy of the school shapes its curriculum as well as the teachers' practices. The participants self-identified as language teachers and they were selected for Duff and Uchida's study on the basis of their reputation as good English *language* teachers. University contexts differ significantly in numerous ways from a language school, and therefore I would like to now consider two studies that share a greater degree of commonality with my studies.

Simon-Maeda (2004a: 414) investigated the relationship between gender and identity in nine female EFL college and university teachers in Japan. Only one participant was Japanese, one was Korean-born Japanese and the remaining seven were foreign teachers with different ethnic and racial backgrounds. Adopting a feminist critical perspective for her analysis, she found that professional identity was formed through the participants' multiple identities as 'daughters, expatriates, racial minorities or socioeconomically disadvantaged', and that many of their struggles were due to cultured expectations of women in a male-dominated work environment. Simon-Maeda found that cultured expectations of the foreign teachers also shaped their identity and that their perceptions of their professional expertise were related to how they strategically positioned themselves within Japanese society and within their workplace contexts.

Stewart (2005) conducted a narrative study of eight English teachers in Japanese higher education (four Japanese, three Americans and one Briton) from the perspective of professionalism and expertise in her PhD thesis. She found that her participants constructed their identity by positioning themselves according to social, institutional and student expectations. She also found that job satisfaction and agency influenced their perceptions of themselves as teachers and professionals. Furthermore, the participants' perceived position in relation to English was more influential over their attitudes toward teaching it.

All three Japanese-based studies reported above have shown that teachers' identities are shaped by the wider social context of Japan as well as the individual contexts of their workplaces. Identities are comprised of previous personal and educational experiences, the people whom they work with and the students whom they teach. What are particularly striking are the differences in the identification process between the Japanese teachers and the native English-speaking teachers.

Although it has been argued that native speakers, especially from the 'Inner Circle' countries that influence English language pedagogy and research, enjoy positions of higher status than non-native English speakers (e.g. Canagarajah, 1999; Kachru, 1989; Medgyes, 1992; Phillipson, 1992), expat teachers are often relegated to marginal positions when working in EFL contexts (e.g. Caesar & Bueno, 2003; Johnston, 1997, 1999).

This is also true of the non-Japanese university teachers portrayed in the studies conducted by Simon-Maeda (2004a) and Stewart (2005, 2006). The teachers in these two studies felt that a prevailing attitude existed that any native English speaker could teach English. This belief has led to feelings of deprofessionalization among some of the participants, who say they are perceived as human tape recorders and living representatives of an exotic and foreign culture to be on display for their students. The notion that foreign teachers are temporary and replaceable (even though many were married to Japanese nationals and intended to reside in Japan permanently) has resulted in discriminatory hiring practices[4] that often include limited and nonrenewable term contracts (e.g. Hall, 1998; Hayes, 2011; McVeigh, 2002). Job satisfaction was related to the connectivity the teachers felt with their university communities, not only in terms of the positions they held, but also in the courses that they were assigned to teach. In many cases, prestigious courses were assigned to Japanese teachers, but less prestigious ones, such as English conversation, were given to the foreign teachers.

Stewart (2005) explained that the different language identities of the English-speaking teachers and Japanese teachers contribute to different perceptions of their professional roles. Japanese teachers mainly saw their expertise resting in knowledge of their academic subjects (translation, phonetics and literature) and through interaction with other experts within the same field. They thought of themselves as 'enablers' leading students toward better understanding of English texts from a Japanese perspective. They favored teacher-centered classes, because they felt that leaving the learning up to the students (an implied criticism of the methodology used by the non-Japanese teachers) was shirking one's duties as a teacher. For them, professional expertise did not lie in their teaching, and they did not feel the need to hold themselves to standards typically espoused in ELT discourse concerning 'good' language teachers.

The foreign teachers, on the other hand, were more committed to teaching according to the standards of Westernized ELT professional discourse and saw themselves as expert teachers. Nevertheless, both Simon-Maeda (2004a) and Stewart (2005) found that the native English-speaking teachers desired to distance themselves from language teaching in order to create a professional identity that was more in alignment with their Japanese colleagues. This was done through attaining advanced degrees, which they hoped would enhance their standing within their communities. It was also done through focusing on developing students' cognitive abilities and skills through critical thinking rather than what they claimed to be superficial and decontextualized language instruction.

Simon-Maeda (2004a) and Stewart's (2005) studies demonstrate that the difficulties foreign teachers have in constructing their professional identities in Japanese higher education is due largely to the complexity of the cultural context. Stewart's study also explicates reasons for the differences in how the foreign and Japanese teachers identify as university English teachers.

Although the differences in Japanese and foreign teachers are interesting, Japanese teachers constitute 97% of tertiary educators in Japan (MEXT, 2006). More light may be shed upon their beliefs, teaching practices and identity when not comparing them to their foreign counterparts. The beliefs and practices of the Japanese teachers warrant further exploration, which is the goal of this book, especially when considering the widespread power that they hold over English language education in Japan as discussed earlier in Chapter 1.

Summary of Chapter 3

This chapter has introduced the literature that deals with teacher knowledge, teacher beliefs and teacher identity. It first summarized the literature from the field of general education, followed by the literature that subsequently emerged from second and foreign language education. Teachers were no longer seen as 'teaching machines' who taught subject matter through researched and academically approved pedagogical practices, but as individuals with their own personal experiences and personal knowledge that impacts every aspect of classroom teaching. The relationship of teacher beliefs and classroom practices was also discussed. Deep-rooted beliefs concerning language teaching and language learning remain stable, and attempts to change such beliefs through teacher education programs may be unsuccessful. Studies of language teacher identity have often investigated issues that influence teachers' sense of identity, such as marginalization, native versus non-native speaker teachers, the status of language teaching as a profession and the student-teacher relationship (Varghese et al., 2005). The studies reviewed in this chapter showed that some non-native speaker teachers experience pedagogical and methodological struggle in their language teaching. The Western applied linguistics methods, which espouse communicative language teaching, were shown to be not only difficult for non-native English-speaking teachers to implement in their classes, but they may also be culturally inappropriate. The chapter concluded with a discussion of teacher identity in the Japanese context, where I focused on three studies that dealt with on the identity development of teachers in post-secondary and higher education.

In the following chapter, I will introduce the research method I utilized for my studies, introduce my participants and describe the data-collection process and analysis.

Notes

(1) For a discussion concerning differences between native-speaking and non-native-speaking teachers, see also Davies (1991), Edge (1996) or Rampton (1990).
(2) The 'Inner Circle' refers to powerful countries such as the United States, Great Britain, Canada and Australia, where English is, and has traditionally been, the language spoken. 'The Periphery' refers to less powerful countries with an outsider status that also use English, but are accorded much less prestige. See Phillipson's (1992) book *Linguistic Imperialism* for a full account.
(3) Bernstein (1971, in Holliday, 1994) argues that two educational paradigms exist: collectionist and integrationist. Education under the collectionist paradigm (which is based upon Western secondary education) had distinct and rigid boundaries between subjects taught and learned in schools. The integrationist paradigm is more commonly found in Western primary schools, where the boundaries between lessons taught by teachers are more blurred.
(4) See Hayes (2011) for an interesting discussion on the hiring criteria for English teachers at Japanese universities. In a series of interviews with 24 Japanese and non-Japanese university faculty on hiring committees, Hayes found that Japanese and non-Japanese applicants were evaluated by different standards in the hiring process and that criteria for both groups of teachers included benefits and constraints that were motivated by gendered and racial ideologies.

4 The Participants and the Data Collection

Introduction

The purpose of this chapter is to outline the data-collection process for the studies that are presented in Chapters 5–7. First I discuss narrative research as a means to investigate teachers' professional lives. Then I provide a brief introduction to the eight participant teachers who are featured in this book, followed by a discussion on how the participants' interviews were carried out, transcribed and analyzed. The chapter concludes with a brief discussion of my own position within the studies, for I am simultaneously an insider and an outsider within the research context.

Narrative as a Research Method

Narrative research, the methodological approach for the three studies in this book, is grounded in the tradition of qualitative research (Lincoln & Denzin, 1994). In particular, it makes extensive use of the actual words that people use to tell their stories in describing their life experiences (e.g. Casey, 1995–1996; Chase, 2005; Creswell, 2007; Riessman, 1993, 2002, 2008). Narrative research has been found to be an ideal tool for analyzing the beliefs, knowledge, practice and identity of teachers in general education (e.g. Clandinin & Connelly, 2000; Connelly & Clandinin, 1995; Elbaz, 1983; Shulman, 1987; Watson, 2006) as well as of teachers in foreign language education (e.g. Bell, 2002; Pavlenko, 2002; Tsui, 2007).

Collecting Teachers' Stories

If identity is 'that which emerges in and through narrative', as Hinchman and Hinchman (2001: xiv) suggest, then the stories that teachers tell are an ideal tool for analyzing teacher beliefs, knowledge, practice and identity (e.g. Clandinin & Connelly, 2000; Connelly & Clandinin, 1995; Elbaz, 1983; Shulman, 1987; Watson, 2006). Narrative research deals with any text or discourse that focuses on the stories of people, usually in the form of autobiographies, biographies, life histories and oral histories (e.g. Casey, 1995–1996; Chase, 2005; Creswell, 2007; Riessman, 1993, 2002, 2008), and makes use of words that 'tell the story of individuals unfolding in a chronology of their experiences, set within their personal, social and historical context, and including the important themes in those lived experiences' (Creswell, 2007: 57). Narrative research is considered ideal for uncovering the complexity of human behavior because it is human-centered, situates itself in practice and explores the perspectives of those under study (e.g. Lyons & LaBoskey, 2002; Webster & Mertova, 2007).

In TESOL and in SLA research, there have been two interrelated modes of analysis for investigating teachers' narratives. The first is *narrative inquiry*, which looks at the meanings that lie underneath the stories people tell (Bell, 2002). The second is *narrative study*, which adds the underlying sociocultural, sociohistorical and social influences in the analysis of a person's narrative (Pavlenko, 2002).

Pavlenko (2002: 213) distinguishes the two as follows: 'Narrative inquiry is usually understood to be an ethnographic approach to eliciting understandings, whereas narrative study has a greater focus on narrative construction from a variety of perspectives'. These two approaches are interrelated and will be described more fully below.

Bell (2002: 209) says that narrative inquiry relies upon the story structures reflected in the stories that people tell in order to comprehend the meaning of their beliefs and experiences that lie underneath. She argues that the positive aspects of narrative inquiry are that it 'allows researchers to understand experience.... get at information that people do not consciously know themselves.... [and] illuminates the temporal notion of experience, recognizing that one's understanding of people and events change'. The difficulty with such inquiry, she cautions, comes with necessarily subjective analysis of the narrative data that imposes meaning upon people's stories, which may not be recognized in some circles as a legitimate (scientific) research method.

Pavlenko (2002: 216) argues that narrative inquiry on its own is insufficient as a research method because it looks at people's stories as factual statements, when they are in reality permeated by sociocultural, sociohistorical and social influences. Because of this, she argues that narratives must be seen as discursive constructions and examined for 'whose stories are being heard and why, and whose stories are still missing, being misunderstood, or being misinterpreted'. In other words, an approach using narrative *study* investigates not only the individual utterances of the person under study, but all the underlying issues as well.

The studies in this book rely upon verbatim accounts of the teacher participants in order to examine the intersection of their personal and working lives, which in turn enables the construction of a sense of their professional identity. I adopt a narrative study perspective in that I also look for sociocultural, sociohistorical and other social influences that are behind the stories that my study's participants tell. A more detailed explanation of how the narratives were analyzed will be discussed in greater detail within the individual studies in Chapters 5–7.

The Participant Teachers

Table 4.1 below provides a brief description of each of the participants in ascending order of age. All names are pseudonyms. They teach in a variety of tertiary institutions throughout Japan in various positions and the physical locations of the universities are omitted to protect the teachers' privacy. Because there are so few female professors in Japan, this is especially important for the female participants who may be identifiable merely by stating the prefecture in which they work. I knew several of the participants slightly prior to the study, but most were introduced to me by friends and colleagues. They were selected for these studies on the basis of their willingness to be interviewed, and in Miwa's case, her willingness to allow me to observe her classroom teaching. That there is only one male teacher in this book is merely a coincidence. Although I had interviewed several other male teachers during the process of my research, Taka is the only one who fit the criteria of the study in Chapter 5, namely being a relatively new university English teacher.

Interviews

In narrative studies, multiple, lengthy and in-depth interviews have often been recommended for uncovering life stories (e.g. Atkinson, 1998; 2001). To collect narrative data from the studies' participants, face-to-face interviews were conducted between December 2007 and December 2008 throughout Japan. The interviews were carried out in a relaxed manner and held at times and in places convenient to the participants.

For the studies in Chapters 5 and 6, I used Seidman's (2006: 17–18) model for in-depth interviews. He suggests that three 90-minute interviews, which occur over a period of several weeks, are optimal for obtaining meaningful data to study teachers' lives. Under his framework, the first interview uncovers life histories, to understand '[a participant's] experience in context'. The second interview reconstructs lived experiences within the context under study by uncovering 'the myriad details of our participants' experiences in the area we are studying'. The third and final interview makes use of the first two interviews by asking participants to reflect back on their experiences to examine how these experiences connect to their present lives.

Taking into account the teachers' schedules and physical locations that were often in regional areas, it was necessary to adjust the number of

Table 4.1 Participant teachers' biographical data

Name	G	Age	Position	University	Research interests	Degrees	Collection method	Featured in chapters
Shizuko	F	32	Part-time lecturer	National, private	American literature	BA, MA	Interview (90 min)	Chapter 6
Taka	M	33	Assistant professor	Private	Adult and community education	BA, MA, PhD**	Interview (450 min)	Chapter 5
Kana	F	35	Assistant professor	Prefectural	English literature/ education/ culture	BA, MA, PhD	Interview (90 min)	Chapter 5 Chapter 6
Miwa	F	35	Assistant professor	National	American literature	BA, MA, PhD	Interview (670 min) Classroom observation (240 min)	Chapter 5 Chapter 6 Chapter 7
Kumiko	F	42	Assistant professor	Private	Literature***, women's studies English education	BA, BA MA, MA, PhD**	Interview (180 min)	Chapter 5, Chapter 6

Table 4.1 (Continued)

Name	G	Age	Position	University	Research interests	Degrees	Collection method	Featured in chapters
Naomi	F	45	Associate professor	Prefectural	American studies and folklore	BA, MA, PhD	Interview (90 min)	Chapter 6
Keiko	F	57	Associate professor	National	American literature TESOL	BA, MA, MA	Interview (90 min)	Chapter 6
Taeko	F	60	Part-time lecturer	Private, national, prefectural	English linguistics*** English education	BA, MA	Interview (90 min)	Chapter 6

* = Current area of interest
** = Unfinished: either withdrew before completing dissertation or currently working toward doctorate
*** = Studied as an undergraduate only
**** = Currently researches on both topics
G = Gender

interviews held for this research. Some participants were only interviewed once, but I still followed the progression of Seidman's (2006) protocol, which is described below.

The interviews were conducted as follows. First, participants were asked to recount biographical details, including their language learning experiences that led them to a career in teaching English. Second, participants were asked to describe their teaching context and their relationships with their colleagues and their students. Third, participants were asked to reflect back on their experiences to examine how these connected to their present lives. Finally, participants talked about what they envisaged doing in the future.

Prior to the interviews, I prepared detailed interview guides designed to generate 'specific concrete life stories' (Chase, 2002: 84). I prepared open-ended questions that would encourage participants to speak freely, but during the interviews they were free to direct the flow of the conversation. As a result, the participants' interviews differed greatly, with various issues raised and discussed. Because the interviews proceeded in a dialogical manner, topics were brought up and discussed by the participants that did not occur to me while preparing the interview guides.

By nature, interviews are asymmetrical modes of interaction where the interviewer retains power over the direction of the interview (Briggs, 2002; Kvale, 2006). Nevertheless, as Josselson (2007) argues, they are unpredictable, subjective and involve, to a certain degree, a collaborative relationship between the interviewer and the interviewee. Meaningful interviews thus involve more than questioning on the part of the researcher and answering on the part of the researched (Mishler, 1986).

Although I did not know well any of the interview participants prior to the interviews, they spoke freely and openly with little prompting from me, which indicates, I believe, a good interviewer-interviewee relationship was established, based on a certain amount of rapport and trust (Arksey & Knight, 1999). That the participants often interrupted their discourse to ask for advice on teaching or language learning may indicate such trust in me as an older native English-speaker and, in many cases, a more experienced teacher.

The interviews might have been easier for the participants had I shared a cultural background with the participants and had I conducted the interviews in Japanese. Although the participants spoke fluent English, code-switching did occur in nearly all of the interviews, indicating some English difficulty for the participants during the course of the interviews. However, since I can speak Japanese, I was able to understand most of the code-switching that occurred.

Furthermore, it is plausible to suggest that *because* the interviews were conducted in English, the participants might have felt more at ease in speaking frankly. Because of the hierarchal nature of Japanese society (see Nakane, 1970), speaking in Japanese, especially when talking to an older person, involves formal and distant language, which could inhibit frank communication. Indeed, one of the youngest participants said one of her greatest difficulties was learning how to speak politely when communicating with her older colleagues, but this was not apparent during our interview, for when it came to a close, she exclaimed, 'This is fun talking about myself'.

Transcription Method for Interviews

Decisions concerning transcription methods, which reflect the specific goals of the research, are among the first interpretive decisions made by researchers, and reflect the theoretical perspective, methodological orientation and substantive interest of the researcher and the subsequent interpretations of the readers (Reissman, 2008). For example, 'conversational analysts' create detailed transcripts, attending to both linguistic and non-linguistic features of language, and they include the length of pauses, false starts, intonation, overlapping utterances and so on (Gee, 2005). Researchers interested in focusing on thematic issues may work with easy-to-read 'clean' or 'sanitized' transcripts that appear to be more like a written text than a spoken one (Elliot, 2005).

I transcribed each interview immediately after the interview, and in the case of multiple interviews, before the next one, and I used the following transcription process for this study. First, I made a version that included all of the participant's utterances, including false starts, hesitant language, language fillers, such as 'you know', as well as any code-switching into Japanese. Then, retaining this copy, I created a second, 'cleaned-up' version. Most false starts, conversational fillers and simple grammatical mistakes were eliminated. This version was sent to the interview participants immediately after each interview to confirm the accuracy of the final renditions. As the participants may be unaware of the grammatical idiosyncrasies of spoken discourse, the original version might have made them feel self-conscious and hesitant to use English in the subsequent interviews.

My studies focus more on *what* teachers say they do than *how* they describe what they do; therefore, I have used the second version of the interview transcripts as described above. For readability in the analysis and interpretation section that follows, the transcripts were dealt with in the following ways. The participants' narratives were written in sentence form with appropriate punctuation. I kept the participants' narratives as close as possible to the original, but eliminated excessive conversational fillers (such as 'you know'). Simple grammatical mistakes were repaired, such as by adding an 's' to plural words and correcting verb tense. However, basic sentence structure and word order was not changed. Table 4.2, an extract from the first interview with Kumiko, shows how this was done:

The following extracts from the interviews provide some examples of the transcription process:

(1) 'Well... ...uh... yeesss, certain passages they will understand'. (Miwa)
(2) 'I am basically a nerd [laughter]. A literature **nut** kind of person'. (Miwa)
(3) 'They didn't like that. *Maa, shigatta ga nai, na* [Well, that's just too bad]'. (Kumiko)

I did not measure the exact length of pauses or deal with overlaps, although noticeable pauses are accounted for. As indicated in Example 1, a short pause in the conversation is indicated as '...' and a longer pause of more than 10 seconds is indicated as '... ...'. Omitted sentences or phrases are

Table 4.2 Example of interview data

Original transcription version	Revised transcription version
And when I was a high school student, the score of English, I mean the score of the English was pretty good. My grades, my grades of English is pretty good even though I don't like English. I don't know why. But just you know, even though I don't like English, but I can get a good grade. So you know my parents think, thought, 'Oh she is **good** at English' but actually I didn't like English so much. La la la. I don't hate English, but it is not my favorite subject you know. Yeah, but you know it is just...maybe I was not critical when I was young. I just followed my parents' way.	And when I was a high school student my score of English was pretty good. My grades were pretty good even though I didn't like English. I don't know why. But even though I didn't like English, I could get a good grade. So my parents thought, 'Oh, she is **good** at English'. [...] English was not my favorite subject. But, you know, maybe I was not critical when I was young. I just followed my parents' way.

indicated by three dots enclosed within brackets: [...]. Intonation was dealt with when it seemed to be particularly important, and it is shown by lengthening the word through its spelling (yeesss) or with boldface when a word was emphasized. Emotive feelings are described in brackets, as shown in Example 2. When a participant spoke Japanese, the original is shown in italics with its English translation in brackets, as shown in Example 3.

Process of Analysis

All of the interviews were read through thoroughly a number of times. The data was first sorted to create a profile presenting a chronological biography for each participant. Seidman (2006: 119) argues that creating profiles of interview participants is a useful starting point for examining interview data and that he has 'found that crafting a profile or a vignette of a participant's experience is an effective way of sharing interview data and opening up one's interview material to analysis and interpretation'.

Next, I used a qualitative software analysis program called NVivo to 'make sense of the data' (Silverman, 1993). I analyzed the transcripts by coding them into two categories that NVivo calls 'free nodes' and 'tree nodes' that can be conceptually linked to other nodes and to other data stored in NVivo (see Bazeley, 2007, or Gibbs, 2002, for comprehensive explanations of NVivo software).

The initial analysis of the data followed a data-driven approach where the interviews were examined line-by-line in order to generate theory from the data (e.g. Glaser & Strauss, 1967; Strauss & Corbin, 1990). Main tree nodes, dozens of sub-nodes and analytical memos were created. This stage of the data analysis enabled me to become thoroughly familiar with the data and to link various themes to each of the participants. An example of the tree node of 'Teaching' and some of its sub-nodes is shown below:

- Teaching
    - Attitudes toward teaching
    - Balancing teaching and research
    - Beliefs about self as a teacher
        - Allowed to make mistakes
        - I'm a *sempai*
        - Teachers should know everything
        - Teachers should not make mistakes
    - Beliefs about teaching
        - Connecting material to outside world
        - Back to basics

- What is important for students to know
- Students need to think for themselves
  o Difficulties in teaching
    - Teaching is boring
    - Hard to choose appropriate materials
    - Can't identify as language teacher
    - Lack instincts for teaching

Classroom Observations

Data for Chapter 7 also includes that which was obtained from three classroom observations of Miwa, who is also featured in Chapters 5 and 6. A more detailed description of how these observations were carried out will be presented in Chapter 7, but a brief description is as follows: Each classroom observation lasted 90 minutes, and was held in November and December 2008 at a university in the Tokyo area. Each class was audio recorded and extensive field notes were taken. Interviews were conducted with the participant after the initial analysis of the audio data, and the field notes were used to clarify and expand upon the initial findings.

My Position within the Studies

Before proceeding further, it is necessary to acknowledge my own position within this study, for I am simultaneously an outsider and an insider within the research context. From an insider perspective, I too am a university English teacher, familiar with many of the day-to-day workings of the Japanese university system. I have worked in several university contexts, as a part-time teacher, a contracted teacher and ultimately as a tenured associate professor. As a person who has lived in Japan for more than 30 years, with a Japanese husband and Japanese children, I am also quite familiar with many of the constraints of Japanese culture. As noted above, although the interviews were conducted in English, I could still understand the discourse when the participants code-switched into Japanese.

From an outsider perspective, most notably, I am a native speaker of English. As such, I never had to consciously struggle to attain proficiency in the language that I teach. Furthermore, my educational background differs from the participants in that I never had to endure Japanese 'examination hell' to gain access to higher education. I began teaching English in Japan at a time when native English speakers were rare, and I was able to obtain a tenured position teaching English at a university not because of my educational qualifications, but because of my 'native-speakerness'. I was what Thornbury (2002) called a 'backpacker' teacher who had the type of personality and a certain amount of drive to become a professional teacher. As I developed an interest in second language learning, I went to graduate school. I studied applied linguistics as developed from Western research centers, which subsequently have been criticized as politically motivated (Pennycook, 1994, 1998) methods to spread 'linguistic imperialism' (Phillipson, 1992). In other words, I had learned teaching methodology based upon studies originating from British, Australasia and North American (BANA) universities, but my participants grew up in and were teaching in a context that relies upon Japanese-derived methodology to teach tertiary, secondary and primary (TESEP) courses (Holliday, 1994).

These two positions as an insider and outsider are likely to have colored not only how I re-storied (Josselson, 1996) the participants' interview data, but also how I approached the research in the first place. Therefore, as Bell (2002: 210) argues, it is necessary to take care while interpreting the data, because my subjective interpretations will have imposed meaning on the participants' lived experiences. She cautions that narrative study involves 'close collaboration with participants and a recognition that the constructive narrative and subsequent analysis illuminates the researcher as much as the participants'. My interpretation of the stories that the participants tell when recounting their professional lives are therefore likely to be a reflection of my own stories as well.

Summary of Chapter 4

This chapter first discussed the usage of narrative as a research method to uncover the details of teachers' lives. The eight teachers who participated in my studies were briefly introduced, and the two data-collection methods (interviews and classroom observations) were laid out. I concluded the chapter by positioning myself within the studies as a simultaneous insider and outsider to my research context. The next chapter, which investigates how professional identity develops in new teachers, presents the first of my three studies.

5 Developing Professional Identity

Introduction

This is the first of three chapters comprising the analysis section of this book. In this chapter, I examine, in detail, how professional identity is developed in four teachers that are relatively new to teaching English in Japanese universities. These teachers are embarking upon their careers at a time when tertiary education in Japan is undergoing a great deal of reform, making them an important target group to research. University reforms, which began a decade ago, include privatization of national universities, establishment of a rigorous assessment system for receiving public funding and emphasis on transparency and accountability in higher education institutions. The Japanese academy has been shaken by the recent questioning of the traditional role of professors, well known for their apathy toward teaching and preference for conducting research (e.g. Amano & Poole, 2005; Goodman, 2005; Newby *et al*., 2009).

Because of this new academic climate, individual universities have also introduced internal reforms. Poole (2003, 2010) describes the changes at one university, which included integrating the English curriculum and streaming students according to their level, as 'remarkable' because they challenged the autonomous role that universities and professors had previously enjoyed in all teaching matters.

University teachers are now often required to take part in numerous activities that result in less time for research. For example, teachers are now asked to participate in various recruitment activities (such as open-campus days), which are often held on weekends or during school holidays; to accompany students on study-abroad trips; to develop and proctor numerous entrance examinations and to provide remedial courses for incoming students. Furthermore, because of widespread budget cuts, university professors are also increasingly called upon to fill important roles as administrative committee members. One of the older professors in Poole's (2003) study, for example, was so unhappy with such reforms that he opted for early retirement in order to continue his research in a think tank rather than follow his university's directive to focus more on teaching.

A further difference between older and younger teachers concerns academic backgrounds. Prior to the 1990s, few Japanese university teachers had completed their doctorate degrees, and in fact, the only requirement to teach at a university was to have a BA, although most had MAs (Nagasawa, 2004). Those with PhDs usually obtained them mid-career and often from abroad (Hada, 2005).

The reason why so few Japanese professors held PhDs in the past was that it was quite difficult to obtain one from a Japanese university. PhDs, particularly in the field of science, were awarded by a person's alma mater only *after* years of published research and the submission of a dissertation. Earning a PhD through thesis submission is called *ronbun hakase*. Tertiary reforms also included the expansion of graduate school programs. In 1955, there were only 213 universities with 131 PhD programs, but in 2005, there were 569 universities with 409 PhD programs (MEXT, 2006).[1] This expansion enabled more students to obtain a university-based PhD called a *katei hakase*. Completing a PhD in Japan is still extremely difficult (Hada, 2005), but applicants seeking tenured positions today are nonetheless generally required to have a PhD. As a result, like many young scholars, three of the participants in this study went to foreign universities for their doctoral studies. One participant even maintained her enrollment in her Japanese PhD program while earning her PhD abroad in order to have its prestigious name on her resume. Her belief that this would enhance her employment opportunities is not incorrect, as one of the characteristics of Japanese academia is academic 'inbreeding', where universities tend to select staff from their own pool of graduates or from universities that are equal or higher in academic rank (MEXT, 2006). Nevertheless, obtaining advanced degrees from abroad is also seen to be advantageous since such degrees not only signify a high level of scholarship, but also the ability to conduct research at an international level. Such academic qualifications, Matsuda (2002) argues, may affect new teachers' positions within a Japanese university faculty, which traditionally has been arranged by seniority rather than scholarship.

Thus, the educational experiences of younger teachers entering the profession today may be significantly different from those who have been involved in university teaching for many years, and they may have a completely different outlook toward English language teaching. These teachers were educated by professors under the old system, but they are embarking upon their careers in the midst of change (Goodman, 2005). Their professional identities are bound to be shaped by numerous factors that are likely to be different from university teachers whose careers commenced some years or decades ago. Therefore, this is an important group to research if we want to not only have a better understanding of English language education at the tertiary level in Japan, but also of the direction that English language education could take in the future.

The research questions that guided this first study are the following:

(1) What are the principal activities that Japanese teachers of English in higher education engage in as a part of their work practices?
(2) How do Japanese teachers of English in higher education construct their professional identity as they become members of the community of practice of English teachers?

Identity

This section looks at the theoretical framework that underpins how I interpret the teachers' stories presented in this chapter and again in Chapter 7. Research into the concept of identity has followed numerous threads. Scholars originally saw identity as an individual and innate sense of self (Erikson, 1968; Mead, 1934). Some years later, beliefs, attitudes and values that shape who and what we are were theorized as being the result of what Bourdieu (1991) calls *habitus*, the context in which we live, through our interaction with others in the form of playing roles (Goffman, 1959) and how we position ourselves and others through speech and actions (Davies & Harre, 1990, 1999; Harre & van Langenhove, 1999). Membership in groups (Hogg & Abrams, 1988; Tajfel, 1978), where common goals or common traits are shared, enables us to understand not only who we are, but also who we are not.

Another perspective of identity is provided by Wenger (1998) and Lave and Wenger (1991), who argue that identity develops through day-to-day experiences that occur through participation in the multiple groups to which we belong, which they call 'communities of practice' (CoP). These groups are sometimes officially organized (such as membership in the Parent Teacher Association [PTA] or being on a particular sports team), but most often they are informal and are unnamed (such as belonging to a group of employees who always have lunch together). People are implicitly aware of who belongs and who does not belong to such communities. The degree of involvement, or 'modes of belonging' (Wenger, 1998), differs among members of these groups, with some people operating as insiders in some groups, and as peripheral members in others. It is the degree of negotiability within such groups that enables members to claim meaning of their membership that can lead to identities of participation or identities of non-participation.

The theory of CoP has been recently utilized in several studies to consider the identity of teachers in general education (e.g. Duff, 2002;

Kimble et al., 2008) and in language education (e.g. Clarke, 2008; Singh & Richards, 2006; Tsui, 2007). It has also been the theoretical framework in several studies investigating the process of adopting the necessary discourse to become recognized as members of an academic profession (e.g. Morita, 2004; Simon-Maeda et al., 2006). In particular, these studies have drawn upon Wenger's three modes of belonging that influence identification and negotiability. These modes are: engagement, imagination and alignment, and each is divided into identities of participation and non-participation. The following section discusses Wenger's theory of identity in greater detail.

Wenger (1998) Theory of Identity as the Theoretical Framework

Wenger (1998) posits that identity forms from belonging to and engaging with the various groups to which people belong, called *communities of practice* (Lave & Wenger, 1991). Belonging to such communities involves the duel process of *identification* and *negotiation of meaning*, both of which are comprised of degrees of participation and non-participation.

Identification is a fluid relationship between individuals and the society in which they are engaged. It evolves through day-to-day lived experiences and is both participative and reificative. The physical process of participation involves *identifying with* members of a community and reification involves the process of *identifying as* a member of the community.

Negotiation is as important in identity formation as identification, for as Wenger (1998) explains, people may be deeply invested in their various communities, but not given a voice. Therefore, the degree to which people are able to 'contribute to, take responsibility for and shape the meanings that matter within a social configuration' (p. 197) is important. Negotiability involves power and reflects peoples' positioning within the communities in which they engage. There are two aspects of negotiability: *economies of meaning* and *ownership of meaning*.

Economies of meaning produced by individual members of communities indicate that not all meanings share equal value or status, and they are interpreted differently. Ownership of meaning demonstrates the degree to which participants in a community can appropriate meaning and claim it for themselves. Wenger says 'the degree to which we can make use of, affect, control, modify, or in general, assert as ours the meanings that we negotiate' (p. 200) becomes an essential part of who we are.

Now let us look at Wenger's three modes of belonging under the categories of *identification* and *negotiability*. The first mode of belonging is *engagement*. Under the category of identification, engagement formation is 'in the doing' and refers not only to how people invest themselves in what they do, but also to who they do it with. Under the category of negotiability, engagement refers to the joint processes of production and adoption of meaning within a community of practice. The degree of distance between production and adoption of meaning is closely related to members' marginality. When members' meanings are recognized and adopted within a community, mutual engagement leads to a shared ownership of meaning. On the other hand, the non-adoption of members' meanings leads to non-participation and marginalizes those members.

The second mode of belonging is *imagination*. Imagination in identification enables people to create an internal picture of the world in which they engage. This identification works through association and opposition that allow people to connect to, or distance them from others. Imagination through participation creates a sense of affinity with a group but imagination through non-participation, on the other hand, may result in a sense of marginalization. Imagination in negotiability enables people to reify the role they play within an organization. Imagination forms from personal observation and interaction with others, as well as, through the informal stories, parables, and fables shared among members of that organization. Imagination enables participants to appropriate the meanings that emerge from these interactions. People may be unable to appropriate meanings if they do not have access to practice, for example, through being a peripheral member. Full membership in a community enables people to see where they lie within the whole. However, as Wenger explains, as members of multiple groups, we often are peripheral members without the need to focus our attention on appropriating meanings for ourselves. In other words, he says 'we cannot understand everything: we must focus our attention and our efforts on the meanings that really matter to us' (p. 205).

The third mode of belonging is *alignment*, which involves power. Under the category of identification, people assume an identity through affiliation with a larger group. It is a combination of allegiance and compliance; active participation creates a willing allegiance toward a group, but non-participation may be coercive and require submissiveness of its members. How we define ourselves is strongly affected by what forms of allegiance we offer to the practices we are members of, and 'makes us "larger" by placing our actions in a larger context' (Wenger, 1998: 196).

Alignment in negotiability, according to Wenger, is the strongest mode of belonging that influences economies of meaning. Alignment can give rise to shared ownership of meanings when agreement within a group is reached through negotiating and sharing. On the other hand, alignment that is demanded may be achieved through forceful means. With such a lack of negotiability, an identity of non-participation may be formed where there is an 'inability to adapt to new circumstances, a lack of flexibility and a propensity to breakdowns' (p. 206).

All members of a community of practice engage in participation as members of that community, but the degree of participation, Wenger argues, is related to a trajectory motion that 'connects the past, the present and the future' (p. 154). These trajectories, influenced by a number of social and individual factors, demonstrate that identity is fluid, developing and always changing. Trajectories influence the type of activities people engage in within their communities. They are aligned with degrees of participation and non-participation and they assist in giving meaning to their memberships through imagination and alignment.

The types of trajectories Wenger describes are the following: (1) peripheral trajectories, where participants will not gain full participation; (2) inbound trajectories, where newcomers may eventually obtain full participation; (3) insider trajectories, where full members renegotiate their identity as members; (4) boundary trajectories, where members of communities link to other communities of practice and (5) outbound trajectories, where members leave a community and move out or into another community (Wenger, 1998: 154–155). Within any community, participation on all trajectory levels occurs, and people hold multiple communities of practice memberships, occupying different trajectory positions within their different groups.

In sum, this section has briefly described the theoretical framework employed for this study's analysis by outlining Wenger's (1998) social ecology of identity, which shows how identity forms through degrees of participation while engaging in activities as members of the various communities of practices to which we belong. The next section briefly reintroduces the participants and reviews how the data were collected and analyzed.

Participants and Data Collection

The four teachers who are featured in this chapter are Taka, Kumiko, Kana and Miwa, and they have been selected from the pool of participant-teachers because of their status as relatively new full-time university English teachers.

A more complete discussion of the data collection and data analysis was described in Chapter 3, but a brief recap is as follows. The teachers were interviewed using Seidman's (2006) protocol, which is designed to uncover the lives of teachers. The interviews were digitally recorded and transcribed. Because the goal of this study is to look at what teachers say, rather than *how* they say it, the transcripts were tidied up to correct grammatical inconsistencies while retaining the individual discursive styles of the teachers. For readability, punctuation was added to construct complete sentences.

The interviews were uploaded to qualitative data analysis software called NVivo and analyzed using Wenger's (1998) framework of social identity to establish thematic categories that demonstrate how the teachers construct their professional identity as university English teachers. The data were examined for the three modes of belonging as described by Wenger: engagement, imagination and alignment. As tenured and full-time university English teachers, all were found to be involved in three common areas of engagement: *engagement in teaching, engagement in the workplace* and *engagement in the wider social context*.

The first mode of belonging is *engagement*, defined by Wenger as the common enterprises that people do as members of a particular group. The activities carried out within these areas of engagement are similar among the four participants. Under the first category, *engagement in teaching*, they prepare for and teach classes; they examine and evaluate students' ability and performances and they interact inside and outside of the classroom with students. Under the second category, *engagement in the workplace*, they work with colleagues and administrators in the day-to-day activities that are necessary for the smooth running of their universities. Under the third category, *engagement in the social context*, they interact with others outside the context of their university. Engagement in these three spheres of activity creates identities as university English teachers because this is the work that university English teachers do.

The second mode of belonging is *imagination*, which enables people to interpret the experiences they have with others in their communities of practices. Imagination provides people with interpretive tools for placing themselves within the broader context in which they exist and explains why people have different perceptions even when engaging in the same enterprises. As university English teachers, my participants engage in similar activities in their various work contexts, but the way they see themselves, their students and their colleagues differs. Wenger argues that imagination of participation and non-participation can connect people to, or detach people from, identities created through engagement, and warns that imagination of non-participation 'can be so removed from any lived form of membership that it detaches our identity and leaves us in a state of uprootedness' (p. 178).

The third mode of belonging, *alignment*, enables people to place their practices within a larger group or community. The teachers in this study align their practices with various people and groups: students, teachers and colleagues as well as with the universities where they work. Alignment is manifested through acts of allegiance toward a group or through acts of resistance that demonstrate distance. Alignment creates a sense of identification *with* a community, but on the other hand, misalignment creates a sense of *not* belonging.

Analysis and Interpretation

In this section, I examine the participants' narratives to see to what extent Wenger's theory is able to reveal professional identity formation through the three modes of belonging as described above. I look at each category of engagement separately to view the teachers' imagination and alignment within these areas. I begin with the category of *engagement in teaching*. As this area was discussed most during the interviews, this section forms the bulk of the chapter. Under this category, I will show how the participants' educational and personal experiences influenced their imagination of themselves as teachers. The second category to be discussed is *engagement in the workplace*. Although the participants are all legitimate members of their workplaces, they occupy different trajectories that influence their imagination and alignment toward their colleagues and their universities. The third area, *engagement in the wider social context*, will show how boundary crossing (Wenger, 1998) plays an important role in bridging their identities as teachers, university workers and scholars.

Imagination and Alignment in Engagement in Teaching

For the four teachers in this study, engaging in teaching-related activities forms the bulk of their work. They not only teach English language (and occasionally their own specialty as well), they also spend a significant amount of time on class preparation and student evaluation, and they cultivate relationships with students, both inside and outside the classroom. Their imagination in engaging in these activities plays an essential role in constructing their identities as teachers. Wenger (1998: 178) says imagination is important because 'it is through imagination that we see our own practices as continuing histories that reach far into the past, and it is through imagination that we conceive of new developments, explore alternatives and envision possible futures'. This section introduces three significant themes of imagination that emerged from the participants' interview data. The first theme examines the influence of the participants' former teachers in how they themselves self-identify as teachers. The impact of former teachers on the teaching practices and beliefs of new or future teachers has been best described by Lortie (1975: 61), who argues that the thousands of hours of direct contact with teachers in an 'apprenticeship of observation' plays a significant role in how teachers view teaching. We shall see that positive images of former teachers contribute to positive impressions of teaching as a profession and negative images of former teachers contribute to negative impressions of teaching as a profession. These images are appropriated and renegotiated by the participants to create images of themselves as teachers.

The second theme concerns the participants' imagined relationships with their students, where being well-liked and popular seems as important to their satisfaction of being teachers as being considered an 'effective' teacher. Here, memories of self as a student provide an interpretive lens for the teachers to judge their own relationship with their students, but these memories are negotiated and renegotiated in order to construct their current identities as teachers.

The third theme, which is important because it reflects the participants' pedagogical goals for their students, concerns imagination of what the participants believe their students are capable of learning and what they believe their students should learn. Here, we shall see that what the teachers consider to be important for their students to learn may not necessarily be related to language pedagogy.

Influence of former teachers

The first theme to be discussed is the influence that *positive images of former teachers* have on constructing teacher identity. Taka is the only one of the four participants who had always intended to become a teacher. At university, he was a member of the education department, where he studied to become a social studies teacher. After graduation, he taught Japanese language instead, and during his stay in Australia as an exchange student, he took a TESOL course and became interested in English language teaching as well. His comment that he would be 'happy teaching any subject' as long as he can 'handle it' indicates a vocation for teaching. He spoke very highly of his former teachers and described them as influential forces in his character formation. He perceives teaching as an opportunity to make a difference in the students' lives. The following comment, in which he uses the word 'important' (emphasis mine) seven times, illustrates his feelings.

> When you have an influence on other people you...as I feel...I am **important** to their lives. The feeling of me being **important** matters to others' lives...or I'm **important** to myself. That kind of feeling is **important** to everybody, and I found the way. To find myself as

important is through talking with other people. Especially when other people accept me as an **important** person, then I feel much more comfortable and happier. So teacher, is part of teacher job is being like those people. Being **important** person, giving a new perspective or new experience through class time.

For Taka, who was not an industrious student himself, teachers are more than transmitters of academic knowledge to students. He feels the information they share with students about their beliefs and attitudes toward living are essential to prepare students for the real world. For him, teachers were more than just those who *taught* him, but those who helped him become the person that he is, and this is the philosophy that he carries with him to his classes as well.

On the other hand, *negative images of teachers* contribute to a disliking for the teaching profession. The negative images that Kana, Kumiko and Miwa hold of their former teachers include 'scary' (Kumiko and Kana), 'violent' (Kana), 'boring' (Kumiko, Miwa), 'spinsterish' (Miwa), 'merely proficient at teaching students to pass entrance exams' (Kumiko), 'unwilling to listen to students' (Kumiko), 'unable to speak English' (Miwa), 'unable to inspire students' (Kumiko), 'unwilling to vary their teaching methodology' (Miwa) and 'disliked by students' (Kumiko, Kana and Miwa).

These images may explain in part why these women did not intend to become teachers. Kumiko, who has a teaching license, only took the course because she was persuaded to do so by her parents. Kana was enrolled in the teacher education program because a teaching license was 'a good thing to have' but dropped out when the opportunity to go to the UK on a scholarship interfered with the teaching practicum. Miwa did not take the teacher training course at all because she was afraid that she would be persuaded to become a teacher rather than being allowed to go to graduate school.

In spite of an initial aversion toward teaching, these women are teachers now. These negative images of their former teachers, therefore, help shape their self-images of themselves in opposition to their former teachers. Kumiko, for example, disliked her university English teacher because he was scary and he 'screamed' at the students, giving her a 'bad image of teachers'. To combat this bad image, she encourages her students to think of her in a different way:

> I don't like teachers since I was a child [laughter]. So, that's why maybe I just don't like to identify as a teacher. Yeah. So. So I always tell my students, you know, when **you** meet me **outside** the school, don't call me teacher. **Sensei!** [teacher]. Don't call me *sensei*, you know. Because I don't like being a teacher outside the school. You know, it's **OK** if you

call me teacher **in** school, [strong emotion] it is just I don't like being called as a teacher.

Miwa's negative image of her high school teacher is related to her perception of her teacher's inability to teach effectively and her poor English ability. Miwa believes that students have the desire to 'learn from somebody who **knows** everything'. This belief is reflected in the importance she places on knowing every detail of the reading materials that she teaches her students. She covers minute grammatical and lexical points in her classes because she believes passing on her knowledge to the students enables them to gain a deeper understanding of English.

In sum, images of former teachers influence how the participants view teaching and how they choose to present themselves as teachers to their own students. Such strong images of former teachers that shape the self-perceptions and teaching practices of these participants may fade as their professional identities develop over time, but it is likely that these images will remain an influential aspect of their professional identity.

Influence of current students

Now, let us look at the following three themes concerning how the teachers' professional identity is shaped by their imagination of their students.

(1) The teachers' imagination of their students in relationship to themselves as students.
(2) The teachers' imagination of what they believe their students think of them.
(3) The teachers' imagination of what they believe their students can and should learn.

The first theme concerns the teachers' imagination of their students. Their attitudes toward their students are influenced by their powerful memories of themselves as students, and these memories are shaped by a wide array of experiences, as well as their educational, sociocultural and gendered backgrounds. The perceived distance between the teachers' former 'student selves' and their current students seem to determine, to a certain extent, the degree of tension in their teaching. Teachers are better able to align their teaching practices with their students when they feel that they share some commonalities with their students, and when they feel there is too great a gap between their former 'student selves' and their current students, tensions in teaching occur.

First, let us look at the tensions experienced by Kana and Miwa, whose backgrounds do not seem to share much in common with those of their students. They have trouble relating to their students because they feel that many of them are wasting the opportunities that are offered to them. Unlike their students, who seem to perceive a university degree as a right rather than a privilege because of their affluent backgrounds, Kana and Miwa studied hard to justify to their families their reason for being there.

They both grew up in regional areas where educational opportunities for female students were somewhat limited because of the sociopolitical attitudes toward women. Miwa needed to convince her family, none of whom had ever gone to university, that the expense of a university education would be worthwhile. Kana's chances of entering a university were extremely low because of the academically low-level commercial high school she had attended. For these women, university was an important time of self-discovery because they could study their favorite subjects to their hearts' content. Since they knew their families suffered from financial hardship in sending them to university, they both made sure they made the most of their opportunities.

At the same time, they both needed to overcome the disadvantages they felt they had in comparison with their classmates who came from wealthier families and who attended better secondary schools. Kana worked hard to overcome the 'inferiority complex' she had because the other students seemed much better at English. She developed confidence in herself after studying abroad during the summer between her second and third year, using money she had saved from a part-time job. Upon returning to Japan, she sought out more opportunities to use English such as joining the English-speaking drama club and making friends with foreign students. In addition to improving her communicative ability, she also put in many hours studying. Her comments below indicate the importance she attached to making the most of her university education.

> I thought I am not wasting the tuition they [her parents] are paying. I have to make the most of it. And I like the studying. I didn't understand why the others are playing around missing classes and try to escape. You know, why, even if some lectures are so translation lectures, they said they don't like it. Basically it is just like translating *Midsummer's Night Dream*, Shakespeare, sentence to sentence. I still regarded it as still studying something I can't study by myself. It is a difficult text. I need a teacher to explain. Even if it is boring. I'm still learning something. Because practical English I can do myself, I can write or express or whatever I can do alone. But something like literature, I need a teacher

because my English is not good enough. So even if it is translation based, it is still study.

Miwa also felt somewhat at a disadvantage when she came to university in Tokyo and found many of her classmates to be proficient at speaking English because they had gone to private schools and they had had experiences traveling abroad. Nevertheless, she worked to raise her skills, and she is proud that she was able to do so even though she was not 'in a privileged position as a student' like many of her classmates who had received a 'special education'.

Although Miwa was an English language major, she took as many classes offered by the literature department as she could. She enjoyed the classes offered by her Japanese professors that focused on detailed grammar and lexical items because she felt that the key to reading original literature lay in developing a deep understanding of English as a language.

Because of her experiences as a student, Miwa wants her students to develop an understanding of English from a deeper perspective, and she says that if they do not, they will merely become 'secretaries or office workers'.[2] Miwa feels a conflict because many of her students are unwilling to make what she feels to be the necessary effort to master English. She feels dissatisfied spending class time on materials that should have been studied at home. The following comment, where Miwa compares herself to her students, shows how differently she perceives their attitudes toward study are:

> I didn't have problems in finding motivation to read [...] I remember I was reading *Newsweek* and *Time* when I was in the freshman year. Of course I had to look up the dictionary very often, but I could still read it and understand it...by myself. I didn't need anybody explaining what the expression means or anything back then. But most of the students I teach, they need guidance in that area, too.

Kana has had only one year of experience teaching in a Japanese university, and Miwa only two. As they gain confidence in themselves as teachers, they may feel less baffled by what they feel is their students' lack of interest in study. For now, however, comparing their students to themselves is one way that they make sense of the difficulties that they have with teaching.

Now, let us turn to the cases of Taka and Kumiko. They seem to have a greater degree of empathy toward their students. Like Miwa and Kana, they also believe their students lack interest and motivation, but their understanding of them may be due in part to having more experience as language teachers: Kumiko taught part-time for 10 years and Taka for five before obtaining tenured academic positions. However, an examination of their narratives indicates that they feel affinity for their students because they perceive they share a number of similarities with them.

Unlike Kana and Miwa, who felt driven to make the most of their educational opportunities while students, Kumiko and Taka had a much easier time during their college days. They came from financially secure, middle-class backgrounds, where it was taken for granted that they would go to university. For them, university life was a time for self-fulfillment and self-exploration, so they went to parties and participated in extracurricular activities.

When asked about his university studies, Taka laughed and said, 'Study? No! No! No! Play? Yes! Yes! Yes!' He was so busy with his involvement in the mountain climbing club that he did not even attempt to search for a job during his senior year, and he was unable to enter the workforce after graduation. Supported by his parents, who felt happy to give him an extra year because they had anticipated that he would be unable to enter university on his first try, Taka spent one year in the United States as a Japanese language teacher. He said that year provided essential 'rehabilitation' to prepare him for a job where he would eventually have to 'sit at a desk'.

Taka's history as a happy-go-lucky student enables him to empathize with his students, whom he describes as unmotivated and with inferiority complexes due to their previous lack of academic success. He understands that they 'like to do something outside of the classroom and are busy with other things'. Compared to Miwa, who feels frustrated that she has to teach what she feels the students should study at home, Taka does not mind doing this. He understands that it would be 'better' for the students if they did put in more effort in self study, but he knows they will not. Therefore, he willingly devotes class time in teaching activities that he feels are nevertheless a 'necessary part of language learning'.

Taka also understands his students' feelings of academic inferiority because he suffered from such feelings as well. Although he attended academically prestigious schools, he said that he constantly ranked toward the bottom of the class. Furthermore, he was always compared to his brilliant older brother who came in first in everything he attempted. Taka's feelings of inferiority are evident in his explanation given below for being able to enter such prestigious schools, where he attributes his success to luck rather than to his ability:

I consider myself lucky. [...] Obviously any reasonable person would say I am lucky. There is no explanation for it. You know, for me getting into those places...hmm. Really. Because those examinations are solely based on the academic results of that particular test. My history of studying prior to that exam was far below the level of having a good chance of getting through.

[Diane] So the luck was that they happened to ask the questions you knew how to answer?

Absolutely. Where else could I find the explanation for that? [Diane's laughter]. I'm lucky. I'm not being just modest or anything. Really. Ask any of my friends.

Taka's experiences of learning to communicate in English with a phrase book while traveling influenced his attitudes toward teaching and learning language. As a student traveling in Mongolia, he learned he could communicate by using simple words and gestures. On a later trip abroad, he memorized many useful phrases before going to Thailand, which he was eventually able to use in conversation. Because he was successful at learning English this way, he spends time in the class on listening and repetition exercises, and encourages students to take chances to be able to communicate in any way that they can. He wants his students to see that they could get by in English if they learn a few 'tricks'. Because Taka did not like to study, and he knows his students do not like to study, he tries to boost their communicative abilities in ways that may be more appealing to them than by, for example, studying a reading text in depth.

Because he found a way that personally worked for him, Taka wants his students to discover their own way to study English as well. He says, 'I'm not just an instructor. I'm a *sempai*[3] at learning a new thing, learning languages. I know many different ways to try to learn new things, so I could provide them, I could show them'. By sharing his successes and failures with his students, he feels that he can 'develop a trust relationship' that will result in providing them with confidence and motivation.

Kumiko, with the most teaching experience of all the participants, shapes her teaching practices in recognition of her students' busy lives outside of her class. The influence of her TESOL graduate courses that focus on critical pedagogy is evident in her pedagogical decisions. A lecture given by a well-known TESOL researcher who spoke of unreasonable demands teachers often make of students resonated with her, for she remembers feeling that her teachers often asked too much of the students. Instead of requiring the students to do less however, she aligns herself with them by doing the same work they do. For example, when she assigns an essay for homework, she writes one as well. That essay becomes a model for her to explain writing organization and a vehicle for her to express her opinions to the students. She says that her approach toward teaching has enhanced her relationship with her students, who often approach her after class to discuss the class topic in more depth.

In sum, the relationship between the teachers' perceptions of themselves as students and the way that they align their teaching practices with their current students shapes their teaching practices. When the perceived distance between their images they hold of themselves as students and the images of their current students is great, they have more difficulty aligning their teaching practices with their students than they do if the perceived distance is small.

The second theme that emerged from the data analysis concerning the teachers' relationships with their students centered on *what they believe their students think of them*. Their confidence in themselves as teachers is heavily influenced by explicit and implicit positive and negative feedback from students.

All of the teachers claimed to want to be well liked by their students, but some have a stronger desire to be popular than others. Kumiko, for example, feels she is a good teacher because she receives positive feedback on student evaluation forms and her classes are always full. She is also very proud of the friendly relationships she has cultivated with her students. She spends time with them between classes and even occasionally has dinner and drinks with them. The importance she attaches to her students' opinions of her is evident in the following comment, where she describes her pleasure when she found students had written positive comments about her on a website:

> So, the students...oh, when I see the *ni* [2] channel? Have you seen the *ni* [2] channel? I see the *ni* [2] channel in my university and I search my name. And some students wrote 'Ah Kumiko *Sensei* is just like a friend' so you know, I really like that comment, yeah. You know.

Being popular with students however is not without drawbacks, because tension can develop in the teacher-student relationship. In positions of authority, the participants understand the difference between being 'a friendly teacher' and being 'friends with the students'. Taka was relieved that his students that he took to Canada did not 'cross the line' between this relationship, but Kana has felt she was being taken advantage of when some of the students she was friendly with started skipping class and not turning in their assignments.

Kumiko's comment below is interesting because it illustrates her complex feelings in how she desires to be seen by her students:

> I want to be friendly with my students. But you know ... in **some**way, in **some**way, I want them to respect me as a teacher. But just they are kind of mix up, and they are you know, they just come to my office, and say *sensei kiite yooo* [hey, Teacher, listen!] listen to me. They start to talk but I [laughter] have to work sometimes, you know. So it is kind of difficult to say you know, 'leave my room'.

All of the teachers mentioned instances where they felt they had received negative feedback from students. Explicit negative feedback occurs on student evaluation forms where students complain that the content is too difficult or the materials are too boring. Miwa experienced negative feedback from a student when she complained to the administration about the grade Miwa had given her for the course. Most negative feedback, however, is implicit and is reflected in students' poor behavior: they do poorly on quizzes and exams, they are passive or sleep during class or they skip class altogether.

It is important to point out that positive and negative feedback can occur from the same students at different times. For example, positive feedback may be displayed when students seek teachers during office hours to chat with, but negative feedback may be displayed when the same students do poorly on a test. If identification as a teacher is strongly connected to the transmission of knowledge, negative feedback in the form of poor test scores may undermine confidence as a teacher, especially for newcomers such as those in this study. On the other hand, if identification as a teacher is strongly connected to building personal relationships with students, low test scores may not have the same negative impact on a teachers' professional identity.

Now I turn to the third theme that emerged from the data analysis, namely the influence of current students on the teachers' professional identity development. Here, I discuss the teachers' *imagination in relation to their students' learning*, and in particular, what the participants imagine their students *can* and *should* learn in their classes. Surprisingly, none of these teachers are particularly optimistic that their students will achieve English proficiency as a result of their English teaching. The main reason why the teachers feel that the students are unlikely to succeed at English is that they feel students fail to make sufficient effort for self-study. Miwa believes the reason for this is that her students are 'just in love with the image of themselves being able to speak and listen to English', but are unwilling to make this vision a reality by putting forth the effort to study grammar and vocabulary. She attributes this to students' beliefs that they have already 'done it [hard English study] in high school' while preparing for university entrance examinations. Furthermore, without a clear purpose of *why* they are learning English, Miwa feels they will not make much progress.

All four participants also questioned the necessity for all tertiary students to learn English. Although English proficiency is viewed as an essential skill for securing a good job in Japan, as discussed in Chapter 2, the *name* of the university from which one graduates is more important (Beauchamp, 1987; Ishida, 1993; Ono, 2001). Because Miwa and Kumiko's students attend good universities where their graduates can expect to find employment upon graduation, they don't necessarily need to develop their English skills at this time unless they have personal motivation to do so. Taka's students at the academically low-level university where he teaches are unlikely to obtain employment in the type of company where it would be necessary to use English, and Kana's students, who live in a regional area of Japan, are unlikely to ever have the opportunity to speak English after they graduate from university, let alone use it for work.

Not having strong motivation or a clear purpose for learning English may contribute to students' passive behavior in class, which is another reason given why the teachers are pessimistic about their students' English language learning. Kana attributes this passivity to Japanese culture, which she says encourages silence and demonstrates a lack of ambition and confidence. She tries to combat this by raising the students' self-confidence by encouraging them to speak out and by praising them for any effort they make. Still, she feels irritated by their passivity and wants to tell them 'come on come on, you are young and energetic and you are wasting your energy'. Miwa has similar feelings and complains that it seems as if her students 'almost took a vow of silence' in their determination to 'just sit there'. For her, the 'toughest part is to make them work, make them at least be there. Not just physically, but mentally'.

Japanese universities have long considered English to be a subject that is essential to study to increase one's liberal arts knowledge, but not one that is taught as a practical skill (e.g. Terauchi, 1995). This reasoning may explain why the participants in this study are not particularly bothered by the likelihood that their students will not learn English language from their classes. However, they do believe that through English study students should be able to expand their knowledge of the world while developing their own character. How the participants do this in their classes will now be discussed.

In spite of being somewhat pessimistic about their students being enabled to learn much English as a result of their teaching, the four teachers do have pedagogical goals for their students that extend beyond linguistic matters, and they attach importance to these goals. They want to prepare their students for the real world by encouraging them to develop their critical- and independent-thinking skills, to gain a broader perspective of the world, to develop more self confidence and to improve communication skills (in Japanese).

Kumiko dislikes classes that focus solely on language teaching, such as those that prepare students for the TOEIC examination, and complains that the required textbook is **'really very, very booooring'**! Her aversion to teaching grammar is explained below:

> Most of the time I ask my students to read the articles in English and then we have a discussion about the issues. And then I ask the students to write a paper. So in **that** class, I don't teach grammar. I mean, I don't focus on grammar very much. I just want them to understand the content. And **then** I want them to express their opinions about the issues. So I don't focus on the grammar very much. I'm not sure... [hesitant]...mmm...Actually, I'm not interested in teaching grammar very much. Yeah. Because, you know, to express their opinion – of course grammar is important of course. But I like to focus on expressing their opinions more than correcting grammar. So...

Kumiko prefers teaching classes where students are encouraged to develop their opinions. She says it is not English that the students remember once the class is finished, but the content of what they have learned. This is why she uses controversial topics, especially those that focus on gender, as a backdrop for her writing classes:

> I think the controversial topics inspire students because students don't know much about the issues deeply or very much. But they know some knowledge about the issues. You know, for example, when I introduce domestic violence, they don't understand deeply, but they know the term. Information about domestic violence. So they, mmm, they seem to enjoy it. And especially I want the female students to understand gender issues. Of course I want the male students to understand issues too. But **especially** female students. I **really** want them to understand gender issues.

Kumiko feels that knowledge concerning gender discrimination in Japanese society is essential for her female students, who constitute 30% of her students. She says they have been able to enter a good university due to their academic efforts, but she wants them to be prepared for the sexual discrimination she is sure they will face when they attempt to enter the job market. Her male students can also benefit from learning about the impact of gender in society. She says some are 'very, very conservative [laughter] and kind of right wing', but she enjoys debating with them when they challenge her with statements such as, 'Women should stay home, because that's their role, because they bear baby and that's the natural way', 'Between same sex, marriage is not natural' or 'I think a woman loves a man is natural'. Her classes are about more than teaching language. They also introduce students to alternative ways of thinking.

Miwa, who also considers herself a feminist, teaches her students about the impact of gender on society as well. For her, choosing such topics for reading and discussion enables her to connect her personal and academic interests to teaching English language. She justifies herself in the following comment:

> I notice I think one of the things I have to tell you about being a teacher is that mostly probably I told you that I'm not really happy about being a teacher. I feel like I have to do, a kind of mission. I have to. I'm a feminist and my specialty is gender studies and women's literature. I have to teach young girls how to respect themselves, and how to insist what they truly are, you know, in relation to men and in society. So, when I'm in the position of instructing and teaching them, I sometimes pick the materials that have that kind of element in it. So that they can learn something from it.

Like Kumiko, she wants to show her students alternative ways of seeing the world. However, she feels discouraged when they fail to see 'beyond the surface' or to 'get the point of' what she is teaching. In one class, for example, the topic of date rape was covered. She felt discouraged by one female student's assertion that women need to assume responsibility when placing themselves in compromising situations that could lead to date rape. Miwa complains that this type of mentality, where 'women are always responsible', is prevalent in Japan, so she is all the more determined to bring gender topics to her classroom in order to encourage students to think critically about such issues.

Kana echoes this sentiment and wants her students to learn how to apply what is learned in one context to another. Without developing these skills, she is afraid they might be 'easily taken to a cult'. Critical thinking will help them become less passive, which she perceives to be a cultural trait that is especially predominant among her female students. She feels that developing such skills is essential for students if they want to learn how to express their own opinions.

Taka also feels that his students do not know how to articulate their ideas because they are used to being passive followers of teachers and because they have lost confidence in themselves due to their lack of success in their academic study. Therefore, he puts priority on helping his students learn how to think for themselves. He says he does this by using EFL materials related to the students' interests, such as horoscopes, magic and survival techniques. He hopes that through these materials the students will improve their English skills, but more importantly, he wants them to increase their self-awareness and self-confidence. Furthermore, he hopes to expose students to wider perspective of the world by teaching them 'how people are living and what is important for some people – what is not important for some people', and to learn that the choices they make in life are ultimately up to them.

All four teachers also place priority on improving their students' communication skills *in Japanese* as well as in English. This is not surprising when considering the importance that MEXT places on Japanese language as a way to learn English, as discussed in Chapter 2. But it is somewhat surprising to find that this attitude exists among these young teachers, who are all fluent users of English themselves. Kana, for example, believes that English study can empower her students because it introduces an alternative communication style. Although her students may not learn much English, she feels they may be able to learn better Japanese communication skills through studying English. She feels that English will help her students overcome some of the limitations of Japanese, which she says encourages humility, passiveness and silence.

For these four teachers, focusing on pedagogical tasks that they perceive to be unrelated to English language teaching, may provide an important source of professional satisfaction for them, especially if their academic backgrounds are not related to language pedagogy and if they do not self-identify as language teachers. Moreover, by considering wider pedagogical goals, the teachers are able to connect their academic interests to the classes that they teach.

Imagination and Alignment in Engagement in the Workplace

In the previous section, I discussed how the participants utilized their imagination and alignment while engaging in teaching, which forms the bulk of the work that they do. The teachers' imagination of their former teachers and their current students plays a strong role in how they perceive themselves as teachers and how they make pedagogical choices in the classroom. Teaching, however, is only one aspect of the work that university teachers do. In this section, I turn to the second category of engagement discussed in this study, which is *engagement in the workplace*. Engagement under this category concerns university work that falls outside the scope of teaching or otherwise dealing with students. It involves interaction with colleagues, membership in the *kyojukai* (professor's council) and working on committees. Engagement in the university workplace involves power and the participants' placement on their workplace trajectories (Wenger, 1998), or, as Poole (2010) puts it, their position as an *uchimuki* or a *sotomuki* player determines how that power is distributed.

Kumiko and Taka are on what Wenger (1998) terms the 'inbound' trajectory of their universities because they have tenure and can remain there until they retire. Although Kana is on the inbound trajectory at her university because she has a tenure-track position, she is not guaranteed a permanent position unless she is promoted to associate professor within five years. Her trajectory, therefore, has some constraints and cannot be considered to be completely 'inbound'. Unlike the other participants, Miwa has a contracted position and is on a 'peripheral' trajectory where her participation in university affairs is limited, but not necessarily marginalized.

Newcomers to academic careers, such as the teachers in this study, are considered as 'legitimate peripheral participants' (Lave & Wenger, 1991), and they are not expected to participate fully in their workplaces until they become more familiar with their jobs. Wenger (1998) notes, however, that not all community members on an inbound trajectory reach what he calls the 'insider' trajectory. Being an insider involves power because insiders make decisions that govern the rest of the community. Thus, only a few are admitted to a community's core decision-making membership. Nevertheless, Kumiko, Taka and Kana, as members of their university faculties, are expected to learn what it takes to become full, participating members of their universities. However, joining the insider trajectory is complicated and reflects the individual sociopolitical contexts of each university. Because the context differs for each participant, their imagination and alignment while

Developing Professional Identity

engaging in the workplace will be discussed separately and individually in the following subsections.

Kumiko

When Kumiko joined the economics department of a large private university in the Kanto area four years ago, she became one of four women out of nearly 100 teachers in that faculty.[4] She said that her male colleagues welcomed her warmly and they treated her 'almost like a daughter'. As a tenured teacher, she participates equally in departmental affairs and she is being assigned more and more administrative duties. However, unlike a male colleague who joined the university at the same time, she was not invited to join the *habatsu* (inter-university political factions that compete for power). She attributes this exclusion to deep-rooted sexism and says, 'If they think I'm an important person, they'd try to get me in the group. But they don't'.

Kumiko thus holds identities of participation and non-participation in her university, which complicates how she aligns her practices there. Exclusion from the political factions ensures that even as a member on the inbound trajectory, she will be unable to join the insider trajectory as a member of its inner circle. She will never have the opportunity to become the president or a dean, nor will she be assigned any influential decision-making position. However, Kumiko, like the other women in her faculty, has chosen not to see this marginalization as a limitation, but as an opportunity for personal freedom. Free from internal politics, Kumiko can devote more time toward activities that she considers more important. In other words, Kumiko shapes her professional identity around a *sotomuki* discourse (Poole, 2010).

The most striking example of how Kumiko has appropriated the meaning of non-participation within the university power politics is her decision to continue with her doctoral studies. When she was hired, she was asked to resign from the PhD program because of the university's policy of not allowing its teachers to be students at the same time. Although she agreed to do so, when she later learned that one of her female colleagues quietly completed her PhD, she decided to do the same. Thus, leading a secret life, she attends doctoral classes in the evenings and on weekends, and she has begun collecting data for her dissertation. Although she is somewhat fearful of being discovered and consequently being fired for breaking the rules, she is determined to continue because once she has a PhD, 'no one can take that away'.

Kumiko now feels this decision was a wise one, for having a PhD would not only enhance her standing in the wider academic community, it also enables her to envision a future beyond her current workplace. Some day, she imagines working for an English department, teaching English majors and training future English teachers.

In spite of feeling somewhat marginalized within the broader framework of the university, Kumiko enjoys a relationship of participation within her faculty in areas that matter to her, especially in teaching. In her third year there, she proposed to teach a lecture course on gender. This proposal was originally met with strong opposition from members of the sociology department, who felt that such a course fell outside the realm of the English department and that she should confine herself to what she was hired to do: teach English. However, the proposal was ultimately accepted and her course has currently become one of the most popular in the university, with an enrollment of over 400 students. The success of the course has resulted in some jealousy among the faculty members, and Kumiko has been warned by a close colleague to downplay her success. He told her she should 'be modest and to say, *"taishita koto nai"* [oh, it's not a big deal]'.

According to Wenger (1998), one of the crucial aspects of belonging to a community is having one's ideas accepted and adopted by members of that community. Kumiko's success in convincing the members of her department of the importance of having a class in gender shows that she is being taken seriously as a member of her faculty. Therefore, although she may feel marginalized with regard to some aspects of her workplace, she is a full participating member in other aspects.

Kumiko has appropriated her exclusion from the university political groups to focus on her own research and her teaching, but her success and popularity as a teacher does not go unnoticed among her colleagues, who good-naturedly chide her when they see her wearing jeans, sitting in the grass and eating pizza with the students. They jokingly tell her she should be 'more like a teacher'. Because of positive student feedback and full class enrollments, some of Kumiko's colleagues may have become envious of her. The tension between maintaining a harmonious relationship with colleagues and being the type of teacher she wants to be indicates that her alignment within her workplace is not uncomplicated.

Taka

This section examines how Taka, the only male teacher in this book, utilizes imagination and alignment within his university. He also teaches in the Kanto area, but unlike Kumiko's university that is quite large and well known, Taka's is a small private women's university. This university was established nearly 100 years ago and has a unique history compared to other private women's universities in Japan, which are usually conservative, family-run businesses existing to further the social prestige of the family (Kempner & Makino, 1993). Taka's university, however, is run by the professors who wield a great deal of power, which Taka credits to a legacy left from the student radicalism of the 1970s. He says that when the students of that era became faculty members of his university, they instilled a democratic system where all the teachers have an equal voice, and the power of the family who owned the university accordingly became very weak.

Taka began working at his university at the time when it was undergoing a great deal of transformation. The balance of power within the university is shifting because the younger professors are coming into power while the older radical professors are reaching retirement. Taka, as the youngest member of the faculty, is being mentored by those who are now gaining power, and he aligns himself with this group. They bid for his allegiance by telling him off-putting stories of the 'way things used to be' when the older group ran the department. Wenger (1998: 203) explains that stories told by more experienced members of a community to newcomers are ways to promote belonging, because such stories 'transport our experience into the situations they relate and involve us in producing the meanings of those events as though we were participants'. This sense of belonging is evident below, where Taka describes his participation in the university's outreach programs to attract potential students. These programs have only recently been implemented due to the previous strong opposition of the older professors. This extract (boldface is my emphasis) is particularly interesting, because even though he has only worked at this university for one year, it is very clear which side he is aligning himself with.

> ... **We** couldn't start new things until recently because **they** tried to discuss every single merits and demerits and if demerit if **they** could find some demerits then ... **they** tend to uh, ... decide not to do. But uh, uh because some of **those teachers** uh ... now have left and **we** could start doing something new, including three or four new promotions kind of things. And one is well, very straight forward speech contests. That was the first time for **us** and **we** invited ... high school students as well as alumni university students and **we** gave one day speech contest that was quite successful. **We** got help from the Toastmasters club.

An identity of opposition toward the older group of professors is again evident when he describes department meetings as a waste of time because of endless pointless discussions. Again, his colleagues seek his alignment by telling him stories of how much worse things were in the old days:

> Those people sometimes evoke the argument... To me it's sometimes pointless to argument for argument's sake kind of argument ... well I see sometimes. And after those meetings we have, my colleagues would say, uh [sigh], 'like 10 years ago, we had a much more problems that this... is only..., seems to get these days and that was nothing'. Oh, Ok. [laughter]

Although he feels unaligned with the older professors in the academic community, he says the upside of the democratic atmosphere they had created is that everyone, even newcomers, is accorded importance as full participating members of the faculty. This was against his expectations, because when he started working, his friends advised him to just 'Shut up and say "yes" for the next three years.... For the first three years, say nothing but yes'. He was not only given the right to speak up, he was expected to do so. This made him feel at home and feel 'important', and he says, 'They will listen to me. That's kind of uncommon practice in Japan. For a 32-year-old'. Therefore, compared to his friends who work at other universities, he feels his situation is 'heaven'.

One incident, however, indicated that Taka might have been a little overconfident believing that he is a full participating member in his department. He was asked to offer his opinion concerning a decision that would have a far-reaching impact on the school during a confidential meeting of an important committee he had been elected to. In doing so, he used what Japanese would consider strong language. At that time, some professors chuckled, but at the next meeting, he was reprimanded by a senior professor whose proposal had not been passed. Although he offered a 'sincere apology', he felt baffled by the contradiction of being reprimanded for his comments after having been invited to speak frankly.

This experience made him realize that 'the whole first year of working is one long initiation' and that engagement in the workplace is more complex than first appears. Nevertheless, unlike Kumiko, who does not completely align herself with her university, Taka strongly identifies as a member of his. By aligning himself with the group that is coming into power now, he is positioning himself to join the insider trajectory if all goes well. Through the shared activities and shared experiences with those who are slightly above him in the hierarchy of the university, he is constructing an identity as a potential, fully participating *uchimuki* member (Poole, 2010) member.

Kana

Next we turn to Kana, who is one of the youngest members of the International Relations department of her university in a conservative regional area of Japan. She had just completed her first year teaching in Japan after having lived abroad for 11 years, and teaches not only English, but also her academic specialty, comparative culture.

Kana needs to learn not only the ins and outs of her workplace, but also how to be Japanese again after having lived abroad for many years. She is learning that all is not as it seems on the surface in her university, which she describes as being contradictory in its openness and formality. In an atmosphere of openness, some professors encourage students to become involved in shared activities, such as playing musical instruments together on the weekends. She says activities of this sort are unusual between professors and students in that conservative area of Japan. However, she is aware of many conservative aspects of that university as well.

While living abroad, she became accustomed to speaking to people of higher and lower status in an equal manner. However, such a communication style has made her readjustment to Japanese society difficult because she feels she has forgotten how to communicate using *keigo* (Japanese polite language). She is afraid of using it inappropriately with the older and conservative professors and inadvertently causing offense. She says she feels 'really nervous' when she speaks to someone she doesn't know well, so to avoid appearing impolite, she plans what to say in advance. She says, 'I try not to be rude, but using *keigo* all the time – sometimes I get mixed up. Am I using *keigo* to myself'?

Although Kana does the work of a tenured teacher, her position is somewhat precarious because her five-year contract will lead to a tenured position only if she is promoted to associate professor within that time. She says that she likes working at this university so she will do what it takes in order to stay. However, she feels gaining this promotion would be 'very, very hard because some professors say something a little bit sexist, which is **never** heard of in Australia'. This fear contributes to her nervousness when dealing with her colleagues. At the same time, however, she admits that she is responsible to a certain extent in enabling sexist communication with her colleagues by communicating in an indirect way with her male colleagues, and says '. . .it is kind of my fault, too. It is being submissive. It is how I was brought up being'. She tries 'not to be submissive', but resorts to indirect teasing and making jokes, even with male colleagues she is comfortable with, in order not to appear aggressive or rude. She is afraid to talk to some of the other professors, because they appear stern and she feels they expect her to be more subdued. When she has to speak to them, she is 'really nervous, you know, really formal'.

Kana feels that she needs several years to observe what is going on in her university before she will feel completely at home. Until Kana obtains tenure, her demure and feminine approach with her colleagues may be the best way to ensure acceptance when the professors, who may not want an outspoken younger female teacher taking a permanent position, eventually vote for her promotion.

Miwa

Finally, we look at Miwa's engagement in the workplace, which differs from the other teachers due to her employment status as a contracted teacher. She was hired only to teach and thus does not engage in any other university-related work. Although she is expected to move to another position in a few years, her exceptional educational background has her securely placed on the inbound trajectory of university English teachers in Japan. Everyone, including Miwa, believes she will find a good job soon. Her limited participation in the workplace is not seen as marginalization, but as a period of apprenticeship (Lave & Wenger, 1991) where young academics gain valuable work experience without administrative responsibilities. Everyone is seen to benefit from such contracted positions: universities can have teaching staff at a reasonable cost, and inexperienced academics can gain valuable job experience while having sufficient time for writing and publishing papers in order to build a resume.[5]

Lave and Wenger (1991) and Wenger (1998) argue that one aspect of becoming a member of a professional community involves learning from the more experienced members of that community. However, for Miwa, it seems that there has been little guidance of *English language teaching* from more experienced members of the community. When she began teaching part-time two years prior to the interviews for this study, she received little guidance. Her initiation into English teaching merely involved being handed a textbook and asked to teach everything in it so that her students would be able to pass a standardized test at the end of the semester. At another school, she was asked to teach a course entitled 'English Presentations' even though she had no knowledge about this area. She said this was a difficult assignment for her because:

> Everything is new and everything is kind of…it's first for everybody. I don't really know any format or any rules for presentation [amused voice] and they gave me brochures of their core requirements for

presentation class so I learned from that. I learned from other people's syllabi [laughter]. So that's how I figured it out.

When asked if she had anyone she could turn to during the first months of teaching, Miwa said that she used to ask her Japanese professor for advice, but she felt uncomfortable asking him questions that were related to language pedagogy and not literature. After part-time teaching for one year, she obtained her full-time job and became more comfortable in the classroom. Nevertheless, being isolated from other teachers and having had insufficient support when she started teaching has resulted in feelings of conflict during the transition period from being a PhD student and a scholar of American literature, to an English language teacher at Japanese universities. Although Miwa's position can be viewed as a period of apprenticeship, there has been very little guidance from other teachers to help her develop expertise. Therefore, she feels she is left to 'figure everything out' herself.

Imagination and Alignment in the Wider Social Context

The third and final area of engagement discussed in this chapter concerns the participants' engagement within the wider social context. As Wenger (1998) argues, the boundaries of communities are blurred and people hold multiple memberships in a number of communities that constitute their identity. For the teachers in this study, these communities include professional membership in academic societies, study groups and various social groups.

Two main areas of engagement in the wider social context emerged from the data analysis and will be discussed in this section. First, the participants engage with like-minded scholars by attending and presenting at conferences, publishing research and taking part in study groups. Engaging in such activities contributes to a sense of professional identity that is apart from teaching and apart from the workplace. Second, the participants engage in personal activities with people outside of academia, which gives a sense of personal identity. This area of engagement will only be touched upon briefly because the time limitations of the interviews prevented a deeper exploration of it.

Engagement with other academics

The first area of engagement under this category involves interaction with academics with like-minded interests. This interaction generally occurs outside the workplace, because the participants often do not share similar academic interests with their colleagues. Kumiko, for example, works for an economics faculty, where the majority of the professors specialize in business-related areas. Her research interests also differ from her English-teaching colleagues as well. Therefore, she maintains some aspects of her professional identity through outside organizations. She has membership in various feminist organizations and edits a bilingual pedagogical journal that focuses upon teaching in the Japanese context.

Taka says the university he teaches at is like a 'continuous version of high school'. It is a teaching institute where a teacher is clearly a teacher and the students are clearly students. This is very unlike his alma mater, where there are blurred boundaries between teaching and research, and teachers and students work together to create mutual identities as scholars. Although Taka has taken a leave of absence from the PhD program, he still attends weekly study sessions convened by his academic supervisor.

Participation in academic communities outside of the university where people work provides Kumiko and Taka with what Wenger (1998) calls 'generational encounters', where 'newcomers can be integrated into the community, engage in its practice and then – in their own way – perpetuate it' (p. 99). This participation also provides networking opportunities that could prove useful over the course of their careers. Kumiko and Taka say they are satisfied with their jobs, but they also say that they would consider moving to a different university if they had the opportunity to teach their academic specialties to students who are interested in doing research.

Engagement with those outside of academia

This section discusses how teachers utilize their imagination and alignment with those who are outside the domains of teaching, university work and professional organizations. Engaging with people outside of their working lives contributes to both personal and professional identities. An identity is built through the discursive practices of others (Gee, 2000). This will be discussed in greater detail in the next chapter of this book, but two areas will be briefly touched upon here. The first concerns how people outside of academia treat the teachers. Because their professional identities are still closely bound to their identities as students, they have yet to become accustomed to the deferential treatment they receive from others. Taka realized that his position as a university teacher accorded more respect from a Canadian library staff member than when he conducted research as a student. He describes the difference in treatment in the following comment:

> I was treated as not as a student any more kind of position. That was also...quite an experience for me. Uh, up until then, I was kind of 'Hello my name is Taka from that university and I'm a student and they

gave me a student "you are student" kind of look.' But this time, I was a kind of professor kind of look. I got a professor kind of look.

Miwa also felt she was accorded more respect as a *shakaijin* (member of society) than when she was a student. She felt somewhat guilty joining the workforce in her mid-30s because of financial difficulties, and she did not like to tell people that she was still a student because she felt that her age and her position did not match Japanese societal expectations. Now, however, as a member of a prestigious university (even if only with a contracted position), she feels she is no longer seen as a 'regular private nerd' (a student) but given greater status as a 'professional nerd' with a full-time university job. This status is important for her because she feels it gives her a certain amount of respect in the community, especially from men whom she says generally look down on women. She is aware that her position at her university is temporary, so she is looking forward to the day when she can say to those who discriminate against her because she is a woman, 'I'm a professor. You can't treat me like that'.

Although being a university teacher often results in special treatment from others not in academia, there is a downside, because people's communication styles shift from being friendly to being deferential. Kumiko complains that this makes it difficult to cultivate friendly relationships with people. She therefore often tells people that she is an English teacher, letting them assume that she teaches at a less-prestigious language school rather than a well-known university.

Miwa says she would tell people she teaches at a university if she were asked, but she clarifies, 'That is what I do to earn money. So that's the definition of what I do for a living, just for a living. I don't think that is the same as what I am'. If someone should ask her what she *is*, she laughs and says she would reply, 'I am basically a nerd. A literature **nut** kind of person. And well, that sums up...most of the things'.

Engagement in non-work-related activities

The final aspect of engagement to be discussed in this chapter contributing to a sense of professional identity is that which occurs through the teachers' interests and hobbies. As previous studies of teacher identity have revealed (e.g. Elbaz, 1983; Gatbonton, 1999; Golembek, 1998), teachers' personal experiences and knowledge are reflected in all aspects of their teaching. These participants lead rich personal lives that contribute to who they are as people, as teachers and as scholars. Miwa feels that the person she really is is a combination of all her experiences and the things that she can do:

For example I'm in academics, and I love reading, I love literature. But I still can bake cookies. [laughter] And I can knit. And I love those things. And I can play musical instruments. [...] Yes, uh huh. And I'm enjoying all of them. Except the athletics field [laughter].

Kana, who feels shy and uncomfortable when standing in the front of the classroom in front of students, draws upon her love of acting and dancing for confidence. When asked if she sees herself as a scholar or a teacher, her answer was quite surprising. 'No... [hesitant] no...A scholar. I like researching and things like that...[hesitant] Half scholar, half dancer. I do dancing'. Laughing, she explains how dancing has influenced her perceptions of herself as a teacher:

> Dancing is my passion. Dancing is what I found in Britain. [...] That changed me a lot. I'm not a language person. I am not. I cannot put things. I'm not a born lecturer. Someone who is a born lecturer can talk [...] I'm more physical, I think. I'm not a language based person. I'm not skilled in languages. But I feel like I can express with my body. [...] I'm normally shy. I don't want to talk in front of people. I get worked up and nervous. [...] To begin with, [...] when I ask questions and things like that. I come close to students. Before that I was too shy. Students are strangers basically. You don't know the individual very well. It is like, I think standing up as well. [...] Before I was nervous about where my hands are going to be and things like that. Clumsy as well. [...] But since I began dancing, I think it is like acting. Because as a teacher, you have to present, you have to kind of look enthusiastic even if you are not enthusiastic. You have to kind of, I don't know, hold the space, make the atmosphere. I think I am using my dancing...

To sum up, the participants' identities as university English teachers extend beyond their classrooms and universities into the wider social community where they are members of multiple communities of practice and where boundaries are crossed in order to construct and support aspects of their professional identity. Professional organizations enable the participants to reify their identity as academics in ways that may not be available through their teaching or interaction with colleagues. The discursive practices of others (Gee, 2000) also play a strong role in constructing self-identity as a university teacher. And, not least, the participants' personal interests, which may not appear to be directly related to their working lives, also play a role in influencing their identities as teachers.

Conclusion of Chapter 5

The first study presented in this book has considered the professional identity development of four relatively new Japanese teachers of English in Japanese higher education. Wenger's (1998) theory of identity, which asserts that identity forms while individuals negotiate the meaning of their participation as members of what he calls 'communities of practice', provided the theoretical lens to analyze the participants' narrative data. The two questions that have guided this study were the following:

(1) What are the principal activities that Japanese teachers of English in Japanese higher education engage in as a part of their work practices?
(2) How do Japanese teachers of English in higher education construct their professional identity as they become members of the community of practice of university English teachers?

The first question was answered through a content analysis of the participants' interview data. The three common areas of engagement that constitute the work of these teachers were: engagement in teaching, engagement in the workplace and engagement in the wider social context. How they utilized their imagination and alignment within these three categories in constructing their professional identity, which concerns the second research question, differed. These differences were discussed in detail, and it was found that although there were a number of shared identity traits, the participants' degree of identification as teachers, university staff and members of the wider community differed according to how meanings of these identities were negotiated and how they were individually appropriated.

The first category, *engagement in teaching*, formed the bulk of the discussion, since teaching was the area of engagement the participants seemed to be occupied with the most. Although they all teach English to Japanese university students, how this teaching is conceptualized and carried out was related to their individual educational and life experiences, which provided them with images of teachers and teaching and of students and learning.

For example, the positive and negative images the participants held of former teachers played an essential role in how they chose to construct their own identities as teachers, and how they aligned themselves with the teaching profession. Taka, who was the only participant in this study with positive images of his former teachers, believes that teachers have the power to influence and shape students' lives. These beliefs are reflected in his attitude that teaching is an important profession and that he sees himself as an important person in his students' lives. Negative images of former teachers, on the other hand, result in the teachers engaging in teaching practices, which are perceived to be in opposition to those of the participants' former teachers. Kumiko, for example, remembers her teachers as scary and unreasonable, so she works hard at cultivating an image of being her students' 'friend', and Miwa remembers her English teacher in junior high school as somewhat incompetent, so she considers in-depth knowledge of English language to be of utmost importance in teaching.

In sum, the power of former teachers in shaping the participants' images of themselves as teachers is strong, but how the teachers choose to identify depends on whether or not they align themselves with the images they hold of these teachers. The participants also rely on images of themselves as students to negotiate the meaning of their teaching and how to relate to their students. By positioning their 'student-selves' with their current students, Taka and Kumiko were easily able to align their practices with their students because they could empathize with their students' disinterest and lack of motivation to study. On the other hand, Kana and Miwa experienced discomfort as teachers because when positioning their student-selves with their current students, they found a large gap that they were unable to comfortably bridge.

The participants' narratives examined under the category of engagement in teaching are congruent with Tsui's (2007) findings that identity is 'relational as well as experiential' (p. 678). Through the act of teaching, the participants' simultaneously construct an identity that is in alignment with or in opposition to those people who influence their perceptions of themselves as teachers: their former teachers and their current students. It is not surprising that these teachers, whose experiences as students are still fresh in their minds, draw upon these memories in constructing identities as teachers. These powerful images may diminish over time as the participants gain more classroom experience, but it is likely that these images will remain a part of their core identities as teachers.

The second category of engagement discussed in this study was *engagement in the workplace*, which included the day-to-day activities that take place in the university workplace that fall outside the realm of teaching. Although all of the participants are legitimate members of the community of practice of university English teachers in Japan, they do not all have equal access to the inbound and inner trajectories in the universities in which they work. Access to these trajectories was first dependent upon the individual terms of their employment contracts, which influence the degrees of participation and non-participation experienced in the workplace.

Accordingly, Taka and Kumiko with tenure, and Kana who is on the tenure track, have access to the inbound trajectories of the workplaces that Miwa, who only has a contracted position, does not. However, as we have seen, due to the varied sociopolitical contexts of each university, the teachers' access to the insider trajectory, which involves power, differs. The teachers' identities of participation and non-participation in their workplaces influence how they identify with – and how they align their practices with – their universities.

Taka's narratives revealed that even though he is a newcomer in his university, the sociopolitical atmosphere there ensures that he is given a voice and is taken seriously by the junior and senior members of the faculty. This acceptance invokes feelings of importance in him. In addition, he is also being wooed by the group of teachers who will soon be coming into power, and he aligns himself with their practices by taking part in their student recruitment activities and by empathizing with their stories about how terrible things 'used to be' when the senior professors were running the programs. Taka thus participates in the university on two levels – as a tenured member of the faculty and as a member of the group about to assume power. Taka admits that the atmosphere at his university is unique and that he would be unable to as easily assume an identity as a full participating member if he were employed at a different university.

Kumiko's identity of participation in the university workplace significantly differs from Taka's. She also has tenure, but because of what she feels to be gendered exclusion from the powerful factions of her university, she does not see herself as a potential member of its insider trajectory. However, Kumiko has appropriated the meaning of this exclusion to focus on activities that mean more to her: her research and her teaching. She may not align herself with the political workings of her university, but within her faculty she feels that her ideas, particularly those related to teaching, are taken seriously and it is there that she has an identity of participation. The course on gender studies that she proposed and that was approved after strong opposition from some of the professors is a case in point.

Professional identity gained through engagement in the workplace is complicated because of the multiple groups that are established within the individual universities. How new teachers are accepted in these groups is dependent upon numerous factors that make up its sociopolitical context. Such factors include, but are not limited to, the university's history and background, its size, its geographical location and its areas of academic focus.

Under the third and final category of identity development discussed in this study, *engagement in the wider social context*, it was found that interaction with other like-minded scholars and academics in study groups or professional association enabled the participants to nurture their professional identities in ways that they could not achieve through teaching or through working with their colleagues. Engagement in the wider social context helps prevent academic isolation and provides recognition by likeminded scholars. Kumiko, for example, belongs to numerous feminist organizations. Such memberships help her maintain her identity as a feminist while dealing with the day-to-day demands of her work. This is true also of Taka, who attends study sessions held by his professor in order to balance his identity as a language teacher at an academically low-ranking university with his identity as a researcher.

How the participants draw on personal idiosyncrasies to construct their professional identity is also interesting. Kana's reflection of envisioning herself as a 'half scholar, half dancer' was most surprising, but merging these two identities together enables her to overcome her shyness and awkwardness in the classroom. This clearly illuminates the humanist notion that teachers are more than 'teaching machines'; they are people with complex private lives that are carried with them into the classroom and utilized while teaching.

This is a small-scale study, and its findings, which concern only four teachers, are not intended to generalize to the wider population of university English teachers in Japan. Nevertheless, the stories told by each of these teachers in the course of the interviews shed light on how professional identity is constructed by newcomers to the field of English teaching in higher education in Japan. The study has shown how the process of identification as a university educator is complex and shaped by sociopolitical factors as well as by personal ones. It also involves crossing the boundaries of the multiple groups to which the participants belong. The study has illuminated how the day-to-day practices these teachers engage in enable them to create and recreate who they are and what they do as teachers in an ongoing reflexive relationship.

Notes

(1) Hada (2005) warns that even though numerous universities have established graduate programs in the past decade, because of the hierarchal nature of Japanese universities and their connection to industry, MA holders and PhD holders from prestigious universities will have an advantage in the job market over those from less prestigious universities. As a result, applicants for lower-level universities may fall, and it will be difficult to maintain their programs.
(2) It is likely that Miwa was referring to the Japanese term 'office lady'. As discussed in Chapter 2, a stratified educational system and sociopolitical attitudes toward women

prevents them from entering the workforce in career positions, but instead, mainly channels them into doing routine clerical work as support staff for male employees.
(3) The Japanese term *sempai* is commonly used to refer to someone who is older and more experienced.
(4) Chapter 6 of this book discusses in greater detail the position of women in Japanese universities.
(5) Contracted positions for young Japanese academics can be viewed as inbound trajectory positions because the chances of them finding a good position are high. However, this is not the case with native-English speaking teachers who are also hired in contracted positions who find it difficult to secure tenured positions and may be on the peripheral trajectories of several universities, with one contract after another. See Simon-Maeda, 2004a and Stewart, 2005, for discussion on how these contracted positions influence the identity of non-Japanese.

6 It's a Man's World

Introduction

This chapter investigates the intersection of gender with other aspects of identity, such as age and social background, in the professional identity of all seven female participants in this book. Teachers at universities in Japan, as elsewhere, are considered to be members of a prestigious occupation. However, as discussed in Chapter 2, the number of female teachers is very low. The percentage of full-time female faculty at national universities in the early 2000s was only 6.6% (Normile, 2001), although a target had been set by the Japan Association of National Universities to raise the number to 20% by 2010. Currently less than 14% of tenured faculty in Japanese higher education is female. The employment profile between male and female teachers is even more striking when examining the type of tertiary institutions where women are employed. In 2005, in four-year universities, female professors accounted for 11.2%, associate professors for 17% and assistant professors for 24.1% of the total faculty. On the other hand, at two-year junior colleges, which are generally considered lower in academic status than four-year universities, the percentage of tenured female faculty rises to nearly half, at 46.5% (Fujita, 2006).

Not only are women underrepresented in Japanese academia, they comprise less than 10% of managerial and lawmaking positions as well, and in 2010, the Global Gender Gap Index ranked Japan as 94th out of 134 countries in terms of women's participation in public life (World Economic Forum, 2010). Action is being taken by the Headquarters for the Promotion of Gender Equality in Japan to ensure that women will represent 30% of leading positions by 2020 (Fujita, 2006). However, it is difficult for Japanese women to gain a foothold in professions, including that of university teaching, because as Liddle and Nakajima (2000: 317) conclude from their longitudinal case study of 120 Japanese professional women, gender ideologies of Japan 'view women as naturally peripheral to the world of work, and define them primarily by their relationship to domesticity, reproduction and the family'.

Why is it important to look at the identities of female educators in Japan? As Simon-Maeda (2004a: 431) pointed out in her study of Japanese and non-Japanese women teaching EFL at various Japanese universities, a critical examination of *all* teachers' stories enables English language educators to examine TESOL more closely by uncovering 'the field's political and ideological underpinnings and rework them toward more progressive ends'. When we look at the narratives of the women in this study, we will see that ideological themes do indeed shape many aspects of their careers – from choosing English as a subject to study, to going to graduate school, to entering the profession of college and university teaching and to taking part as members of the community of practice of university teachers of English (Wenger, 1998). Even a cursory examination of the data provided from this study's interviews indicate that gender clearly impacts these teachers' sense of self-identity, which in turn influences what they do in the classroom.

As discussed earlier, there have been relatively few studies investigating teacher identity in the Japanese tertiary context, and those that did mainly focused on both Japanese and non-Japanese teachers. Duff and Uchida (1997) investigated the transformation of sociocultural identity of two Japanese and two non-Japanese teachers in a language institute, and how culture was transmitted through teaching. Simon-Maeda (2004a) investigated the gendered struggles of nine female university English teachers, seven of whom were non-Japanese (including one composite participant from the foreign lesbian community), one was Japanese and one was an ethnic Korean-Japanese. Stewart (2005) analyzed the narratives of four Japanese and four non-Japanese teachers from the perspective of professionalism and expertise. These studies have confirmed that identity is closely related to sociopolitical contexts and that it is always shifting rather than static or fixed. However, they have also demonstrated that there are distinctions in identities between the Japanese and non-Japanese teachers. Non-Japanese teachers feel marginalized within their workplaces because they perceive that they are seen as 'walking dictionaries', cultural ambassadors and temporary/replaceable teachers. Perceptions of what English language teaching constitutes also differs between these two groups: non-Japanese teachers' expertise lies in their pedagogical and cultural knowledge, but Japanese teachers' expertise lies in their abilities as scholars in English-*related* fields such as English literature or English linguistics and/or their knowledge *of* English language.

While Simon-Maeda (2004a) has investigated the professional identity of female university teachers in Japan, the current study both follows her study and refocuses it: this study is a narrative study that seeks to explore the details of women's lives from their gendered perspective; however, its focus is solely on female Japanese teachers. Their wide range of ages may reveal changes that have taken place over the years in how women have gained access to their careers as university teachers and differences in their educational backgrounds. Furthermore, unlike the Japanese teachers in Stewart's (2005) study who taught for academically prestigious universities in the Tokyo area, the teachers in this study teach at universities varying in status throughout Japan. Indeed, it is important to look at the full range of teachers because their professional identity may differ in significant ways from teachers who teach their academic specialties only in academically higher-ranking universities.

The research questions that have guided this study are the following:

(1) What, if any, is the impact of gender in the professional identity of female teachers of English in Japanese higher education?
(2) What, if any, are the main similarities and main differences in the professional identity development among female university teachers of various age groups?
(3) How do female teachers in Japanese universities appropriate and negotiate their professional identity in a social context that is predominantly male oriented?

Analytical Framework: Gee's (2000) Perspective on Identity

In a theory of identity that shares a number of similarities to Wenger's (1998) theory of identity which was utilized as the theoretical framework for Chapters 5 and 7, Gee (1996: 99) argues that identity develops through what he calls Discourse (written with a capital D to distinguish from 'discourse', which he defines as text longer than a sentence) that reflects thinking, speaking and acting. In other words, he says that Discourses provide people with a 'sort of identity kit which comes complete with the appropriate costume and instructions on how to act, talk and often write so as to take on a particular social role that others will recognize'. Gee (2000: 99) later succinctly defines identity as 'being a certain type of person in a given context' and offers four useful perspectives to view how people see themselves and how they are seen. These perspectives are: (1) identity that is formed by nature (N-identity); (2) identity that is bestowed from institutions (I-identity); (3) identity that develops through interaction with others (D-identity) and (4) identity that occurs when one affiliates with a group or a system (A-identity).

The interview data in this chapter was analyzed using Gee's conceptualization of identity. His construct has recently been used as the theoretical model to understand how identity is developed in several areas of educational research, such as the identity development of secondary school students (e.g. Blank, 2008; Brown et al., 2005); of university students

(Johnson & Watson, 2004; e.g. Nguyen, n.d.; Watson *et al.*, 2005) and of teachers (e.g. Bullough, 2005).

Gee's different perspectives of identity are cultivated, recognized and identified through interpretive systems, which can come from traditionally approved roles, through the discourse of others or through membership of groups. Individuals rely on all four perspectives in order to let themselves be seen and to let others see them as a means for forming identity.

First, nature-identity (N-identity) reflects the unchangeable biological properties of people, such as sex, age and ethnic background. It develops because of the attributes society places on these biological properties, and not necessarily because of the attributes themselves. It is only when importance is placed upon these attributes that they play a role in shaping identity. Mere biological traits (such as, to use Gee's example, having a spleen) do not influence identity *unless* some importance is attached to it. A person's sex is also a biological trait, but the state of being male or female is ascribed a great deal of importance by society, and is often referred to as gender. This study examines the intersection of the participants' N-identity of gender and Gee's other three identity perspectives in their professional identity as university teachers of English.

Second in the theory is Institutional-identity (I-identity), which develops from an institutional perspective. This type of identity is bestowed by *authorities*. This identity comes from authorization, rules, laws and tradition, and includes hierarchal relationships within people's workplaces, respect given to people as professionals and power. In this study, I-identity is related to the capacity in which the participants are employed and to the type of tertiary institution they are employed at. For the women in this study, there is a distinct interconnectedness between the N- and the I-identities because of the gendered societal expectations for women that have influenced their access to gaining credentials that would enable them to develop I-identity as university teachers.

Third, Discourse-identity (D-identity) refers to individual traits in people that are recognized by others. Under this category, discursive practices through interaction with others construct and sustain identity. D-identity can be seen as an ascription or an achievement depending on how actively a person recruits and negotiates their identity with others. Gee describes D-identity by giving the example of a teacher, which is most pertinent to this study. He simply says that identification as a teacher is possible because society ascribes a person with the identity as one and treats them as such.

Finally, Affinity-identity (A-identity), the fourth perspective in Gee's theory, evolves through group membership and is similar to Wenger's

(1998) theory of identity that claims identity evolves through engagement in the various communities to which we belong. A-identity also comes from shared experiences and practices that 'create and sustain group affiliations, rather than on institutions or discourse/dialogue directly' (Gee, 2000: 105). Group members, Gee argues, have primary allegiance toward the practices of a group, and a secondary allegiance toward the members of the group. In other words, people may identify as members of the academic department with which they are affiliated because of the shared practices that are necessary in order to belong to that department, but they may not share affinity with the people they work with.

These four perspectives of identity are not four discrete categories, but ones that interrelate in complex ways. Gee says that the separation of identity into these four categories enables understanding of what 'kind of person' (p. 109) people are within certain contexts. People constantly engage in a combination of these identities to be seen as a certain type of person:

- Speaking (or writing) in a certain way.
- Acting and interacting in a certain way.
- Using one's face and body in a certain way.
- Dressing in a certain way.
- Feeling, believing and valuing in a certain way.
- Using objects, tools or technologies (i.e. 'things') in a certain way (Gee, 2000: 109).

The Participants

The seven female teachers who are featured in this chapter range in age from their early 30s to their 60s and cover three educational generations. Taeko (60) and Keiko (57) belong to the postwar baby generation and attended university in the 1960s. Kumiko (45) and Naomi (45) went to university during the 1980s, when the Japanese economy was booming and tertiary education was still expanding. Miwa, Kana and Shizuko, members of the second wave of postwar baby boomers, went to university when the numbers of students vying for places in good universities were at their peak in the 1990s, but began teaching when the numbers of students were at their lowest. As will be seen in this chapter, each educational generation has had its own distinctive impact on the students who lived through the practices and policies of those times.

The ultimate decision of each of the seven participants to become university English teachers was due in large part, as we shall see, to their flexibility in thinking and their ability to overcome numerous difficulties related to the sociopolitical ideologies in Japan that shape women's lives. Flexibility was essential to readjust and reevaluate their life plans and careers. Straying from the normal social path, they needed a certain amount of what Taeko called 'guts'. It is this combination of flexibility and guts that enabled these seven women to gain entry into the prestigious profession of university English teaching in Japan. These characteristics may of course be necessary for all teachers in higher education, for this is not an easy profession to enter. To reiterate what was demonstrated in Chapter 2, sociopolitical constraints limit women's access to education and to employment in Japan. As we shall see in the discussion that follows, these women's ability to negotiate and renegotiate their identity as daughters, wives, mothers and sisters gave them the edge in gaining the academic credentials that they could eventually convert into a high-status career.

Analysis and Interpretation

In this section, I examine the participants' narratives to see to what extent Gee's (2000) theory of identity reveals the identity formation of the seven women in this study. As previously mentioned, the stories told by these women show instances of identity that overlap and intertwine with each other, and do not therefore divide into four clear-cut categories. However, it is the aim of this analysis to make clearer distinctions by looking at identity from Gee's four perspectives described in the previous section. Such an analysis will enable a clearer understanding to emerge of how the professional identity of these women has been formed.

Therefore, the analysis begins with a discussion of the participants' N-identity of gender. Here we examine the familial and social influence in shaping and guiding their initial access to university English study, which is at the heart of their identities as teachers of English. At some point in their lives, the participants took decisive actions to improve their academic qualifications. These actions were the results of 'critical events' or 'critical moments' (Webster & Mertova, 2007), which included life-changing events, such as going abroad for the first time, the breakup of a marriage or job dissatisfaction. As a result of these actions, the participants gained the academic qualifications to enable them to become university English teachers and to claim an I-identity as such. Next I examine how the participants' professional identity as university teachers is influenced by their D-identities. The perceptions of others, as we shall see, play a strong role in how these teachers see themselves and how they choose to present themselves to others. Numerous D-identity themes emerged during the interviews, but only a few, particularly those that are related to gender, will be touched upon in this section. The three main areas of discussion will be the participants' perceptions of themselves and the perceptions of others as (1) role models; (2) independent women and (3) as university teachers.

The final section focuses on the participants' A-identity that forms through their membership in groups. The main group discussed in this section is the participants' individual workplace community, although this section will briefly touch upon the difficulties found in balancing membership in family groups as well.

Nature-Identity

My analysis begins with a discussion of the impact of gender on the participants' professional lives. Gender falls under Gee's (2000) first perspective of identity: N-identity. A person's sex is a natural state of being, but identity as a man or a woman is the result of gendered sociopolitical attitudes. As discussed in Chapter 2, Japanese men and women have different access to education and employment in Japan, and as we shall see in this section, being female played an instrumental role in their academic choices that constituted the first step in becoming university English teachers.

English as a 'feminized' subject to study

The most striking issue that emerged from the narratives was the gendered perception of English as an area of study. This was reported by the participants as holding true both for them and their parents.[1] The study of English seemed to be based on one of two rationales. First, parents persuaded their daughters to major in English, especially if they felt their daughters' first choices were inappropriate. Second, English was seen to be a useful 'backup' plan, which parents felt could provide a source of income for their daughters if necessary.

The power of parental persuasion in choosing English is clearly shown in Kumiko's narrative. She said she originally wanted to study art, but her parents thought that because she was 'good at English', she should major in it and become an English teacher instead. Although she said she 'didn't hate English', it was 'not her favorite subject'. Her comment below illustrates how obediently she followed her parents' wishes:

> I...was very, very interested **ART**, so I wanted to go an art school. But my parents were so against that. So my parents recommended me to go a girls' high school and a girls' university and major in English literature.

> That was kind of common at that time – a common and popular way...for girls. You know...girls go to women's universities and major in English or in English literature. And after, they work for maybe three or four years, they can get married and they can....Well, that's my parents' perception...so I kind of followed their way. I went to a women's high school and women's university and majored in English and American and literature.

Kumiko's parents also felt she should get a teaching license because it would be handy to have. She did not intend to become a teacher, but she was unable to resist their demand. She said, 'Maybe I was not critical when I was young. I just followed my parents' way....I didn't tell my parents I didn't want to be a teacher. I tried to be secret'.

Kana also faced opposition from her parents when she wanted to become an actress. She successfully auditioned for a theatrical troupe while still in high school, but her father and her uncles, who were adamantly against her moving to Tokyo to become an actress, argued that she would become 'nothing better than a Ginza bar hostess'. She abandoned her plan and decided to attempt to pass university entrance examinations instead. Although she went to a low-ranking commercial high school that prepared students to enter the workforce and not university, she was good at English. Within a very short time, she crammed for the test, and against all odds, she passed the entrance examination of a well-known private university in her prefecture. Although her parents, neither of whom were college graduates, supported her decision to try to go to university, there were some gendered strings attached to her plan, as the following anecdote illustrates:

> My family was like...for example, my brother could take university exams around Tokyo but I was not allowed because I'm a woman. I was just given the chance to go to university in [local prefecture], because I could go to university from home. So that kind of things, I was brought up. Without realizing. I was in the kitchen, but my brothers were out of the kitchen.

Miwa, who comes from a rural fishing village where few people, particularly women, go to college, had to convince her family to send her to university in Tokyo. Miwa, as the first person in her family to go to university, felt that literature study would appear to be too frivolous to warrant her parents to pay for an expensive private university education. To persuade her parents that the financial outlay would be worthwhile, she drew upon the popular gendered beliefs that English language skills would result in a high-paying job. She explained:

> My **love** for literature was always strong. But then again, it was kind of a weak reason to convince my parents. Even though I got into the literature department **and** the language/English department as well, I thought...well, from my family not so many people are going into college so it's not really natural. I thought it was sort of a luxury for me to go into college. So if I said only literature, it sounds really like um.. ... um... in a sense... studying literature...does not.. um.. um...
>
> *(Diane) Get a job? Or have a practical end to it?*
>
> Right there is no practicality. So if I couldn't say yes, I want to study literature. So I decided to get into the English language department so that I could have more options later.

Taeko and Keiko, the two oldest women in the study, majored in English because they felt it would again provide the greatest opportunities, but it was not their first choice. Taeko considered studying math. Her mother and her sisters were teachers, so she thought, 'At that time, teacher is the only job I could think of as a woman...so math teacher? English teacher? Those are the two choices. Then I thought English is better for my future [...] I chose to be an English teacher'. Had Taeko studied math, she would have faced competition from male students, both as a student and later as a job hunter. She came to feel that English, as a subject predominantly occupied by other female students, was a less competitive path with more opportunities.

Similarly, Keiko wanted to study Japanese literature. However, her father, who was a high school teacher, convinced her that English was a better choice because 'you can get a lot of money [laughter] by teaching privately'. Keiko followed his advice and majored in English at university, even though she felt it was 'too difficult' for her.

Impact of studying abroad

Several of the younger participants had studied abroad as undergraduates. This experience became a turning point that broadened their outlook and awakened various career dreams. Kumiko, for example, decided that she wanted to become a television announcer after she had spent a summer learning English in the United States as an undergraduate. After working a few years, she accumulated enough money to apply to the journalism department of an American university. Her parents strongly opposed this, but because of her financial independence, she was able to reject her parents' demands:

> *Mooo*, [really] it is a very famous story. You know my mom, **cried**, for three days you know [laughter] because she ... wanted me to ... uh get married and take up children and so she was really shocked. My father is kind of, step back...and see the situation guy. But my dad...he didn't agree with me, but didn't disagree with me either. So you know, he said, 'What's wrong? What's the matter'? And yeah, but finally you know, I told them...I had money.

Kana had two overseas experiences as an undergraduate, a summer in the United States and a summer in the UK. Her first experience in the United States was funded by money she had earned from a part-time job, and her second experience was after she received a Lion's Club scholarship to study in the UK. These two experiences fueled her interest in overseas study, so she did not take part in *shushoku katsudo* (job-hunting procedures), which involve seminars, tests and interviews that are essential for third- and fourth-year university students to do to obtain employment. Instead, Kana applied for scholarships to return to the UK.

Miwa said her experiences abroad as an undergraduate differed from most students:

> I didn't go to language schools like all the people do, but real classes. I took English classes which were really tough...probably the toughest days for me because I had to study all the time, and then you don't get the scores you think you would get. Just because of my language skills.

Studying American literature side-by-side with American students was challenging because of language difficulties, but at the same time, it solidified her connection to literature and made her all the more determined to go to graduate school to study literature.

As discussed earlier in Chapter 2, studying abroad is considered a high-status activity for Japanese women to engage in. For the women in this study, studying abroad was a life-changing event that proved to be more than simply a pleasurable experience. It led them toward concrete career goals that entailed further education.

Summary of nature-identity

This section has shown how the gendered sociopolitical attitudes toward and expectations of women in Japan shaped the participants' and their parents' attitude toward embarking upon English study, which was a foundational step in these women's careers.

Choosing to study English achieved two purposes. First, it could enhance the participants' cultural capital and signify them as members of the middle class, which could enhance their marital prospects (Amano, 1997), which seems to be the reason why Kumiko's parents were insistent on her majoring in English. At the same time, it was also perceived to enable women to have a livelihood independent from male competition. Next, the experience of studying abroad acted as a catalyst for the younger women in this study, who went to school during the time Japanese women became economically able to travel abroad, to break away from parental authority and to make concrete decisions that would influence their futures. In other words, studying abroad was one of the foundational steps for these women in gaining necessary independence and self-sufficiency.

In sum, the participants' gender – their N-identity – played a crucial role in the first stage of their professional identity as university English teachers. In the next section we shall see how gender carries over into Gee's (2000) second perspective of identity: I-identity.

Institutional-Identity

What will be examined in this next section are the two gendered educational paths that the participants took in attaining the postgraduate qualifications that have ultimately provided them with an I-identity as a university English teacher.

Going to graduate school directly from university

The first path is that taken by the two youngest members of this study, and it involved going to graduate school immediately after finishing university. Kana won a two-year scholarship from a Japanese foundation to study in the UK, where she completed two MAs during that period, one in children's literature and one in comparative education. She subsequently won a scholarship for doctoral studies. Because she was unable to secure employment in Japan upon graduation, she taught cultural studies in Australia for a few years. In 2008, she found a position in Japan at a prefectural university near her hometown.

Miwa's graduate education took place in both Japanese and foreign universities. She entered a prestigious national university in the Kanto area to study literature and completed her MA and all of the doctoral coursework there. Like many students from that university, she decided to go abroad to complete her PhD because her Japanese university rarely awarded PhDs in literature. She maintained her enrollment in that university because as discussed previously, being a graduate of such an elite university is a career asset. She returned to Japan after living in the United States for seven years and taught part-time at several universities before getting a full-time three-year contract position at a prestigious university. As explained in Chapter 5, Miwa's position is considered to be a career 'stepping stone' even though it is not a tenured position. Although both Kana and Miwa managed the expenses of graduate school through scholarships, grants and various types of financial aid, they put off earning an income until they entered the workforce in their early 30s, about 10 years later than most Japanese people start working. In fact, they began working when many women their age have already exited the workforce in order to marry and begin raising children (Brinton, 1988; Kobayashi, 2007a).

The years spent studying toward a doctorate may in fact be something of a gamble, for there is no guarantee of a career upon successful completion, even though a PhD is now considered essential for obtaining tenure (Hada, 2005). Had Kumiko and Miwa been men, pressure from their families to choose a more secure career path by entering the workforce at an earlier age may have been stronger. For women, there may not be the same expectations to obtain stable lifetime employment, and therefore these women may have had more freedom in pursuing advanced degrees than many men might have had.

Going to graduate school later in life

The other five teachers followed the second path toward graduate school. These women went to graduate school after various twists and turns in their private lives, reflecting sociopolitical attitudes toward women in Japan concerning education and employment.

Naomi taught English at a high school for several years, but quit after winning a Rotary scholarship to study in the United States. Although the scholarship was for only one year, she decided to stay for two in order to complete an MA, supporting herself with her own money for the remainder of her time there. After returning to Japan, she taught English part-time at several universities in her home prefecture before being hired for a tenured position in the Department of Culture in a prefectural university far from where she was brought up. Several years ago, she took an unpaid leave of absence to fulfill the residency requirements for a PhD from an American university. She returned to Japan after a year and completed her PhD while working full-time. She is currently an associate professor.

Keiko, as mentioned earlier, attended a prestigious university in Tokyo, and after graduation worked as a high school teacher there and then got married. Ten years later, however, she returned to her home prefecture with her children and entered the graduate school of that prefecture's national university. She changed her major from American literature to English literature upon the advice of her undergraduate supervisor, a woman, who informed her that the professor specializing in American literature at the university she was applying to was 'infamous for sexual harassment'. This time was difficult, not only because of the shift from American literature to English literature, but because she was studying together with younger students while balancing the demands of motherhood.

All of the male colleagues in Keiko's graduate class found tenured positions upon graduation, but Keiko and the other women could not secure such positions, even though qualified university English teachers were in demand at that time because that was during the period when numerous new private universities were being established. Therefore, she enrolled in a doctorate program, but a year later, after the English literature department at a junior college in a nearby prefecture hired her, she discontinued her studies. She taught at that college for 10 years. She accompanied her students to England several times, and completed a second MA in TESOL while on sabbatical. In the late 1990s, she moved to the science department of the prefecture's national university, where she now holds the rank of associate professor.

Kumiko went to the United States several years after completing her BA, where she majored in journalism and minored in women's studies. Because of her increasing interest in gender, she went on to complete an MA in women's studies. After returning to Japan, she was unable to find a university lectureship, but through the introduction of one of her Japanese professors, she took a position teaching English at a girls' high school. Unhappy there because she was required to teach grammar and translation while policing the girls' behavior, she quit when she obtained a part-time position teaching English at a university a year and a half later. With a foothold in part-time teaching, she was offered many English classes. Unlike the regulated teaching at the high school, she was free to teach what she liked, so she focused more on content rather than on language, admitting that at that time she 'looked down' upon teachers whose specialty was 'merely' language. She began to feel after awhile, however, that she was being passed over for tenured positions by teachers who had TESOL qualifications. To improve the chances of getting tenure, she enrolled in the graduate school of an American university with a campus in Japan. She was surprised to find that TESOL was more interesting than she had imagined, so after finishing her MA, she enrolled in the university's doctorate program. This shift in academic focus paid off, for Kumiko obtained a tenured position in the economics department of a well-known private university in the Kanto area where she is now an assistant professor.

Shizuko's undergraduate background differs from the other women's because her undergraduate degree is in *Japanese* literature. She decided that she wanted to change her life after working for a few years. She realized she was not cut out for clerical work, which she found to be boring, demeaning and low paid. Although she didn't particularly like English study in university, she says:

> I recognized that if I use, if I'm fluent in English, I am a good... person...I mean, I am a person who can earn a lot of money [laughter]. So that's why I started learning English [...] to get a nicer job [laughter], to get promoted.

She saved money and went to a community college in the United States to improve her English conversation skills and to study American literature. She returned to Japan and moved to the prefecture in which her brother, an English literature professor, lives. She married his friend and entered the graduate school of that prefecture's national university, where she obtained an MA in American literature. She has been teaching part-time at two universities in her area and is currently developing skills to become a freelance translator with her brother.

Taeko made an enormous change in her life in her late 40s when she went back to university to obtain the necessary credentials to help her find a job after getting divorced. She says she was a 'typical' housewife and mother for more than 20 years. At the same time, however, she engaged in 'feminine' paid and volunteer work: she taught English to children from home and she volunteered as a guide for foreign tourists. To enhance her employability, she decided to improve her English ability by enrolling in undergraduate classes held at an American university on a nearby US military installation to study 'in English'. When she learned that her alma mater was beginning a new graduate program in English education, she decided to 'try' for that as well. She successfully passed the entrance exam, later learning that she had scored the highest of all the applicants. Going to graduate school at that time was so unusual for a woman her age that there was even a write-up about her in the local newspaper. She was busy the next two years commuting between the American and Japanese university, and because of the double course load, this was the toughest time for her. She said she was able to survive such a grueling schedule because she 'had guts'.

After completing her MA, Taeko wrote research papers and applied for positions in many colleges and universities, aware that the window of opportunity for her to obtain a tenured position was narrow because of her age. Other than getting a non-renewable contracted position for three years, she was unable to secure a permanent placement. The slowdown of the Japanese economy, the decrease in the number of students going to university and the university reforms worked against her. When she reached her mid-50s, she became resigned to the fact that she would remain a part-time teacher, and decided to focus on teaching and materials development. When asked if she felt it was her gender that prevented her from getting tenure, she said:

> I don't think so. It was my age...I applied several times for universities. But my experience and my age didn't match. That's my observation. Age and experience. Because when I am 50, I should be in the position of professor....But my experience is very short. As a teacher with only three years of experience. Even though I tried several times [to get a job] I knew it would be very unlikely.

Taeko does not attribute her inability to attain a tenured position to her gender, but instead to her late age of entry into the profession. However, it is difficult to ignore that giving up her job to stay home for 20 years as a housewife and mother, putting her career on hold while engaging in 'feminine' activities, made it extremely difficult to reenter the workforce.

Summary of Institutional-identity

This section on 'Institutional-identity' has outlined the process of these women in obtaining the academic qualifications that are necessary to become university English teachers. Although these women may have initially been guided toward English by their parents, they came to realize that English proficiency was an asset that would provide better job prospects. Developing English proficiency was an important step to becoming a university English teacher, but the good (and in some cases, highly prestigious) universities that these women attended as undergraduate students were equally, if not more, important than language skills in laying the groundwork for becoming a university teacher. As discussed in Chapter 2, the university one attends determines, to a great extent, a person's future in Japan. The cultural capital they obtained as graduates from their universities was convertible into graduate school entry at prestigious national universities (Keiko, Taeko, Miwa and Shizuko) and to study-abroad scholarships (Miwa, Kana and Naomi).

Advanced degrees from prestigious Japanese universities, especially in regional areas, opened doors for Taeko and Shizuko, the part-time teachers, and enabled Keiko to find a tenured position. Those with MAs and PhDs from universities abroad are seen to have a different kind of advantage, because it signifies an ability to do research and publish at an international level (Matsuda, 2002). This advantage is particularly evident now with the current demand for applicants for tenured positions to hold PhDs (Hada, 2005). In other words, access to and attaining these degrees from well-known tertiary institutions gave these women I-identities as scholars, which led them to be hired by their respective universities, giving them their current I-identity as university teachers.

Where does the N-identity of gender fit into the developing I-identities of these women as university English teachers? Although academic degrees signifying scholarship and ability are necessary for both men and women, as noted in Chapter 2, female university teachers are clearly in the minority (MEXT, 2006). This suggests that women are either not gaining the necessary qualifications or they are being excluded from the profession or both. With more and more young women like Miwa and Kana entering the profession with PhDs, there may be an increase in the number of female teachers. Nevertheless, Keiko's difficulty in finding a tenured position tells us that the academic climate accepting female university teachers has not always been receptive.

Another issue to consider in how these women gained their I-identities is in the roundabout paths that some took to attain their academic degrees. English was perceived as something of a 'backup' plan that the women would be able to fall back on should the need arise. By contrast, it would be quite unusual if a Japanese male student were to undertake an area of study, even English, with a 'just-in-case' scenario relating to its future utility. Nevertheless, these women actually *utilized* English as a backup plan (or as in Shizuko's case, cultivated an ability in English) for employment reasons, supporting the literature that argues Japanese female students' motivation to study English differs from that of male students (Kobayashi, 2002).

A further issue to consider here is that the sociocultural pressure for men to secure lifetime employment means it may be harder for men to leave their jobs to pursue an advanced degree, which may or may not result in a job upon completion, as Kumiko, Shizuko and Naomi did. Japanese women have traditionally been expected to exit the workforce for marriage and family obligations, but today, due to the trend of late marriage, many women are accorded a period of time to pursue personal interests between paid work and marriage by studying abroad (Burton, 2004; Kobayashi, 2007a; Matsui, 1995). Although it has been argued that for many Japanese women, the time and money spent studying abroad does not result in better career opportunities for them upon returning to Japan (Burton, 2004; Kobayashi, 2007b), the women in this study were able to do so. This is especially true for Kumiko and Naomi, who returned from the United States with MAs in the early 1990s when it was still rare for Japanese to have advanced degrees from abroad. They were able to convert that educational capital gained from obtaining a foreign MA first into obtaining part-time teaching positions and then to tenured positions. The two youngest women, Miwa and Kana, who proceeded to graduate school immediately upon graduation, may have been somewhat free from parental pressure to find a permanent job because of lower career expectations for them. As mentioned above, advanced degrees do not guarantee tenure, but they are useful for securing part-time work, which is perceived to be a very good job for supplementary income – again, a useful 'backup' for women – even though completely supporting oneself or a family from part-time teaching would be difficult.

Although these women have gained official recognition as university English teachers, we shall explore in the next section how they maintain and nurture their identity as such. In occupying a relatively high-status position, the perceptions that they have of themselves and that others have of them is critical in constructing their D-identities.

Discourse-Identity

Now let us consider Gee's (2000) third perspective of identity, Discourse-identity, which is created through discursive practices and reflects personal attributes and personalities that are ascribed to people. This section highlights several issues from the interviews that connect the women's D-identities, which are reflected in their interaction with others, to their N-identities of gender and to their I-identities as university teachers. First, I discuss several ways in which these women's identity as role models is reified through the recognition of others. Second, I discuss the existence of a conflict in how they wish to be seen by others and the reality of how others see them. Third, I show how some of the women deliberately downplay their status as university English teachers through their discursive practices with those connected to academia in an effort to cultivate a friendly relationship that otherwise might not occur. Finally, reflecting Japanese women's tendency to be modest, I show how Miwa downplayed her ability and intelligence with her male graduate school cohorts.

Discourse-identity as a role model

The first area to analyze using Gee's (2000) third perspective of identity concerns the teachers' D-identity as role models. All of the women in this study identify as role models for not only their students, but for other people around them as well. They see themselves as role models for their female students, projecting themselves as women with successful careers, and they want to encourage their students to envision brighter futures for themselves. As non-native English speakers, they also see themselves as role models for students struggling with learning English, for they have been through the same process (Medgyes, 1992).

Taeko identifies as a role model for others, drawing upon an identity as a person who has guts and who was able to accomplish what might have seemed impossible. She feels her personal experiences can inspire others. As a language learner, she didn't have the benefit of travelling abroad or studying under native-speaking English teachers, so she sought out local opportunities to master English. When she needed to support herself, even as a middle-aged woman who had been out of the workforce for more than 20 years, she went 'back to school'. She said that her friends are amazed that she could change her life completely, by going from a housewife to a university teacher, which is 'not a usual thing'. At school reunions, they celebrate her accomplishments, and one friend, who was encouraged by Taeko's success, decided to return to university to get an MA herself.

Being seen as a successful English language learner and as a fluent English speaker comprises a substantial component of Taeko's D-identity. Like many students even today, Taeko learned only *about* English but not how to actually *use* it. The first time she communicated in English was years later, as a housewife, when she volunteered as a guide for foreign tourists. By memorizing the handbook and arming herself with its important phrases, she eventually learned to communicate spontaneously. Recognition as a fluent English speaker is reinforced in her being asked to teach English conversation classes, because at many universities, these courses are often designated for native-English speakers. Drawing upon her own language-learning success, she made this the theme of her graduate study and of her subsequent research. She also has developed her own teaching materials based upon her language-learning/teaching philosophy and was later approached by a publisher to compile these materials into a textbook, which was published the previous year.

Being recognized as a successful woman is important for the intersection between Taeko's I-identity and her D-identity. Even though she is a part-time teacher and has no university to affiliate herself with, she still feels she is a person that others look up to, and has even created other identities for herself as a politician (she ran for city mayor) and as a volunteer in an international peace movement.

Miwa also sees herself as a role model. She feels that her background shows students that it is possible to master English if they study hard on their own. Her students ask her if she lived abroad as a child because of her fluency in English. She tells them, 'No. I couldn't speak. I was raised in Japan. So...the only education I got is just the regular education you can get in Japan'. She wants to encourage them to recognize the opportunities that they have at hand to master English, and says to them:

> If you work, if you try hard, then hard enough, at least you can communicate in English in the future...even if you didn't get the [English] education at the lower level, elementary or junior high school in an English speaking world. You still can speak. Still can communicate. Probably that's the kind of thing I can give them.

Feminists and career women

The women's perceptions of themselves as independent career women and feminists are complicated by treatment from and attitudes of others. Kumiko, for example, struggled with her relationship with her parents after she returned from the United States, no longer as their docile daughter, but as a politicized feminist. Her life choices shocked her parents. She moved into her own apartment, and did not live with them; she refused to marry her boyfriend, preferring instead to live with him in order to be able to maintain her surname[2] and she fostered a child rather than having a baby of her own. Kumiko says that she did everything 'her parents didn't like', leading her mother to eventually say to Kumiko's aunt, 'I give up. About Kumiko. I give up'.

Obtaining a tenured university position has been instrumental in changing Kumiko's parents' attitudes toward her to a certain extent. Kumiko says, 'They are happy [hesitant] and they are kind of proud of me'. Kumiko goes on to explain that their pride in their daughter is fraught with mixed feelings. 'They are kind of worried about me'. They seem to be of the old-fashioned school that believe a woman's happiness lies in marriage and family, and they feel that since she has 'too much education to get married', she will end up alone and unhappy in her old age.

Kumiko's struggle with her identity as a feminist and independent woman is not only evident in her relationship with her parents, but also in her workplace as well. She is experiencing a gendered ideological struggle at her university because of paternalistic treatment from older male professors. As described below, she does not wish to be ill-treated, but such patronizing communication styles bring up contradictory feelings in her.

> We have very few female teachers, so they treated me as a kind of princess [laughter]. They are so nice to me. Maybe I'm a woman. That's the reason. Because the year we entered the university, we had, you know, three male instructors. Newcomers. Others in our college are really old, like 50 years old or 60 or 70 years old. So they are so nice to me. They think of me...as a daughter. Yeah, they are so nice. [laughter] *demo, maaa*...[but, well...] it's in one way, a kind of discrimination. Because I'm a woman, they treat me nice. Mmm. I feel complex feelings. You know they treat me nice because I'm a woman. But you know, I don't want them to treat me as **bad**.

Kumiko believes that these professors who treat her as a 'princess' do so as a way to make her feel comfortable as a female minority in the faculty. Nevertheless, this treatment detracts from the I-identity bestowed upon her as a tenured teacher at that university. It creates an emotional struggle, because Kumiko would like to identify as a feminist teacher, and not as a princess or a daughter to the male professors, however kindhearted their intentions may be.

Kana also struggles with the discursive practices of the male professors in her university. She feels nervous communicating with them, but ignores them when they 'say something a little bit sexist' and complains that such behavior is '**never** heard of in Australia'. Nevertheless, she adopts a feminine, indirect and subdued way of communicating with them as a way to avoid offending them, going against her self-identity as a strong and independent woman. She knows she is enabling sexist behavior through her submissiveness, but she said she cannot help it because, 'It is how I was brought up being'.

Being a university teacher: The attitudes of others

It is interesting to note that some of the teachers feel uncomfortable disclosing to strangers that they are university English teachers. In Japan, where the hierarchal nature of society influences communication styles among people, there is a shift in conversational tone from informal to formal, in deference to these women's suddenly recognized status as members of a prestigious occupation (see Nakane, 1970). The women say that they feel uncomfortable when praise is heaped upon them because of what they do, because this praise rings false with the implication of disbelief that women can be university teachers in the first place.

Kumiko adopts a humble position to avoid this situation, and is purposely vague when talking to strangers about her work, as the following exchange illustrates:

> If I say I am a college teacher, they are kind of ohhhhh, they kind of back and change their attitude...you know, until then, they were very friendly. But after I say I'm a college teacher, *ahhhhhhhh, dakara... subarashii desu ne* [ahhhhhhh. So. How wonderful.] You are fantastic. I just don't like that praise. So when I was a part-timer, you know, lecturer, at that time, I said I'm a part-timer. So part-timer in Japan could mean anything, yeah, like working in a supermarket as a part-timer. I always said to them, I'm a part-timer. But now I have a full-time job so I say I have a full-time job.
>
> *Diane: So you don't say 'I'm a teacher'¿*
>
> No, I don't. I'm not going to say teacher. Oh, I say, *chotto, eigo o oshieteru desu* [I teach a English...somewhat]. They think elementary school or conversation school. They just imagine that. And sometimes they ask where do you teach. [...] Then I have to say, oh college. If they ask several questions then I have to say.
>
> *Diane: You wait until they really want to know¿*
>
> *So so so* [yes, yes, yes]. I kind of try not to say.

Miwa also says she does not want to be judged as a 'person who has a PhD or who teaches English at college or anything like that'. She especially dislikes the shift in the patronizing attitudes from men, who generally 'judge you as a woman'. The following comment illustrates how conversation becomes insultingly solicitous when they learn that she teaches at a famous university:

> They regard women so low to begin with, so when they see women they think they are better than – women, in general whatever that is. So when they see someone with more credentials in a sense. They are like, 'Oh I'm sorry...uh huh. My education is not as good as yours'. So they change their attitude.

Nevertheless, Miwa is relieved to have made the transition from student to university teacher. As a student, she was uncomfortable in telling people her age. As a woman over 30 years old, she felt people expected her to be married or employed. Now that she works for a prestigious university, she feels that her years of study are now publically recognized as having been worthwhile:

> At least I'm teaching at [name] University. Then they [other people] just listen. They can think of me as an 'authorized nerd' in a sense. [laughter] I was just a regular private nerd, but now I am an authorized nerd. [laughter]

However, Miwa knows that her current job is temporary, and she needs the security of a tenured position to be fully recognized as a woman with a professional career:

> When you are a woman, people kind of.... you know, 'you are just a girl' kind of attitude all around. Especially from older men. So, someday I have to be a professor and say [laugh] 'I'm a professor, you can't treat me like that'.

When the women's school friends, particularly those of Kumiko and Kana, discover what they do for a living, they are also surprised. However, the expressions of disbelief are not necessarily connected to their gender (although it is certainly possible that there are gendered attitudes at work). They seem shocked because the young women they remember as students did not seem to be the type that would become university teachers. Kumiko said that her friends 'can't believe that [I'm a university teacher]. It's kind of an unbelievable thing, because I was not a very good student, you know. But now, I'm a college teacher [laughter]. Many say, mmmm... many say to me "you changed"'.

'Promoting' self to others

Gendered attitudes toward self and toward others also seem to influence the women's D-identities. When Miwa was asked if she felt that being a woman would have an impact on her chances of finding a tenured position, she said she felt gendered attitudes toward hiring men 'because they needed to support a family' might still exist, but the greatest obstacle for her would be her lack of ambition:

> It is probably something to do with my lack of ambition. [laughter] I **love** literature and love being in this position [having a job as a

university teacher]. But I'm not particularly in love with, you know, appealing my ability, appealing how smart I am. It is not in me. So maybe that's what you need to get a better job. So I'm kind of ambivalent about it.

Diane: Well, that is really interesting. So your lack of ambition is because you do what you want to do? And you don't want to do something because it might get you up in the field?

Right. Probably what I have to learn is to be ambitious. I have to learn how to impress people with what I have, what I can do. But sometimes, it is about power. How to, uh, decorate, how to present your power. But you know, I'm Japanese. [laughter]

In the following extract, we can see Miwa's hesitation in promoting herself as a graduate student, particularly in the company of her male cohorts:

Well, I think it is kind of too honest to say this, but when you are in graduate school you notice all the guys there. They are smart. But they seem to depend on mentally how smart they are, and their identity [laughter], identity issue is centered on their smartness. Their intelligence. But [hesitant] I kind of envy them that they can think in that way. And you know, I was probably a lot smarter than a lot of people, but not smart enough to be **that** confident. [...] I [hesitant], I kind of pity them, too. I **envy** them, but I kind of pity them.

Because...I think it is kind of sad to get your self-esteem from **just one** aspect of your own self. [...] There are always smarter people [laughter]. Well, umm, no, I was...it takes courage for a difficult question. I just can't pinpoint just **where**, the person...the kind of person I am, um, combining all the experiences I have had and all the things I can do. [...] For example, I'm in academics, and I love reading. I love literature. But I can still bake cookies. [laughter] And I can knit. And I love those things. And I can play musical instruments.

Miwa attributes her hesitation to sell herself to her own personal inclinations, but Japanese gendered beliefs that women should be modest and self-effacing may be an underlying reason why she was reticent in promoting her own abilities in graduate school. It may have been easier for Miwa to cultivate an identity as a 'literature nerd', a person who is mainly interested in reading, in order to separate herself from the competitive atmosphere of her graduate class. However, it is necessary for her to assume a more proactive position and to promote herself in order to obtain tenure and secure her position as an academic in the Japanese tertiary system.

Summary of Discourse-identity

This section has discussed the tripartite overlapping of the N-identity of gender with I-identity of being a university teacher and the D-identity that forms through the discursive practices of others. Through the stories the women told, we can see how they wish to present themselves to others and we can see how others perceive them to be. In some instances, there is harmony with these discursive practices, and in other instances, there is conflict.

All of these women see themselves as role models, but Taeko's self-perception as such is particularly strong and plays a very important role in how she perceives herself as a woman with guts as well as a university English teacher. Her presentation of herself as a woman who mastered English on her own and who overcame the odds to attain a career as a university teacher is clearly seen to be accepted and recognized by others who work with her.

Kumiko, Kana and Miwa self-identify as feminists, but the discursive practices of those around them force them to compromise. Especially in the workplace, they renegotiate their identities in order to maintain a level of personal comfort, and they renegotiate their identity as feminists in order to fit in as Japanese women in Japanese society and to maintain a good relationship with their colleagues.

Conflict was also evident in the way the women identify as university teachers and in the way they present themselves to people who are not connected to the university world. A consequential conversational style shift occurs when Miwa and Kumiko's interlocutors become differential and polite when they learn they are speaking to someone in a high-status position. This conversational shift thus leads to feelings of discomfort. Although it is true that a person with a prestigious occupation is accorded respectful language when speaking in Japanese, such a sudden shift indicates ingrained sexism in people by exhibiting a certain amount of disbelief that a woman could have a better education and hold a higher position in society than a man.

Miwa's description of her time in graduate school where she sat back and observed her male cohorts promoting their abilities and intelligence is particularly interesting. She claims her dislike in promoting herself is due to her personal inclinations and that she only wants to concentrate on literature studies. However, her reticence may also be connected to the sociocultural expectations of women, who are supposed to be modest and supposed to place themselves lower than men.

Now that we have seen how these three areas of identity interrelate and overlap with each other in constructing the women's professional identity, let us now turn our attention to Gee's final perspective of identity, which entails self-identification through degrees of affiliation toward the groups (mostly their university workplaces) to which the women belong.

Affinity-Identity

This section analyzes the data for Gee's (2000: 105) final category of identity: Affinity-identity (A-identity), which is rooted in the 'distinctive social practices that create and sustain group affiliations, rather than on institutions or discourse/dialog directly'. Identity in this category evolves from practices that symbolize membership in a group, or what is also called a community of practice (Wenger, 1998). Allegiance for, access to and participation in these groups are essential elements for creating a sense of belonging to the communities in which practices are shared.

All university teachers experience a number of shared experiences that signify membership in the community of practice of university English teachers in Japan. Professionally, they are teachers of English language, scholars in their academic field, members of university departments and members of academic societies.[3] Personally, they belong to numerous affinity groups that include family and friends and that revolve around personal activities.

In this section, we examine three particular aspects of how the women's A-identities intersect with their N-identities. First, we discuss their affinity toward their universities even though they are a gendered minority in a male-dominated workplace. Second, we look at a connection between their affinity toward their workplace and a decreasing respect for English as an area of study. Third, we look at conflict in the division of affinity between one woman's private life as a housewife and future mother and her burgeoning career as a university English teacher.

It's a man's world

The first area to be discussed under the category of A-identity is the women's gendered minority in their workplaces, which determines, to a great extent, the degree of allegiance the women have toward their workplaces. The tenured participants' narratives revealed that they experience gendered isolation in the workplace: Keiko, for example, is only one of six female professors out of 52; Kumiko is one of eight out of

100 and Naomi is one of two out of 50. Naomi describes the situation as follows:

> I find men definitely are in charge of everything. I can't say that this is a distinct difference, a regional difference or not. But it's just the situation that I happen to encounter.... There tends to be different unspoken rules between men [all the women in the room laugh] but something that I can't understand or get [laughter]. Something is happening underneath that I cannot see.

In Japan, workplace relationships are cemented with behind-the-scenes, after-hours socializing, from which women are often excluded. Kumiko, for example, was not invited to any *habatsu* (factions that compete for power) sponsored social occasions at her university, although a male assistant professor who was hired at the same time was. She attributes this exclusion to the 'deeply rooted sexist beliefs of the male professors' that she says consider women as 'unimportant' in the politics of her university. As discussed in Chapter 5, Kumiko appropriated this exclusion as a means to secure more time for herself to pursue her own interests. Nevertheless, it has impacted the degree of allegiance she holds toward her workplace.

Poole (2003: 264) found that male professors have more affinity toward the universities for which they work than do the female professors. He says that the women were excluded from administrative practices that lead to roles of responsibility, but they did not 'necessarily want such positions, knowing full well the time commitment involved', and he cited one woman saying, 'as a woman, I am not asked to participate in a lot of meetings and committees. This can be seen as either positive [more time to focus on research and teaching] or as negative [being excluded]'. What Poole does not identify is that these women, like Kumiko, may choose to concentrate more on their own research activities *because of* the exclusion from the power politics of the university. It is also worth considering if this exclusion is related to the notion of Japanese lifetime employment, which in return demands loyalty and devotion from employees. If lifetime employment (or, in the case of university teaching, tenure) has traditionally been exclusively for *men*, attitudes toward female university teachers may be laden with gender bias that still perceives tenured women as temporary and replaceable females and not valuable enough to entrust with important university work. Men, on the other hand, may see such committee work as a way to 'make and implement changes' (Poole, 2003: 264) within the university, but the women in Poole's study, like Kumiko in this study, instead concentrate on their own research and building up their own resume. They envision a future in a different university; however, this may not always be feasible or even possible. Furthermore, even if the women do move to a higher-ranking university on the basis of their research, they may still encounter gendered exclusionary practices at work in their new universities.

Keiko, for example, with 20 years of university experience, has been teaching at her prefecture's prestigious national university for the past 10 years. Surprisingly, she is still an associate professor. Considering that seniority strongly influences academic promotions, with the average age of promotion to professor between 45 and 50 years old (Evanoff, 1993; MEXT, 2006), one suspects that conservative gendered attitudes are the reasons for why Keiko, age 57, is not yet a professor. Keiko's position seems to validate Sodei's (2005) assertion that Japanese female academics lag behind their male counterparts.

Being in the minority as an English teacher

Keiko says that she was more comfortable when teaching for the English department of the women's junior college than she is now, teaching at a more prestigious national university. This is not only because there were many women professors there, but also because there were many English teachers. Currently she belongs to a humanities chair in a faculty of science, which she shares with teachers specializing in areas such as Japanese history, anthropology and German. She has noticed a shift in students' and colleagues' attitudes that now question the necessity of English study. She explains:

> They don't...they don't support English studies. And...language communication by English is compulsory at the moment. But the other Japanese history teachers said 'we want to abolish it' or something like that. So that is very severe for me. [...] They have a kind of inferiority complex. Until now, English was so popular. So English teachers were valued in college education. So at the moment, they have a bad attitude toward me. So that is not good.

This change in attitude toward English has made it very difficult for Keiko to motivate her students to study hard. She feels that as potential scientists, they will need English for their careers. She tries to maintain a good relationship with her students, who are mostly male, but she finds it difficult because they 'are not so obedient' and they are difficult to supervise because they tend to ignore her advice.

Keiko's affiliation toward her university thus is influenced by two criteria: she is one of a handful of women in the faculty of science, and she is one of two professors who specialize in English. English has traditionally been considered a 'feminine' subject, with many female students being intrinsically motivated to study it (Kobayashi, 2002). As such, one wonders if the attitudes of the male professors who wish to 'abolish it' from the curriculum reflect disdain for a feminine subject. Furthermore, it would be interesting to know whether or not her male students are equally dismissive of their male teachers' study advice as they seem to be of hers.

Balancing personal and professional identities

As discussed in Chapter 2, balancing married life and professional life may be one of the greatest obstacles for working women in Japan, and has been cited as a reason why many women quit working after marriage (Amano, 1997). In Japan, if women are married, they generally refer to themselves as 'housewives' whether they work outside the home or not, because marriage for women involves the doing of household chores and the managing of a family.

Shizuko, who identifies as a teacher, a translator and a housewife, prefers engaging in activities related to teaching and translating, rather than those connected to the home. Her academic shift to English literature from Japanese literature has given her access to a prestigious, high-paying career that she loves. She claims an identity as a teacher, and she feels strong allegiance toward the practices that goes with it. Still a novice at teaching, she invests a great deal of time in classroom preparation, as is evident by the detailed penciled-in teaching points in the textbook she uses.

Shizuko's comments below demonstrate how she handles the demands of her multiple identities:

> If my semester is over, my lifestyle is quite changed. I wake up and I make breakfast [laughter] and I do the laundry and do translation work. And I am always in the house, you know. I don't like staying in the house. So once the semester starts, I give my students lots of energy to...so I, even if I am frustrated, once I change my mind, my mind is from my students.

She goes on to say:

> To tell the truth, I want to have a baby, but I want to continue to work. [...] I have a dilemma now. Maybe after teaching one more year, I want to have a baby. [...] In Japan, for now, it is so difficult to have both.

It may be difficult for Shizuko to do both teaching and child rearing, but her strong allegiance toward teaching may make it easier for her to cope. Furthermore, because teaching is a high-status job, she may have more approval from her family and from society to continue working. Shizuko optimistically believes, 'When I get more confident, then I have a child. That's the plan'.

As a part-time teacher, Shizuko may not have too much difficulty in carrying out her plans. But Poole (2010: 134) provides an interesting example from his case study of a Japanese university that illustrates the difficulty in balancing the demands of a family and the demands of a university. He describes a conversation held between the president of the university, the head of the administrative office – a vice president, and himself while the three of them were having dinner and drinks together one night after a meeting. The president complained that one of the female professors was acting 'irresponsibly' when she – a mother of three children – backed out of a weekend lecture she was supposed to take part in because that weekend coincided with her children's once-a-year school sports festival. He generalized that the female professors typically were 'opportunistic and engage in university [administrative] work only when it suits them'. Poole asked the president if he felt it was right to expect professors – male or female – to 'sacrifice once-in-a-lifetime experiences with their children for the sake of the university administrative work'. The other professor replied, 'But Poole Sensei, having to miss a child's sports festival is hardly a once-in-a-lifetime experience'! The president went on to explain that even though Poole may not understand because he is a foreigner, the university was correct in its expectations for *all* professors to participate in weekend events, no matter what the cost may be to their private lives. The president then qualified his statement by saying, 'I am not referring to *all* women at EUC. Some women do not shirk responsibilities asked of them, just as some men readily escape as this professor did'. This discussion, which occurred over drinks after working hours when the female professors at the meeting had presumably returned home to care for their families, illuminates the attitude that university responsibilities override those of the home. Poole wrote that although the discussion by these *uchimuki* players at the university was framed in the context of the female professor's gender, what really was the issue was the woman's lack of *uchimuki* dedication toward the university, and the president admitted that such problems could also exist with male professors.

Poole argues, 'the prize in the political games of a modern Japanese university is power' (p. 90), but only those who operate within the inner circle – the *uchimuki* players – and not those who are on the periphery obtain the power. *Sotomuki* players who have concerns outside of the university, such as women who need to balance family with work, will never have access to such power unless they are willing to sacrifice themselves and their families to do so. Male professors may of course have numerous concerns outside of the university as well, but for women, this may be an even greater obstacle for them to overcome if they wish to obtain and maintain insider power within their universities.

Although Poole's anecdote illustrates only one instance, the sentiments expressed by the president and the administrator concerning their perceptions of female professors' lack of dedication to their university may be widespread at other universities as well, especially when considering the low proportion of female academics in Japan. Furthermore, when examining the narratives of the women in this study, particularly those with tenure who are made to feel like gendered outsiders within their workplaces, Poole's example rings with a great deal of truth.

Summary of Affinity-identity

This section has highlighted three areas that emerged from the data analysis, in which the women's gender influences their degrees of affinity toward their I-identities as university teachers. First, feelings of isolation exist for the women with tenure because of gendered exclusion from many of the university activities. This isolation influences the affinity they hold toward their workplaces and, as a consequence, they choose to focus upon their own interests instead.

It was also found that feelings of isolation also exist when one is a minority teacher in a department where the academic focus is something other than English. Keiko reports that a shift in attitudes toward English study has made her feel professionally less important than when she worked for an English department, even though it was at a lower academically ranked school.

Finally, the difficulty in balancing professional and personal affinity groups was discussed by the youngest and least experienced teacher in the study. Shizuko, as a new English teacher, shows a strong affinity toward the act of teaching English, especially since she came to this profession after an unhappy stint as a clerical worker. Nevertheless, she worries about the degree of affiliation she must have for the gendered affinity groups she belongs to.

In sum, holding multiple identities as teachers, scholars, wives and mothers requires degrees of affinity toward each group, and in combination, clearly contributes to the women's sense of professional identity.

Conclusion of Chapter 6

Gee's (2000) conceptualization of identity has provided a useful analytical lens that enabled me to tease apart four interrelated aspects of the participants' identity in order to gain a more complete picture of how they identify as university English teachers. Viewing identity from these four perspectives highlights the complexity of identity and shows that it is in a constant state of negotiation and renegotiation according to the discourse of others and to the social context in which one is placed.

The women's narratives clearly illustrate that their N-identity as females is at the heart of their professional identity. Although sex is merely a biological trait, the attributes that Japanese society ascribes to the female gender have influenced how the women gained access to their I-identity as university English teachers. This access was first provided through initial contact with English, which was considered one of the best choices of study for Japanese girls. In addition, gaining the necessary academic qualifications seems also to be influenced by the teachers' gender to a certain extent; since women are often considered to be temporary and peripheral members of the workforce, some women had the freedom to abandon paying jobs to seek self-fulfillment in higher education, which ultimately led to careers as university English teachers.

However, as the teachers' narratives indicate, although they have attained professional recognition as university teachers, their female gender influences the discursive practices of others. This, in turn, results in some struggle in constructing their D-identities. For example, Kumiko and Kana desire to present identities as feminists, but in order to get along with their male colleagues in the workplace, they have necessarily adopted feminine communicative strategies instead. Kumiko and Miwa say they downplay their professional status because of people's shift in discourse when it is disclosed that they are university teachers. Although Miwa feels discomfort from people's reactions, she notes that displaying her academic and workplace credentials is an effective way to command respect from men.

On the other hand, when self-perceived D-identities are the same as how others perceive these women, professional satisfaction is evident. Taeko, for example, identifies as a 'gutsy' woman who mastered English through her own efforts. Indeed, through extraordinary efforts, she transformed her career from housewife to university teacher, and she is happy when others see her as a role model, for she also sees herself as such.

The final perspective of identity discussed in this section dealt with affiliation as members of a group. Gee (2000) states that it is the 'shared practices' that creates affinity toward a group. As the participants' narratives clearly show, they are in the gendered minority in their universities, and as a result feel excluded from the inner workings of their universities. As a consequence, the degree of affinity that the participants have toward their universities may differ from that of their male colleagues. The women may choose to channel their energies into other activities, but acceptance of oneself as a gendered outsider in the workplace can continue to perpetuate gender bias.

Finally, Shizuko's narrative shows the struggle that she has in balancing her multiple identities as a wife and teacher and hopefully soon-to-be mother. As the most inexperienced teacher in this study, she has just recently learned how to manage her time in the classroom and in class preparation. As a married woman in Japanese society, she also feels obligated in doing the myriad of chores that go with being a housewife. Her ability to continue developing her professional identity as a university teacher with the demands of the other affinity groups of marriage and motherhood competing for her time and energy will be a challenge for her.

The stories the participants have told during the course of the interviews showed that their gendered lives as daughters, mothers, wives and even sisters (in the case of Shizuko) have played an important role in shaping the outcome of these women's professional identity as university teachers of English.

Summary of the Findings

This chapter has considered the relationship between gender and the professional identity of seven Japanese female teachers of English in Japanese higher education. The research questions that guided this study were the following:

(1) What, if any, is the impact of gender in the professional identity of female teachers of English in Japanese higher education?
(2) What, if any, are the main similarities and main differences in the professional identity development among female university teachers of various age groups?
(3) How do female teachers in Japanese universities appropriate and negotiate their professional identity in a social context that is predominantly male oriented?

In answering the first question, it was found that the participants' gendered lives have permeated every aspect of their professional identity. First, as girls growing up in Japanese society, their initial access to English study in higher education was encouraged and supported by their parents, who felt that such an area of study was not only appropriate for their daughters, but was one that would generate a 'ladylike' income for them as adult women. Second, societal expectations that do not consider Japanese women to be permanent members of the workforce may have inadvertently provided the participants with the necessary time it takes to obtain advanced degrees, which in turn provided the necessary qualifications for securing an I-identity as a university teacher. Unlike men who are generally expected to earn a living to support a family, and with the exception of Taeko who withdrew from the workforce for marriage, these women exited the workforce, or postponed joining the workforce, to pursue their studies.

As university teachers, how they are accepted in the workplace is also dependent upon their gender. This is especially true of the tenured teachers who are only one of a handful of female teachers in their departments and, as such, are keenly aware that they are peripheral members of their faculties. For example, the discursive practices of Kumiko's male coworkers, who treat her like a 'princess' or a 'daughter', are intended to make her feel at home, but it is hard to imagine that newly hired male employees would be treated as a 'prince' or a 'son' by the same professors. Kumiko feels a dilemma over this treatment because she does not want to be treated 'badly' by her colleagues. Nevertheless, she recognizes this so-called kindness to be somewhat discriminatory, especially in conjunction with her exclusion from the socializing that takes place in the factions that compete for power within the university. Such exclusion has lead Kumiko, as well as the other tenured teachers in this study, to attend to her own interests. This suggests that these women have a weaker degree of affiliation toward their institutions than they might have had if they felt they were perceived to be more 'important' by their universities.

In answering the second research question, it was found that there were a number of similarities in the professional identity development across the three educational generations of women. The most significant similarity concerned the attitude that English could provide them with a better living. This was true of the women who studied in the 1960s, who could not envision a career beyond being a teacher, and this was also true of the youngest participant, Shizuko, who attended university and obtained employment well after the Employment Opportunity Act was passed in 1986. Shizuko, who felt that the routine clerical work she was assigned to was demeaning and therefore decided to return to university to study English, was motivated by the belief that such knowledge would lead her to a more meaningful and better paid job.

Another similarity across the three educational generations entails the perception of English as a 'fall-back' plan. Keiko, for example, was advised to choose English as a major because she would always be able to make a living by teaching English privately. She was able to do more than teach private English lessons from the home; she utilized her undergraduate degree in English when she returned to her parents' home with her children and entered a national university to attend graduate school. With their support, she was able to convert English into a prestigious career as a university teacher. Kumiko's parents also insisted that she obtain a teaching license because they felt it would be handy for her to have. Although at that time, Kumiko had no intentions of becoming an English teacher, when she was unable to find a university position teaching gender when she returned from the United States, she was easily able to become an English teacher instead. Taeko utilized the English 'capital' she had gained as an undergraduate student in the 1960s nearly three decades later when she returned to graduate school and became a university teacher. Without having English to fall back on, Taeko might have become a grocery store clerk or a gas station attendant like many Japanese women her age who seek employment.

Despite the similarities in professional development among the participants, there are, however, some differences across the three generations of women. The most notable difference concerns the participants' educational credentials. Kana and Miwa completed all of their education prior to being hired with tenure. Kumiko and Naomi obtained, or are working toward, their PhDs mid-career. Keiko, like many older Japanese professors, does not have a PhD (although like many, she has completed some doctoral coursework). It is likely that holding a PhD at the onset of a career will provide Kana and Miwa with academic clout that may ease their path through Japanese academia and may reduce the gendered barriers that were faced by older women like Keiko.

Another area of difference across the generations concerns the opportunity to travel and study abroad. Prior to the 1980s, overseas study was generally the prerogative of the wealthy, and therefore Taeko and Keiko did not study abroad as undergraduate students. There were very few short-term overseas language programs available at that time like the ones that Miwa, Kana and Kumiko subsequently attended. These overseas experiences were found to be instrumental not only with regard to generating a deeper interest in the study of English, but also in enabling them to envision futures that extended beyond what was considered usual for young women at that time. Had they not studied abroad, their lives might have taken an entirely different path.

The third research question addressed how female teachers appropriate and negotiate their professional identities in a predominantly male social context. The women in this study may be university teachers, but they are also viewed as females in a society that is predominantly run by men. Even though the women with tenure are technically employed under the same conditions as their male colleagues, they say they experience 'gender isolation' due to having few female colleagues. The atmosphere in the workplace is distinctly male dominant, and as Naomi said, she sometimes feels like an interloper in a men's club because the 'unspoken rules' are hard to decipher. Although none of the women expressed any desire to join this club, it is evident that such exclusion has influenced their professional identity as members of their institutions. They tend to do what they like; they focus on research and on teaching and ignore the internal politics of the university.

The part-time teachers, Taeko and Shizuko, who do not have an institution to affiliate with, do not experience the same sort of gender isolation in the workplace that the tenured teachers do. It is important to note here that part-time university teaching is a high-status and high-paying part-time job that is considered an excellent 'additional' source of income for Japanese women. Because neither Taeko nor Shizuko is likely to obtain tenure, they have branched into other areas in their professional development to complement their identities as teachers. Whereas part-time work for Taeko and Shizuko may provide them with an enhanced sense of professional identity that they are able to merge with various other interests, some female academics (for example, a woman with a PhD who is unable to find a tenured position) may see their own part-time status as a sign of a 'dead-end' career.

Outside of the workplace, the women also seem to experience some struggle in maintaining their professional identities. This is evident in the discursive practices of others, who abruptly shift their communicative styles once they become aware that they are talking to a 'university professor'. Although it is true that Japanese language requires attention to the interlocutor's status in order to know how to communicate appropriately, some participants in this study feel uncomfortable with this because they perceive it reflects sexist attitudes concerning women, who are generally not expected to have a prestigious career. Interestingly, while Kumiko and Miwa tend to be more reticent about making known their professional status, Taeko, who has taken on an identity as a 'role model' *because* she knows the path that led her to become a university teacher is quite extraordinary, is quite happy to tell people what she now does for a living, knowing the surprise this will cause to her interlocutors.

These women's professional identities are formed in conjunction with other identities as well. For example, Kumiko's identity as a feminist professional woman conflicts with her identity as a daughter. Although her parents are now more accepting of her life choices because she has a secure job, they nevertheless consider her to be 'too educated' to live as an ordinary Japanese woman. Shizuko's struggle may be representative of many young female academics. She is concerned with combining the practical aspects of her private life as a housewife (and future mother) and her professional life as an English teacher and an upcoming translator. Balancing these multiple identities, which are often laden with gendered assumptions concerning women, requires a great deal of flexibility among these women.

This study was undertaken to better understand the lives of Japanese women teaching English in Japanese higher education, but the findings from these women's narratives are not intended to be generalizable to the wider population of female university teachers. Their stories and their experiences are uniquely their own and, as such, do not speak for others. Nevertheless, it is plausible, even likely, that the issues that have emerged from this study will resonate with other Japanese women teaching English in the Japanese tertiary context.

Notes

(1) It may be useful to point out that gendered attitudes toward appropriate areas of study also exist for sons as well as daughters. Hiro (who participated as a questionnaire respondent and in a follow-up interview) revealed that his original interests were in music, but his father strongly disagreed with his son's wish to be in the music club and to study music in school. His father forced him to join the baseball club instead and refused to allow him to study music. Hiro majored in English instead. His interest in music may have been carried over into his research area of phonetics, which also deals with the sounds of language.

(2) Currently in Japan, when a woman marries, she is legally obligated to take her husband's last name.

(3) A-identity involves engagement in practice (Wenger, 1998) and the main areas of engagement that constitute the work of Japanese university teachers were discussed in detail in Chapter 5.

7 Teaching is What I 'Do', Not Who I Am

Introduction

The third and final study in this book explores how the identity of one teacher of English in Japanese higher education is influenced by and reflected in her teaching practices. This study uses Wenger's (1998) theoretical framework, which asserts that identity development is ongoing and is the result of engagement in activities within a particular community. In this study, through classroom observations and interviews, I attempt to explore how notions of identity account for why Miwa, a relatively new English teacher, teaches the way that she does.

As a member of the community of practice of university English teachers in Japan, the majority of Miwa's working time is spent engaging in teaching English as a foreign language (see Chapter 5), and yet, she has no background in language pedagogy, nor does she really enjoy teaching English as a foreign language. Miwa's specialty is American literature, and she mainly identifies herself as a 'literature nerd'. For her, teaching English is merely what she does for a living, and she does not see herself as an English teacher.

Miwa's background is not unusual. Most university English teachers in Japan specialize in English-related fields such as literature or linguistics (Nagasawa, 2004). These teachers are admitted to the community of practice of English teachers in Japanese higher education because of their prestigious academic backgrounds and because they show promise as scholars. In many cases, they have no background in nor are they interested in language pedagogy. Nevertheless, these university teachers usually need to teach English language in at least some of their classes. Without a background or an interest in language pedagogy, it is likely that they draw upon their own personal experiences as language learners or upon the teaching practices of their former teachers when they teach.

Although this chapter considers the case of only one university English teacher, by examining the rationale behind her instructional decisions and methods, some insight may be provided into what kind of teaching occurs at the university level in Japan and why this type of instruction is often followed.

The Participant

The participant in this case study is Miwa, who is also featured in Chapters 5 and 6 of this book. At the time of this study, she was reaching the end of her third year of English teaching. She has a full-time contract at a national university in the greater Tokyo area where she teaches six core English classes per week. She teaches six classes (two of which are literature) part-time at other universities as well. Miwa had recently been offered a tenured position in an English literature department at a national university in a different prefecture, so she will be leaving the Tokyo area at the beginning of the following academic year.

Data Collection

Data for this study was collected in two waves over a yearlong period. The first wave of interviews began in January 2008, following the technique for conducting narrative data collection advocated by Seidman (2006), which was described in greater detail in Chapter 4.

The second wave of the data collection took place in November 2008, when I observed Miwa teaching three of her English classes over a period of several weeks. Each observation was audio recorded and I took extensive field notes during the classes. After a preliminary analysis of this classroom data was carried out, two follow-up interviews were conducted in December 2008. These interviews were designed to reconfirm my initial analysis of the classroom observations and to enable me to question Miwa about her attitudes and beliefs about teaching. These interviews were conducted 'on site' in an empty classroom and 'off site' in a restaurant.

Classroom Observations

This section describes the classroom observations. I observed three of Miwa's English language classes, each 90 minutes long with 25 to 30 students in attendance. Table 7.1 summarizes the lessons from the classroom observations and the students.

The physical layout of the three classrooms was typical of many Japanese university classrooms where the desks are permanently fastened to the floor and face the front of the room. The teacher's desk is on a raised platform and is situated in the center of the room in front of the chalkboard. Although the room is capable of holding 40 students, the maximum enrollment size is 30 students, so there are some empty spaces.

Table 7.1 Observed classes

Lesson	Students' placement according to TOEIC scores	Faculties
(1) Reading and Listening (first-year students)	Lowest level (out of three)	Faculty of Science
(2) Reading and Listening (second-year students)	Highest level (out of two)	Faculty of Arts and Letters
(3) Reading and Listening (first-year students)	Middle level (out of three)	Faculty of Arts and Letters

Field notes

I arrived in the classroom about five minutes prior to the lesson and sat in the back of the room with my small laptop computer, which enabled me to efficiently record extensive field notes, which yielded about 7500 words for each observation. I noted what the students were doing before and during the lesson, and I paid attention to the flow of the lessons and to the procedures that Miwa followed, as well as to her physical movements and mannerisms while teaching. After each observation, the raw field notes were rearranged in a chronological order and were then compared with the transcripts from the audio-recorded data.

Transcription Methods for Observations

The lessons were audio recorded, with a microphone clipped on Miwa's lapel and a digital voice recorder in her pocket. The audio data were uploaded to a computer, and were listened to repeatedly while comparing with the field notes and making memos (Miles & Huberman, 1994) for analysis. Miwa's lessons were taught almost entirely in Japanese, and although I could understand the Japanese that was used in the class and what was recorded, transcribing it proved to be extremely difficult and time consuming. Therefore, I relied mainly on the field notes and memos for the analysis of Miwa's lessons, and I transcribed only a small portion of the audio data. This portion was selected because it included various instructional features, which were representative of Miwa's teaching in the classes that I observed, as well as it being the most comprehensible for me to transcribe. The transcribed portion of Miwa's classroom observation discussed in this chapter came from Lesson #1, where Miwa taught the students a chapter from an EFL book entitled 'Robotics: From Slaves to Readers'. The entire text was five paragraphs, which took 41 minutes to cover, but I transcribed the lesson that focuses on the second paragraph, which took Miwa 10 minutes to cover. This paragraph is shown below:

> Robots are today changing from slaves to assistants, meaning they work together with human beings. Robots assist surgeons in installing artificial hips, and can also assist surgeons in delicate surgery on the human eye. In the future, 'assistant' robots will grow both much larger and much smaller, depending on the task to be performed. Large robots will make new highways, construct steel frameworks of buildings, clean underground pipelines and even do maintenance on lawns and gardens. Tiny robots are being created through the development of microelectromechanical systems and will one day be as small as a millimeter. These micro-robots will be able to travel through blood vessels to deliver medicine. They may be used as 'rooters' to clean out blockages in blood vessels and prevent heart attacks and strokes. They may be placed inside of large robots and other machines to diagnose potential mechanical problems and then fix them. (Fromm, 2005: 42–4)

As the majority of Miwa's lessons were conducted in Japanese, it was necessary to first translate the transcripts obtained from the observations into English. Table 7.2 below provides an example of the original talk in Japanese on the left-hand side, with its translated version on the right-hand side. For readability, the Japanese version is written in Romanized letters rather than in Chinese characters, and unless noted otherwise, all discussion in this study will refer to the English translated version of the transcripts. The English and the Japanese transcripts were coded in the following manner:

- Words and phrases in regular typeface indicate explanations about vocabulary, grammar or the text.
- Words and phrases in boldface indicate the original words and phrases from the textbook that are spoken or read by Miwa with a natural American English accent.
- Words and phrases that are italicized indicate that Miwa has translated something from English into Japanese.
- Extralinguistic activity is noted in English in square brackets.

Limitations of the Study

As with all studies, this one has several limitations. I only observed Miwa's lessons at one university, where the students are considered to be among the brightest in Japan. To gain a more rounded picture of Miwa's teaching practices, it might have been better to observe her lessons at other

Table 7.2 Examples of transcription methods

Original Japanese transcripts	Translated transcripts
Robots are today changing from slaves to assistants.	Robots are today changing from slaves to assistants.
To iuu koto de **assistant,** to iuu kotoba wa tsukatte imasu *ashisutanto. Ashisutanto* desu ne. **Meaning they work together with human beings.** *Ningen no tomo ni hataraku to iuu koto nanda* to iuu wake desu.	The word **assistant** is used in this text to mean *ashisutanto. Ashisutanto,* right? **Meaning, they work together with human beings.** It means *They work together with human beings.*
Sono ashisutanto to shite no rei **Robots assist surgeons in installing artificial hips and they can also assist surgeons in delicate surgery on the human eye. Assist** to iuu assist	Here is an example of this kind of assistance: **Robots assist surgeons in installing artificial hips and they can also assist surgeons in delicate surgery on the human eye. Assist.** The word **assist.**
[Miwa writes the word assist on the board with Japanese explanation] **Assist in** dare dare ni nantoka dare dare o nani nani no shigoto ni oiete kanji.	[Miwa writes the word assist on the board with Japanese explanation] **Assist in** *someone helps someone with something.*
To iuu koto de. **In** to iuu kotoba ga haite iru no desu ne. Nanode. **In** no ato ni wa desu ne. Meishi. Mata wa kono meishi no katachi de saisho **install** – **ing** no katachi natte imasu	According to this – the word 'in' is placed here, and it's followed by a noun. Ok. It's made into a noun – like this: **install** – followed by **ing** makes it a noun.
Sono sugi wa **delicate surgery** to iuu meishi naru kotoba [writes in Japanese on board] meishi no katachi. Desu ne... too iuu wake de ima genzai no desu ne	Next, the words **delicate surgery** shows a noun. [writes in Japanese on the board]. Ok?
Roboto no ashisutanto toshite no shigoto no rei, dono shigoto no rei agarete imasu ka?	So, what examples does the reading give concerning the work that assistant robots do nowadays?

universities as well. It would have also been beneficial to observe Miwa teaching the same group of students for several lessons to see if the teaching that occurred during my observations was indeed representative of her typical teaching practices. However, due to time constraints for both Miwa and myself, more observations were not possible.

The greatest limitation concerned transcribing the classroom observation data. I was unable to secure the services of a Japanese transcriber and the task proved to be very challenging for me because it was too difficult to distinguish all of the Japanese words on the uploaded audio files (although I could understand the gist what Miwa was saying). Thus I took the decision to transcribe the 10-minute portion of the data, albeit a significant segment, described above (which took approximately eight hours to achieve). This segment was chosen not only because the language was easier for me to catch in detail, but also because it clearly demonstrates the teacher-centered approach that Miwa adopted in all three of the lessons that I had observed. During this 10-minute period, Miwa guides the students, step-by-step, toward understanding with grammar and vocabulary explanations *in Japanese*. The IRF (initiation, response, feedback) (see Sinclair & Coulthard, 1975) exchange with the student, which is shown in this segment, is also typical of other instances when she questions students during her lessons.

Analysis and Interpretation

In this section, I examine in greater detail Miwa's teaching methods that I observed in the three lessons, using the data obtained from the observations, field notes, memos and transcripts. First I look at the lesson progression of the three lessons observed. Then I examine the classroom discourse that Miwa engaged in during a 10-minute segment of her reading class. Miwa confirmed the samples of Miwa's lessons offered in these sections in follow-up interviews to be representative of how she conducts the majority of her lessons.

As it has been shown teachers' beliefs and decisions are strongly influenced by the sociopolitical context in which they work (e.g. Duff & Uchida, 1997; Simon-Maeda, 2004a), I next examine Miwa's style of transmission teaching. The pedagogical methods displayed in her reading lessons, which may be representative of teaching that commonly occurs in TESEP cultures (Holliday, 1994), are significantly different from those cited as 'effective' ESL teachers in a BANA culture (Holliday, 1994).

Then a comparison is made of the classroom observations and the narrative data obtained from the three pre-observation and two post-observation interviews to investigate the intersection between Miwa's personal and professional identity and her teaching practices. This section is divided into several subsections that will discuss the impact that Miwa's initial motivation to study English and her educational background has had over her teaching practices and her beliefs toward language learning. Finally, I consider what Miwa's future may hold for her, followed by concluding comments.

The Chronology of the Lessons

In this section, I describe the flow of the three lessons that I observed, which is set out in Table 7.3. The field notes, the audio recordings, the memos and the transcripts all make clear that Miwa relies strongly on the transmission method of teaching.[1] Miwa is always in control and she directs every aspect of the lesson's activities. There is no pair or group work conducted at all during the lessons, even when the textbook calls for students to work in pairs or in groups.

As we can see, each lesson began by immediately 'getting down to business' – Miwa did not greet the students or engage in any small talk. She began Lesson #1 with 'Ok, first we will have a vocabulary test'. Lesson #2 began with 'Today we start with listening component of our class' while passing out a listening sheet, and Lesson #3 began with, 'Ok, let's begin. First I return your vocabulary test from last week'. The lessons are conducted nearly entirely in Japanese. All vocabulary and grammatical lessons are in Japanese, and English is used only when referring to the words or the sentences in the texts. Any exchange with the students is also carried out in Japanese.

During each lesson, the students are quiet, but for the most part, they seem attentive. They appeared to be listening, taking notes and consulting their electronic dictionaries, although some students, particularly in Lesson #3, were sleeping or doing homework for other classes.

Now let us take a closer look at Miwa's lesson by examining the portion of her classroom discourse, which was described earlier in the chapter.

Classroom Discourse

The discussion of Miwa's classroom discourse in this section comes from a 10-minute segment that was transcribed from Lesson #1, where Miwa was teaching students a paragraph from an EFL reading textbook. Miwa translated or paraphrased the entire reading passage during this lesson, suggesting that she wants her students to be able to understand the text in its entirety *in* Japanese. The following excerpt illustrates how Miwa guided her students toward this understanding.

Table 7.3 Chronology of Miwa's lessons

Lesson #1 (Reading) Text: 'Robotics: From Slaves to Leaders'	Lesson #2 (Listening) Text: A dramatized version of Agatha Christie's 'Wasp's Nest'	Lesson #3 (Reading) Text: 'Happy Birthday to a Musical Genius'
Class begins at 9:08	Class beings at 10:40	Class begins at 10:40
Miwa gives a quiz and collects it when students finish.	Miwa passes out a listening sheet with a vocabulary list (in English) and 12 comprehension questions.	Miwa returns the previous week's quizzes to students.
She plays the CD that accompanies the reading from the textbook.	She translates the vocabulary list into Japanese.	She reads the directions from the textbook in English and translates them into Japanese.
She reads the textbook to the students sentence-by-sentence and explains words and expressions in Japanese.	She plays half of the tape. She questions students about the tape.	Students read to find main idea. She calls on students, who answer in Japanese.
Students do the exercise in the book.	She replays the tape, and explains in Japanese what they heard.	She goes over the reading sentence-by-sentence and explains words and expressions in Japanese.
She calls on students to answer and she elaborates on their answers in Japanese	Students answer the questions on the handout while they listen to the tape for a third time.	She calls on students to check their understanding of the text and elaborates in Japanese.
She plays a long listening text about amphibious houses.	She calls on students, who answer the questions in Japanese. Miwa elaborates on their answers in Japanese.	Students do the comprehension exercises.
She explains unfamiliar words in Japanese and then plays the tape again.		She calls on students to answer the questions. Miwa explains and elaborates each answer in Japanese.

Table 7.3 (*Continued*)

Lesson #1 (Reading) Text: 'Robotics: From Slaves to Leaders'	Lesson #2 (Listening) Text: A dramatized version of Agatha Christie's 'Wasp's Nest'	Lesson #3 (Reading) Text: 'Happy Birthday to a Musical Genius'
Class begins at 9:08	**Class beings at 10:40**	**Class begins at 10:40**
She plays a third time and students answer three questions.	She writes sentences on the board that were heard in the reading.	Students do exercises comprehension and vocabulary exercises in the book.
	She repeats English from the texts but explains the meaning in Japanese.	She calls on students to see if they have the correct answer and she elaborates on their answers in Japanese.
	She plays the second half of the CD three times for the students.	
	She has the students answer the questions on the handout while listening for the third time.	She tells students to turn to the discussion question at the end of the chapter. She reads the question in English, but explains it in Japanese. She asks the students if they agree or disagree with the writer. But instead of the students talking, she explains the writer's opinion and the reading.
	She calls on the students to answer the questions in Japanese and elaborates on their answers in Japanese	
Class ends at 10:29.	Class ends at 12:05.	Class ends at 12:10.

'Assistant' robots will grow much larger and much smaller, depending on the task to be performed. *In the future, robots will become both much larger and much smaller.*

They will get bigger, bigger. Robots will get bigger, but they will also get smaller, too. **On**, *depending on... depends on something.* [Briefly explains the grammatical usage of 'depending on' in Japanese]

> **The task to be performed. Task.** *Task/work,* **to be performed.** *Well, this means depending on the work to be done,* **'assistant' robots will grow much larger and much smaller, depending on the task to be performed.** *Depending upon the work, assistant robots will become big or they will become small.*

As with other parts of her lesson, this sentence is translated, then broken down into smaller parts, with particular phrases, such as 'depending on', 'task' and 'to be performed' taught in more detail. Miwa translates new and difficult vocabulary immediately after the English word is presented to the students, for example, '**blood vessels** – *blood vessels*' and '**heart attacks and strokes** – *heart attacks and strokes*'. When an English word is also a word that can be used in Japanese,[2] she re-pronounces it with a Japanese pronunciation to ensure that it is completely understood by students. For example, words like **robot** or **assistant** are changed into *robaato* and *asshitanto*, and they are highlighted as in the following: 'The word **assistant** is used in this text to mean *ashisutanto. Ashisutanto,* right'?

When there was a long and difficult word that has no direct Japanese equivalent, she advised students to figure out its Japanese meaning by unpacking it into its smaller components, as the following extract demonstrates:

> **Tiny robots are being created through the development of microeletromechanical systems. Microelectromechanical** This is a really long word. This type of word – it's best to cut it if you want to understand it. **Micro** [writes the word micro on the board] means something *small.* Until here. **Electro** [writes on board] *electricity.* Then, **mechanical** [writes on board]. It's a really long word. Each part is a word. **Micro** and **electro**, if you cut them. Each one becomes a word. So, this word, **electro** means something to deal with electricity. So, if electricity is with the word **micro**, it means small, *small.* And then **mechanical,** *mechanical* deals with machines.
>
> Look at each as a separate word and you'll be able to understand them when they are together to form a large word. There is no word for **microelectronics** in Japanese. But you can understand **microelectro** *machine.* And the word *system.* That's the kind of thing that they can use small robots for.

During the teaching of this paragraph from the textbook, there were three IRF (initiation, response, feedback) elicitations from students, of known facts from the textbook (see Sinclair & Coulthard, 1975). As we can see from the follow-on excerpt below, a student is asked to demonstrate an understanding of the content of the reading; the student answers it in barely audible Japanese and then Miwa elaborates on the student's answer.

> This is an example of what big robots do. Here, the future tense is shown by the word **will**. This shows the future. What examples are given about what robots big robots will do in the future?
>
> Miss Kiriyama? Big robots?
>
> [Student answers in Japanese, with Miwa saying 'uh-huh' several times during her response]
>
> Yes, that's right. That's right. Uh, *they will build freeways, conduct steel frameworks for buildings.* It is something to do with construction. For example, **clean underground pipelines.** That's *pipelines, underground pipelines, cleaning underground pipelines.* So the word *even* – *even* shows that they can *even* do this sort of work. This shows the kind of things that they can do concerning construction.
>
> That's what the reading means. They can even do **maintenance** on lawns and gardens. This is an example of what large robots can do. Now let's take a look at small robots.

It is interesting, but not surprising that Miwa's question, and the student's response were given *in Japanese*. Miwa said 'uh-huh' several times while the student was answering in order to encourage her to continue and to show she was on the right track with her answer. After the answer was given, Miwa then elaborated on the student's answer in a louder voice, drawing attention back to the textbook. Miwa's question was to confirm the student's understanding of the text through her Japanese translation of it.

IRF exchanges such as this constitute a significant portion of classroom discourse (Wells, 1993). However, educational theorists have criticized such exchanges because they often do not provide sufficient learning opportunities. IRF teaching, which is associated with transmission style teaching, enables teachers to maintain classroom control (Wright, 2005). Bloom (1956, cited in Wright, 2005) argues that teachers' questions can help learners develop lower-order thinking skills (which focus on knowledge, comprehension and application) and/or higher-order thinking skills (which focus on analysis, synthesis and evaluation). Barnes (1968, also cited in

Wright, 2005) argues that in order to develop higher-order thinking in students, open-ended questions without set answers are necessary. As we can see from this excerpt taken from Miwa's lesson, the IRF exchange focuses on lower-order thinking that checks the students' comprehension of the text but does little to engage the student in thinking about the text, let alone help the student improve her English skills.

The previous two sections have described the flow of three of Miwa's English classes and how one portion of her reading lesson was handled. Miwa's classes are teacher-fronted, with her clearly being in charge of what is meant to happen in the classroom. She does nearly all of the talking, most of which is done in Japanese. The only English used in the class is that which comes directly from the texts, and this is spoken only by Miwa. Students are not required to produce any discourse in English at all, but simply to demonstrate their understanding of the text materials in Japanese.

If we only look at *how* Miwa teaches her English lessons without considering her thoughts and beliefs that underlie these practices, we run the risk of gaining merely a one-sided perspective of what she does in the classroom. As Borg (2003) argues, we must go deeper than what is visible in order to truly understand what teachers do. The next section, therefore, looks for explanations for why Miwa teaches the way that she does by referring to interview data and offers a different perspective on understanding the observed lessons.

Transmitting Knowledge to the Students

As we have seen, Miwa clearly takes charge of her classes and what she wants to occur in them. She lectures the students about the material's content; she explains important points and she calls on students to demonstrate their understanding of the text. Transmission teaching such as this depends upon the authority of the teacher, who is seen to be the bearer of knowledge, and as such, teaches or instructs a group of learners who are, by contrast, 'passively' involved (Wright, 2005). Briggs and Moore (1993: 496) call this 'high structure' teaching, where all pedagogical decisions are made by the teacher and students have little or no say in their learning.

The transmission method of education has been criticized because it is said to encourage passivity in learners, who are expected to reproduce later what they have been taught, usually by way of a test. Freire (2000, 1972) calls this the 'banking' concept of education, where teachers make a 'deposit' and later 'withdraw' knowledge from students. In spite of this method being widely criticized, it is nevertheless one of the most common pedagogical methods utilized throughout the world because it is often seen as the basis for a progression of learning and it is considered an effective way to teach large groups of students simultaneously (Wright, 2005).

For language teaching in TESEP cultures, transmission teaching, particularly that which is grammar-oriented, is often viewed as more important for learning than inductive or practice-based teaching methodologies generally preferred in BANA cultures (Holliday, 1994). Holliday explains that this conflict originates from the different notions held of 'teachers' and of 'learning'. In a TESEP culture, it is believed that learning cannot take place without the teaching. This teaching is defined as passing on the specialized knowledge, held by the teacher, to the students. In a BANA culture, however, a learner-centered pedagogy is emphasized, and students are considered active participants in their own learning, which comes through discovery. These differences can lead to the feelings among those from one academic culture that those from the other academic culture may not be doing their jobs properly. For example, Stewart (2005) found in her study of professionalism and expertise of Japanese teachers of English in higher education that one of the Japanese teachers believed that she would be shirking her duty if she just sat back and let students assume responsibility for their own learning. This teacher's comment, Stewart surmised, implied a criticism of the more communicative approaches utilized by the native English-speaking colleagues at her university, whom she felt did not 'teach' their students.

The cultural role of teachers in a TESEP culture is thus significantly different from those in a BANA culture. Teacher-oriented teaching can reflect the respected social position enjoyed by the teachers, and encouraging student-oriented practices could undermine these teachers' authority. Therefore, the potential impact of CLT needs to be examined critically (e.g. Edge, 1996; Phan Le Ha, 2008).

To further illustrate this divide in methodology between TESEP and BANA cultures, let us now examine the differences between Miwa's teaching style, which reflects that of a TESEP culture, and the teaching style of an 'effective' ESL reading teacher described by Richards (1990). The teacher observed in Richards' study had just completed his MA in TESOL and was teaching advanced level students in Hawaii. The teacher's stated goals for his students were to increase their reading speed, comprehension and vocabulary, as well as to provide sufficient opportunity for them to develop an enjoyment of reading through extensive and intensive activities. To accomplish these goals, he designed a variety of classroom activities that involved a combination of activities using top-down and bottom-up processing such as pair work, group discussions and individualized reading activities. Vocabulary focus included writing original sentences and learning vocabulary in context through analogies, derivations, collocations, definitions and paraphrases.

Miwa, on the other hand, focuses on getting students to comprehend the reading passages from the textbook by using strictly bottom-up processing. After playing the textbook's accompanying CD for the students so they could listen to it in entirety once, the reading was dissected by Miwa sentence-by-sentence, word-by-word. Although she did not ask the students to translate it into Japanese, which is the strongest feature of *yakudoku* style of language learning (Hino, 1988), she translated the passage for them in a running commentary *about* the passage.

Unlike the teacher described by Richards (1990), who believes strategy training is an important part of language teaching, Miwa introduced only one vocabulary-related strategy in the three lessons observed, when she advised students to break a long and difficult word into its smaller parts in order to understand its meaning. There was no pair work or group activities done in any of the three lessons observed. When Miwa was not teaching the students, they were either taking a quiz or working independently on exercises in the textbook (or, in the case of the listening class, on the handout). Although students were given an extensive reading assignment for them to complete outside of class, in-class time was spent on an intensive analysis of the reading texts *in Japanese*.

The teacher's pedagogical style portrayed in Richards' (1990) case study and Miwa's teaching style are as different as night and day, and upon first glance, especially from a BANA methodological point of view, it might seem that no meaningful learning could possibly be taking place in Miwa's lessons. However, students in TESEP countries are often not only accustomed to this approach to teaching and learning, they often *expect* their professors to possess important knowledge and to pass it on to them (e.g. Holliday, 1994; Phan Le Ha, 2008). TESEP students see many communicative classroom activities, which are designed to put students at ease and to facilitate learning, as useless and childish activities that fail to bring about 'real' learning (e.g. Li, 2004; Phan Le Ha, 2008; Tsui, 2007).

In Miwa's class, many students appeared to be listening earnestly, taking notes and consulting their dictionaries, indicating their familiarity with this style of teaching and suggesting that the teaching was making an impact on the students.[3]

Holliday (1994) also observed this attentiveness during his research and reports being surprised to discover that students in knowledge-transmission classes appeared to enjoy them just as much as they did his own classes, which focused on more practical aspects of language use. However, it is necessary to point out that the university in which I observed Miwa's lessons is a highly competitive one to enter. These students are not just accustomed to transmission style of teaching; they have excelled academically through it. By contrast, students in other types of academic institutions might not display the same sort of attentive classroom behavior.

The Impact of Beliefs, Knowledge and Identity on Miwa's Teaching Practices

In the previous section, I examined how Miwa conducts her lessons, which seems be in keeping with expectations in a TESEP culture (Holliday, 1994). I will now consider her teaching practices from a different perspective. Here, I examine three areas where Miwa's personal beliefs and knowledge toward language learning and language teaching seem to directly impact how she conducts her lessons. This section is divided into four subsections. First I show how Miwa's initial motivation for studying English, which guided the way that she herself studied English, influences not only how she teaches it, but also what she believes her students should be doing in the classroom. Then I show that a relationship exists between Miwa's self-identification as a 'literature nerd' and the importance she attaches to written materials for teaching. The following section looks at Miwa's attitudes toward students' learning, and finally I examine Miwa's conflicting identities as both a language teacher and a literature specialist.

Miwa's love of literature

At the core of Miwa's personal and professional identity lies her love of literature. In order to understand the relationship between Miwa's love of literature and the way she teaches English, it is necessary to look at her initial motivation for studying English and her own academic history. For her, the main purpose of learning English was to be able to read English novels in the original language. Even though as a university student she chose to major in English language rather than literature (because of its presumed practicality), she nevertheless took as many English literature classes as she could. She spent her undergraduate years simultaneously improving her language skills while studying literature. The majority of Miwa's English language professors were Japanese priests with traditional linguistics or literature backgrounds, teaching from old-fashioned materials using somewhat archaic language. Yet Miwa said she felt that it was 'fun' to learn from them.

Miwa doesn't remember having any teachers whose academic specialty was in English language teaching, but she did attend several classes, such as basic composition, taught by part-time native English-speaking teachers. In comparison with her Japanese teachers, whom she said taught 'language and culture', those classes taught by native-speaking teachers seemed to be mostly superficially useful. Her comment below clearly illustrates mixed feelings toward these teachers and their lessons:

> I think it worked. They tell you the mechanical way of writing. They tell you that they use the material or the textbook from the [United States] for like English Composition 101. And it helped. But I felt like I'm learning **techniques,** not really language or culture. I was learning techniques from them. So yes. We have to have techniques. But sometimes you can just keep on learning techniques. It will be boring. Well, it is a weird thing at [name of] University. Lots of them [the Japanese professors] are priests, so I think their English is sometimes outdated. But that was fun, too.

This comment, where Miwa compares her Japanese teachers, who focus on what she feels to be deeper aspects of English, and her foreign teachers, who teach 'mechanical ways' of English, suggests that she holds two attitudes toward learning English. First there is a deeper and more meaningful approach, which concentrates on developing an understanding of language through the words and expressions used by writers. Practical language skills, on the other hand, which are perceived to be gained through the superficial learning of 'techniques', may provide students with an appearance of language fluency, but not much substance. This is a reoccurring theme in Miwa's professional identity as a teacher and will be revisited later in this discussion.

Miwa's beliefs of the importance of having a deeper understanding of English language are reflected in her transmission style of teaching, where she goes over every point of a reading passage in minute detail. Dissecting the text and explaining each point, she feels, is making the reading material understandable to all her students. This is one way to ensure that her students have an equal chance to learn, *if*, she feels, they make the necessary effort to do so.

These beliefs also explain in part why Miwa, who *is* fluent in English, conducts her classes entirely in Japanese. She said that when she tries to teach in English, students are 'scared and nervous' and are not able to understand everything that she tells them, even if she simultaneously writes what she says on the blackboard. In her words, 'I don't think they will hate me if I do that [speak in English], but definitely they don't enjoy the class as much [if I do speak in English]'. Speaking Japanese ensures that everyone has the same opportunity to understand. She also said that as her classes focus on reading and listening, speaking English would detract from time that should be spent on those activities. These comments also suggest that Miwa considers 'practical' English to be somehow less important than English that is 'studied'.

When asked about her style of teaching, Miwa said the students in the classes that I observed were not ready to understand 'complicated and detailed argument...at that level, I think that they [first] have to get every detail and every expression and every new word they can learn'. In other words, she employs a distinctly bottom-up approach to language teaching because she feels that without knowing 'all the basics', her students will be unable to understand the broader points of what they are reading.

Miwa's style of teaching is related to how she herself learned English. She developed her language skills through the careful reading of articles in magazines such as *Time* or *Newsweek* and from reading novels. She feels that if her students are to master English, then they need to make a similar effort, at least in terms of looking up unknown words in the dictionary and trying to work out the meaning of the reading on their own. If they are unwilling to make this effort, she feels they will only gain a 'superficial' knowledge of English and they will only 'become secretaries'.

The key to learning is in the materials

Because Miwa's main interest in English lies in the printed word, it is not surprising that she believes successful language teaching is connected to the materials. She feels that if she can find appropriate texts that will stimulate her students, they will not only improve their English ability, but will also be able to transfer their interest to the broader context outside of the classroom. As she was able to broaden her own world through English reading, she hopes her students will be able to do the same.

However, finding such appropriate texts is proving to be one of the most challenging aspects of teaching English for her. When she first began teaching, she was given an EFL textbook and told to teach 'everything' from it so that the students would be able to pass a standardized test at the end of the semester. In her second year of teaching, she had the freedom to choose her own teaching materials, so she picked authentic texts that she believed would be of interest to her students. Currently, in her third year of teaching, she uses published EFL reading textbooks as sources for reading texts.

Miwa reported that she found advantages and disadvantages in using both authentic texts and in using EFL texts. The main advantage of using authentic texts for her is that preparing for classes using these texts is intellectually challenging. She chooses materials from her students' academic fields because she believes this will spark their interest in language learning. She said that by choosing these sorts of materials, she is able to expand her own knowledge of the world and learn new specialized vocabulary and expressions as well. She spends a great deal of time preparing for classes by extracting important expressions and grammatical patterns to teach. She also gathers background information concerning the topic to increase her own understanding of the articles. She said she does this 'not to give a big lecture, but to give students a little more information than what is provided just from the journal article'. Although using authentic materials forced Miwa to spend a significant amount of time in preparation, it provided a certain amount of satisfaction for her because she could gain new knowledge.

Although Miwa liked using authentic materials for her classes, she discovered there were a number of disadvantages as well. First, she realized that authentic readings are generally too long and too difficult for students to understand, particularly those with low-level English proficiency. She also found that in spite of choosing materials she felt were interesting, students complained that they were boring. Students' lack of effort to study hard and their lack of interest in such materials led Miwa to choose an EFL textbook in her third year of teaching.

Miwa feels that, in a way, EFL textbooks are much easier to use because it is not necessary to invest a great deal of time or energy in preparation. The short readings in the texts can be covered in one lesson period, and all of the grammar and important expressions are set out in the textbook and in the teacher's manual. Since Miwa had 12 classes per week at the time of this study, minimizing class preparation is a definite advantage for her. Nevertheless, she complains that the readings from the EFL textbooks are 'so boring' for her and they have 'no depth' because 'when you have only two pages to write about something, it is just not that interesting'.

Even though Miwa recognizes that EFL textbooks are generally aimed at students with a 'certain ability', she discovered using them as teaching materials does not necessarily ensure students learn any better than when she uses authentic materials. She complained that students become quite lazy and they will not study on their own by consulting the dictionary when Japanese annotations are provided for them.

Furthermore, as a teacher, Miwa feels 'guilty', almost as if she is 'cheating' when she uses an EFL textbook. In contrast to the extra effort it takes to use authentic materials, she confesses that she 'just teaches whatever it is they [textbook authors] say. I don't feel I am doing a good enough job with that'. Because she relies on the teaching manual to do all the preparation for her, she sometimes discovers inadequate explanations or mistakes in the annotations while teaching, forcing her to ad lib portions of her lessons because she had not prepared sufficiently in advance.

Miwa was also concerned about the authority of textbook writers in deciding what vocabulary and which grammatical expressions are essential to include in the books for the benefit of students to learn. She wondered how the decision is made to include such topics in the book, and she felt that in some cases the textbook writers have 'weird opinions' about topic selection.

As the written word holds so much importance for Miwa personally and professionally, it is no wonder that she places a great deal of importance on written materials for teaching. Selecting appropriate reading materials for students has created a struggle for her: should she use materials that are intellectually challenging for her but too difficult for the students? Or should she use materials that are easy to teach from but are not intellectually stimulating? As Miwa gains more experience and expertise in English language teaching, she may come to recognize more easily authentic materials that are of an appropriate pedagogical level for her students as well as which particular materials may be more interesting for students.

Authority as a teacher

Although Miwa is developing an increasing confidence in her English-teaching ability, she still struggles with self-identifying as a teacher, and she confesses that she does not yet enjoy teaching. Nevertheless, she takes her job seriously and she believes that instructing people is important.

Miwa feels a good teacher is someone who 'knows everything' and who can lead students, step-by-step, to understanding that knowledge. However, being able to do this is much harder than she had anticipated, and she now realizes that as a student she had no idea 'how much teachers are struggling or how much effort they are making in their classes'.

Miwa's confidence in teaching stems from the content of what she teaches. Her excellent English skills and her extensive class preparation (when using authentic texts) ensure that she has a complete understanding of the content when she steps into the classroom. She feels that she has important and useful things to teach her students and she has to 'give them [students] information and all these things they **need** for their future… definitely if they keep everything that I say, everything that I tell them, they can use it. If they want to.' Miwa makes sure that she knows everything in advance that she feels is important for her students to learn, and she teaches the material meticulously in class.

As Shulman (1986) points out, however, teacher knowledge includes not only knowledge of the content being taught, but also knowing how to teach that content and knowledge of the social context in which the teaching is taking place. Although Miwa seems to be confident with the first aspect of teacher's knowledge according to Shulman's classification, it is apparent she has yet to fully develop its second and third aspect. This gap in teacher knowledge is evident in the following comment where she discusses her difficulty in simplifying explanations for students when they do not understand:

> Sometimes I just don't understand some students' problems in understanding certain things. I just try to go back to the basics and ask lots of questions why they don't understand. But the problem is, they cannot answer those questions either. So I don't have any instinct or inclination to understand their inability to answer those questions.

The admission that she has no 'instinct' or 'inclination' to help students understand when they have difficulties in learning is interesting. Such fatalistic comments seem to suggest that she feels that when she has reached an impasse with teaching there is nothing left to do but 'give up.' This attitude may be related to Miwa's belief that it is the students' responsibility to make the effort to understand what they are taught through diligent study, especially since this is what she did as a student. As a teacher, her job is to present the material to be learned in its entirety to the students, but the responsibility of learning lies in their hands, and not necessarily hers.

Miwa feels that when students fail to do well on quizzes and examinations it is because of their lack of effort. Although she does not like to be in a position of authority where she must decide to pass or fail students, she says she will fail students without hesitation:

> It is difficult to grade people. When you see the horrible result of the exam...I just can't help but think, OK, I have to fail this person. But then again, you can't fail too many people [smiling, exasperated]. When someone gets only four points out of 100, what can you do?...I felt that the test might have been hard at first, but there are some other people who get 80 points. That means I wasn't giving them too hard a test.

To provide students with more likelihood of passing her classes, Miwa began giving vocabulary quizzes every three or four weeks. These quizzes demonstrate to her that students are studying and they enable students to accumulate sufficient points to pass the class, even if they do poorly on the final exam. These quizzes are straightforward and involve translation of vocabulary, which is covered in class and often annotated in the textbook. Nevertheless, Miwa complains that some students still fail them, indicating, in her view, a complete lack of effort on their part, and she says these are the same students who are likely to fail the final examination as well. Even though her classes are compulsory subjects for the students, she said:

> If they are really terrible, I think there is no choice but to fail them. I'm not afraid to do so [laughter] but if they are really good and if they show that they are trying hard, I think I'll try to save them. Somehow.

English language teacher or literature specialist?

The final, and probably the most significant area of struggle for Miwa in language teaching lies in her having an academic background that is not related to English language teaching. Because she has a PhD in American literature and a number of academic publications in that field, she is deemed *qualified* to teach English language in Japanese universities, but she had very little prior teaching experience before she began teaching English nearly three years earlier. She has no English-teaching license, and no pedagogical training about *how* to teach language. Feeling pressure to start earning money after completing her PhD and with no guarantee of obtaining a tenured position, she took on as many classes as she could find. Currently she has twelve: six English language lessons at the university where she has a full-time contract, and four language lessons and two literature classes for non-literature majors at other universities.

Although Miwa does not like teaching English very much, she confesses that teaching it is 'better than nothing,' and she does it because she 'has to'. She feels that English language teaching is a lonely business because she always has to stand up in front of so many people and 'talk, talk, talk... always talking and explaining' without expecting any response from the students. She says she would like to have more interaction with the students concerning the text content, but she feels that she ends up just talking about the text herself, which is like 'talking to hear her own voice'.

It is not surprising, therefore, that Miwa prefers teaching literature classes. This is not only because literature is her academic field, but because the students' behavior in these classes differs significantly. She says:

> There is more discussion and interaction and going back and forth in English. But [laughter] in English classes, I'm just talking and talking and talking and explaining things. There is no dialogue. It is just a monologue. Seriously.

Miwa's background in literature drives her desire to help the students in her language classes to be able to 'understand all the nuances and the minor details' of a text, but she complains that the students 'just want to understand what is said and they don't try to go deeper than that'. She attributes this lack of desire to student passivity in class, resulting in her doing all the classroom talking.

Miwa's students' passive behavior in class may be due in part to the teacher-fronted transmission style of teaching that she engages in, which encourages students to listen silently as she teaches. Opportunities provided by the EFL books for students to engage in pair work or discussion were either entirely skipped, or Miwa glossed them over with an explanation in Japanese. The impersonal nature of the classes could also explain a lack of classroom interaction between Miwa and the students. The lessons that were observed began with getting right down to classroom business, without encouraging any interpersonal dialogue with the students.

Miwa admitted that she has no personal relationships with the students in the language classes, saying this is because the classes are 'too big and impersonal'. Miwa cannot do anything about the size of the classes, but she still may be contributing to the impersonal nature of the classes herself by withholding her personal self from the students, as the following excerpt suggests:

> In the English classes, I feel like I'm against the whole class. So if I give them my personal perspective, I kind of feel...I don't want to be responsible for whatever I'm saying. You know, as long as it is about a textbook or a material I'm teaching, that's OK. But I don't want to give them my opinion about these world affairs. [laughter] That kind of concerns me.

Given her feeling that as a language teacher, she is pitted *against* her students, it is not surprising that Miwa openly admits that she would be happier if she could 'give up all those language classes' and focus on teaching literature. A comparison of the field notes taken during the classroom observations indicates that Miwa was much more enthusiastic teaching the listening class than teaching the reading classes. This enthusiasm is connected to the materials, because in that particular listening class, she had students listen to a dramatized short story by Agatha Christie. During the follow-up interview Miwa confirmed the enjoyment she had had teaching this class because she 'loves' mysteries like this.

Even though Miwa does not really like teaching English, she believes that her background in literature can nevertheless offer students an important perspective on language learning that students may miss out on if they only learn English from language specialists. She explains:

> I was a student once, and I learned from literature teachers. And well, probably I could give them [students] more than just the language [teacher] people. Because they just teach language as language. But literature people can say 'this expression can be found in that', and back then – like this, like this', and something like that. So, I think. I don't know what's its new or something meaningful to them. But still.
>
> *Diane: You are opening doors for them?*
>
> [...]Yes. I definitely enjoy it. Probably not all of them but some of them [students] would enjoy it.[...] Well, that's how I learned language.

Miwa's beliefs that English language learning can be divided into two strata, one deep, and full of nuance and meaning, and the other superficial and practical, is again exemplified by the following statement:

> You cannot have all those ELT majors...I think there is something good in learning from literature majors. **I believe. I hope.** Because language is of course something you can use and probably just a tool...

Perhaps Miwa equates ELT teachers with being only one of those who entertain students, because she wondered whether if she were perhaps a 'more entertaining teacher', students would be more inclined to pay attention in class and would respond to her better. However, she explained that this is not her teaching style:

> I can't be those kind of people who just entertain students. So I'm not really trying to be popular with students and I don't really want to be. I don't want to be the person who tries to be popular. But sometimes

students, who are not interested in the subject at all – they just need someone, a charismatic teacher. But I can't do that [laughter].

She revisited this theme later in the interview. The following statement demonstrates her feelings that, focusing on practical English – even if students want to do that – is at odds with the necessary efforts she feels they should make. She said:

> I don't think students really want something valuable. They just want to be entertained or they just want to be spoon fed something really useful without doing anything...Without effort every day, routine work, you don't get anything. But some people make you believe that there are some miracles and miraculous ways to do it, so they like those teachers. But I don't have them, you don't have them. Nobody has them. Also practical things all the time, and they want something they can use right away, but without all the necessary motivation, you don't get to the point.

For Miwa, it is apparent that English learning is a serious matter, and not merely for entertainment.

Miwa's Future

Miwa's current conflict between the necessity of teaching English language on the one hand, but wanting to focus on literature on the other, may be short-lived, because at the beginning of the upcoming academic year, she will be moving to a tenured position in an English literature department of a national university in a different part of Japan. Tenured positions of any sort are difficult to obtain, but especially ones in academic universities like the one where Miwa will move. Because the majority of universities in Japan are liberal arts colleges where the academic quality varies widely (Kinmouth, 2005), many literature and linguistics scholars find tenured positions in academic institutions where they teach mainly English language classes to disinterested students. Miwa, however, will be able to teach literature classes to students majoring in literature. This will help her sustain her identity as a 'literature nerd' while she engages in teaching the subject of her choice. Moving away from Tokyo also enables Miwa to give up her part-time teaching positions. With a greatly reduced teaching load, she is looking forward to centering her teaching life on literature, as the following comment illustrates:

> I can use my time to teach literature and to do my research. I can combine my interest and teaching at the same time. That will save a lot

of my time because I don't have to do only preparation for the classes – I can prepare for the class and at the same time do my research. I think that will be a whole different story.

In spite of the majority of her classes focusing on literature in her new position, Miwa will still have to teach some language classes for non-English major students. Furthermore, in the second semester, she has been asked to teach a required course for students to obtain an English-teaching license. Miwa is worried about this because she does not have an English-teaching license herself, and she has no idea of what is expected of her in this class. She said she was told to teach whatever she likes as long as it 'concerns language and culture', and she suspects that she was asked to teach this class because no one else in the English department wants to do it.

There will undoubtedly be a number of adjustments that Miwa will have to make in order to be accustomed to her new job. In addition to teaching, she will be responsible for other administrative duties as well. Nevertheless, moving to this new university will not only provide Miwa with job security, it sets her firmly on the inbound trajectory (Wenger, 1998) of English literature scholars in Japan. Because her new position is in a prestigious university where the students are likely to be motivated to study hard and where they are interested in literature, Miwa may achieve more satisfaction from her teaching than she does currently. Furthermore, it is likely that she will encounter students who have similar attitudes toward study that she herself had as a student. At her new university, it may not be necessary for her to maintain two separate identities as an English language teacher and as an English literature specialist, because she will actually be an English literature specialist who helps students understand English language in relation to literature.

Conclusion of Analysis and Interpretation

In the analysis and interpretation section of this chapter, I first examined a sample of Miwa's observed teaching that reflects the way in which she conducts her English reading classes. I found it to be very teacher-directed and in sharp contrast to a BANA (Holliday, 1994) approach toward teaching reading. Indeed, seen from a BANA perspective, Miwa's methodology might be considered a dismal failure: the class was conducted entirely in Japanese with practically no participation from the students at all. No group or pair work was carried out and the entire lesson was spoon-fed line by line for the students to swallow.

The interview data analysis showed that Miwa's self-identification as a 'literature nerd' strongly impacts her English language teaching practices. For her, language learning is connected to the printed material. Being able to read deeply between the lines and being able to understand the writers' intentions and nuances cultivates a deeper understanding of English. It is this deeper understanding of English that Miwa perceives to be more important than acquiring mere technical language skills.

In her classes, Miwa does not focus on the translation of lexical items and the instruction of grammatical details merely because this is how she herself was *taught* English. Rather, she teaches this way because this is the method she successfully used to *learn* English herself. She draws upon her own language learning experiences to teach what she feels is most useful for her students. Instead of emulating the language learning 'techniques' that were offered by the native English-speaking teachers in her undergraduate days, she instead focuses on 'language and culture', which was what she learned from her Japanese professors and which represents the most important aspect of language learning for her.

At this stage of Miwa's professional development, she struggles to some degree with knowing what to teach and how to teach it. She also is not quite sure how to engage with students. Nevertheless, she feels she has developed more confidence in her teaching during the past year, supporting Lave and Wenger's (1991) argument that learning is always situated within a context. Although Miwa is hesitant to agree that she now enjoys teaching, she said she is no longer as nervous as she used to be. It is difficult coming to terms with thinking of herself as a teacher after having spent more than 10 years as a student. As time goes by, and as more time is spent in the classroom, Miwa is likely to become increasingly comfortable self-identifying as a teacher, particularly as she will be teaching more within her academic area and less in teaching English language.

Conclusion of Chapter 7

In this chapter, I have considered, through a series of five interviews and three separate classroom observations, how the beliefs of one Japanese teacher of English in Japanese higher education shape her professional identity and how these beliefs about language teaching and learning influence her teaching practices. The study has been guided by the following research questions:

(1) What beliefs does Miwa hold about language teaching and language learning?

(2) How are these beliefs manifested, if at all, in Miwa's teaching?
(3) What is the strength of the relationship between Miwa's beliefs, professional identity and classroom practices?

In answering the first question, it was found that Miwa's passion for literature is at the core of her beliefs toward language learning and her language teaching. She was driven to study English in order to read English literary works in the original language. Therefore, as a student, she felt that her Japanese professors really taught her 'language *and culture*' through fine-grained analysis of the lexical and syntactical details of reading materials they presented in class. In contrast, although she felt that the classes taught by her native English-speaking instructors, such as 'how to write an essay' were useful, she believed they were only concerned with the 'mechanics' or the 'technical' aspects of language. Miwa thus holds two viewpoints toward English language learning and English language teaching. The first one represents Miwa's preferred method of learning, which entails in-depth understanding of language through hard self-study and careful listening to teachers' lectures about language. The second concerns the 'mechanical' aspects of English, which she feels can give the appearance of fluency but, at the same time, is superficial and lacks substance.

These attitudes are reflected in the way that Miwa teaches, the focus of the second research question of this study. Miwa, who feels she has important information to impart to her students, engages in transmission-style teaching in Japanese to ensure that all of her students have the opportunity to understand what is being covered in each lesson. It appears to be that her main aim for her students is to have them foster an appreciation of the written materials she presents. This appreciation comes through *intellectual understanding* of the materials, and not from *practical engagement* with them. A recurring theme throughout the interviews was Miwa's distinction between merely learning 'techniques' and the importance of learning 'language and culture'. Emphasis only on the former, she believes, will limit intellectual development, resulting in students, particularly *female* students, merely becoming language technicians with limited professional futures.

Miwa's beliefs in the importance of words and structure are also reflected in the attitudes she holds toward the teaching materials. She feels that if she can make the right materials selection, students will become motivated to study harder. Even though she feels students should study independently, she spends class time deconstructing the textbook materials phrase-by-phrase and word-by-word and provides a commentary for students while she translates the texts into Japanese. It seems that it is not necessarily the *process* of learning that is important, but the *outcome*, especially when reflected by scores on quizzes and tests. Students are evaluated by the outcome of such scores, and as Miwa says, if they are 'horrible', she will fail them.

Miwa's definition of teachers as people who 'know everything' is at the heart of her teaching practices as well. Her lessons are teacher-fronted, and she engages in bottom-up processing of the selected reading materials in order to provide students with detailed knowledge about the texts. What is particularly interesting is that it seems that Miwa utilizes such a pedagogical method not merely because this was how she was taught herself, but because this was the way that she could absorb important information that her teachers were providing for her. To reiterate, as a student, she *liked* studying this way. As a teacher, it seems that she perceives this to be 'real' teaching of language and culture, and not just 'techniques'.

In answering the third research question, concerning the strength of the relationship between Miwa's beliefs, professional identity and classroom practice, it is clear that Miwa's identity as a literature specialist guides nearly every aspect of her teaching and how she perceives herself as a teacher. As mentioned earlier, Miwa believes the key to students' learning is in the materials. The materials are also of utmost importance for Miwa to gain satisfaction in teaching. When she chose authentic materials that she felt pertained to her students' majors, she was able to learn about new topics and to learn specialized vocabulary. She was happy to 'study' for her classes, but she found that her students did not necessarily appreciate such efforts. Switching to EFL textbooks the following year reduced the amount of time required for class preparation but resulted in less teaching satisfaction.

Miwa's identity as a literature specialist is, however, in conflict with her developing identity as a language teacher. This is not surprising, considering that Miwa has spent more than a decade becoming a literature scholar. This identity was cultivated from years of study, which culminated in a PhD. On the other hand, she became a language teacher the moment she walked into the university language classroom having been told to teach from a textbook so that students could pass a standardized test at the end of the semester. Considering the differences between what Miwa had accomplished academically and what she is expected to do as a language teacher, it is no wonder that she has experienced difficulty during these first three years of English language teaching. Being recognized and hired on the basis of being a literature scholar, but then being asked to engage in work that is unrelated, meant that Miwa had a very wide and a very difficult gap to bridge.

Another area of conflict between Miwa's identity as a literature scholar and her identity as a language teacher entails her viewpoints toward language learning. Miwa's beliefs that language and culture are more important than practical English may be in opposition to her students' beliefs. Miwa has not yet learned how to view the students as language learners with different learning goals from what she herself had had. As a result, Miwa's goals for instilling a love of language and culture into her students may be met with resistance because students' goals may lean more toward the 'technical' ones that she disdains.

It is likely that it will take some time for Miwa's conflicting identities as a literature specialist and a language teacher to merge together into an identity as a teacher of English in Japanese higher education. As Wenger (1998) notes, identity develops through engaging in activities. Even though Miwa does not particularly like teaching English language, she believes that it is an important aspect of her job, which, accordingly, she takes seriously. Therefore, as she gains more experience in 'doing' language teaching, it is likely that she will create a professional identity that becomes suitable and comfortable for her.

Notes

(1) See Wright (2005) for a historical overview of transmission-style teaching in EFL.
(2) The Japanese language has a system for appropriating foreign words into Japanese, known as *gairaigo*. These words often have no equivalent in Japanese, and so they have become a part of the Japanese lexicon. They have been adapted to fit Japanese phonological patterns so that the original English is often not recognized by Japanese speakers.
(3) It is likely that the 'observer's paradox' occurred during the classroom observations. Miwa later reported that the students were 'much better' than they were ordinarily. She said they might have felt that as an older and more senior teacher, I (the observer) was there to evaluate her teaching performance, and thus the students behaved more actively in order to 'help her out'.

8 Conclusion

I began this book with a description of the apocryphal Hiroshi Yamato, an associate professor of English literature in a fictitious Japanese university (Kelly & Adachi, 1992). His method of teaching English involves lecturing on obscure points while students sleep through his lessons. His private and professional world revolves around the professor who chairs the department. His thoughts and opinions are dictated by this professor, and Hiroshi's knowledge of what is going on in the outside world is severely limited. I have come across one or two 'Hiroshi Yamatos', especially in my early years of teaching in Japan, but much more often than not I have met hardworking and dedicated teachers who want the best for their students.

My intent in embarking upon this study, therefore, was to move away from negative discourse about English education in Japanese higher education (e.g. Hall, 1997; McVeigh, 2002, 2004), and instead to explore this field from the perspectives of those who mainly teach it. My aim was to look at Japanese university English teachers from a 'small culture' perspective (Aspinall, 2006; Holliday, 1999) and to investigate their teaching practices, beliefs and identities.

In the introduction to this book, I described the impact that university teachers of English have over English language education in Japan and outlined the reasons why this group of teachers needs to be studied if English language education in Japan is to be better understood. MEXT has revised its course of study several times over the past 20 years in order to improve the communicative English skills of Japanese students, but the goals established by MEXT are unlikely to be successfully implemented due to resistance from secondary school teachers to change their teaching practices. Reasons for this resistance were shown to be directly and indirectly related to the teaching practices and beliefs of university English teachers.

Using two separate but complementary theoretical frameworks to analyze the content of the participants' narratives enabled me to study their identities from two perspectives. This, I believe, enabled me to gain a richer view of how identity is constructed and maintained by the participants in my studies. The first theoretical framework was Wenger's (1998) theory of identity, which asserts that identity forms through engagement in the various activities that members of a community of practice do. This was the theoretical framework utilized in Chapter 5 that looked at how relatively new teachers of English in Japanese higher education come to identify as members of this community. Here the analysis was on engagement, imagination and alignment. The second theoretical framework was that of Gee (2000), who proposes that identity forms from 'being recognized as a "kind of person" in a given context' (p. 99). In Chapter 6, where I examined the intersection of gender and professional identity, Gee's four perspectives of identity enabled me to tease apart aspects of the participants' identity to understand the impact that gender has had on nearly all areas of their professional lives. In Chapter 7, I returned to Wenger's (1998) theory of identity in exploring the relationship between Miwa's identity as a specialist in literature and her English language teaching practices.

Although these were small-scale studies, I believe that taken together, these multiple views of teacher identity present a coherent and revealing picture of English language education at the tertiary level in Japan from the standpoint of those who teach it. Chapters 5 and 7 examined the identity development of teachers who are relatively new to teaching. As newcomers, their careers stretch ahead of them, and how they make the transition from scholars in English-related fields to teachers of English while they learn the ins and outs of their jobs will impact the language learning experiences of their students for many years. Chapter 6, which examined the identity of female university teachers ranging in age from early 30s to early 60s, showed that English language education was, and still is, perceived to be a gendered asset for female students. The women featured in this study were able to develop prestigious careers using English as the starting point. However, the narratives of these seven women also highlighted the struggles that they endure as female minorities in a predominantly male profession.

Summary of Overall Findings

This section summarizes the findings that emerged from the three studies in this book. However, caveats about making broad claims are in order. First, it is important to reiterate that these findings are applicable only for the Japanese tertiary context. Second, they are limited in that they provide in-depth analysis only of the particular participants in the study. Although the findings cannot be generalized to all teachers in all universities in Japan, I do believe they will, nevertheless, resonate with tertiary English language teachers throughout Japan.

English Language Teacher Versus Academic in an English-related Field

The most significant finding to emerge from this study concerns the tensions caused by the participants' competing identities as specialists in their academic fields and as non-specialist English language teachers. If these two identities are viewed as a dichotomy, then there is a struggle in how the participants identify professionally. This is particularly evident in those who see a distinction between who they *are* (specialists in English-related areas) and what they *do* (English language teaching). I do not mean to suggest, however, that the stronger the affiliation toward one's academic field, the weaker the affiliation toward language teaching, or that the weaker the affiliation toward one's academic field, the stronger the affiliation for language teaching. The participants who feel fewer struggles with these competing identities are those who consider themselves as specialists in their fields *and* as language teachers.

The participants who are able to self-identify as both specialists and as language teachers are not necessarily those whose academic backgrounds are closely related to English language teaching. Instead, they are those who have a natural inclination for teaching, who like teaching, who have some knowledge about teaching and who have had a sufficient amount of experience in the classroom. Taka, for example, has an inclination for teaching, and he says that he has always wanted to become a teacher. For him, it isn't so much what he teaches that is important: it is *the act of teaching*. His experience as a Japanese language teacher and his enrollment in the TESOL course while in Australia as an exchange student provide support for his comments where he said he would be 'happy teaching anything', and that if he were not an English teacher at a university, he would probably be teaching 'something else'.

A natural inclination for teaching seems to help reconcile the conflicting identities as a researcher and as a language teacher, but it is also important that the participants actually *like* teaching as well, because a greater enjoyment in teaching also contributes to a positive self-identification as a teacher. Some of the participants may not have been driven to become teachers as Taka was, but once they started teaching, they found they liked it. This is particularly true of Kumiko, who 'settled' for English language teaching when she was unable to find a job as a university lecturer in women's studies after she returned to Japan. Kumiko liked teaching, but she looked down on *language teaching*. However, once she entered a graduate TESOL program for the sole purpose of improving her chances to find a tenured position, she found second language education to be a much more interesting field than she had originally thought. Now Kumiko feels that teaching is one of the most important aspects of her job. Shizuko, who decided to change and upgrade her academic credentials to English in order to get a better job, has found that she also loves teaching. This is an interesting turn of events for her, considering that as a student she did not even like English.

Experience was also found to be an important aspect in the development of the participants' self-identification as language teachers. The newest teachers, Miwa and Kana, have not yet had enough experience to feel at ease in the classroom. Miwa's resistance toward identifying as a language teacher may be connected to her inexperience and to her unpreparedness for teaching. However, her comments during the second wave of interviews, which occurred 11 months after the first wave, indicated that although she did not 'enjoy' teaching yet, she was beginning to feel more comfortable in the classroom, suggesting that over time she may develop a positive identity as a teacher.

Former Hardworking Student Versus Teacher of Non-hardworking Students

The second major finding of this book concerns the way the participants relate to their students, which is heavily influenced by how they remember themselves as students. How the teachers see their students can lead to a sense of conflict, such as in the cases of Miwa and Kana, who find it difficult to relate to the students whom they feel are wasting their educational opportunities. Alternatively, how the teachers see their students can lead to a sense of solidarity, such as in the cases of Kumiko and Taka, who identify with 'lazy' students who claim better things to do than study, because they felt that they too were like that when they were students. Taka, who admits that his university undergraduate years were filled with 'play, play, play', understands that his students will not study on their own, so he figures out ways to boost students' language ability through classroom activities. Miwa also covers activities in the classroom that she believes her students should be doing independently outside of classroom time, but because she was a diligent student herself, she has trouble coming to terms with this type of teaching.

Recognizing that a connection exists between teachers' personal backgrounds and how they relate to their students is important, especially in Japan, where university teachers are generally products of elite educations in prestigious universities but may teach in ones that are academically quite different. The teachers' motivation for and attitudes toward study might be entirely different from their students'. Therefore, teachers need to be aware that holding their students to the same academic standards as themselves and teaching in ways that were suitable for them when they were students might result in frustration for both themselves and their current students.

The Influence of the Teachers' Learning Histories on Their Teaching Styles

A third main finding concerns the pedagogical methods that the participants employ in their classes. These methods are closely connected to the way that they *learned* English, but not necessarily to the way that they *were taught* English in school. Miwa's personal experience with successful learning, which was described in Chapter 7, involved intensive self-study and attention to grammatical and lexical details. This is what has shaped her teaching practices, and not the practical 'techniques' that she learned from native English-speaking teachers in university. Miwa's bottom-up approach toward language instruction, which draws attention to the minute details of the reading text, reflects the success *she* had with language learning, because such an approach suited *her* purposes for learning English. Miwa's approach toward language teaching may be useful for students who have similar learning styles and similar purposes for learning English. However, such an approach may also explain in part why many language learners in Japan do not attain English linguistic competency from attending their classes. Furthermore, Miwa's statement in Chapter 5 where she admits that her students are unlikely to learn much English in her classes is also quite telling.

Teachers such as Taka and Taeko, on the other hand, draw upon their own language learning experiences, which mainly occurred outside of the classroom and in the real world, to shape their pedagogical philosophy, rather than how they had 'studied' as students. Such practical approaches toward language teaching may be more appropriate and motivating for students who do not have an academic interest in language learning. However, like Miwa, neither of these teachers is completely optimistic that their students will attain English proficiency from their classes.

Japanese teachers throughout Japan may identify with both of these attitudes toward language teaching, one that places emphasis on the academic aspects of English and the other on the practical aspects. Miwa's philosophy toward language teaching may be somewhat 'old school', but she is not entirely wrong in wanting her students to engage in English on a deeper level. She wants English to empower her students professionally, and if students only gain a superficial knowledge of English, she is afraid they may not be so empowered. Taka (whose students attend a non-academic university) and Taeko focus on the practical aspects of English in order to empower their students mentally. They believe that students' feelings of accomplishment gained in their classes could motivate them in other areas as well. What is important to consider is that learning a handful of situational conversational techniques may not necessarily be of great use to students in the long run. On the other hand, learning *about* English in depth through a few reading passages may not be of much use either. Therefore, it may be better for teachers (and students) to consider that *both* academic and practical aspects of language teaching and language learning are essential if students are to be empowered through English study.

Women in a Male-Dominant Profession

The fourth major finding in this book is that the professional lives of the female teachers are intricately bound to societal expectations of women in Japan. The study in Chapter 6 did not originate as an investigation into the impact of gender on the professional lives of the women, but evolved into such upon examination of the narrative data from the women's interviews. Every female participant spoke about the tension she experiences in her professional life as a result of being in the gendered minority in the workplace. Their narratives suggested that the path toward becoming an English language teacher is motivated by gendered expectations that have traditionally limited women in the sorts of careers they can aspire to. That there may be a significant difference in the professional identity of male university English teachers and female university English teachers warrants further exploration.

What was found to be important in shaping these women's professional identity in spite of gender difficulties was their individual sense of agency in reconciling the gendered difficulties they encountered in the workplace and in dealing with others, supporting Wenger's (1998) theory that people's interpretation of their placement within a community plays an instrumental role in their identification with the community. Unlike other professions, university teaching in Japan (and elsewhere) enables teachers to enjoy individual freedom to pursue their individual research interests. Although the women in this study experience gendered isolation in the workplace, they choose to see it as opportunity to have the freedom to focus on what they feel is more important for them. In other words, they chose to appropriate their marginalization for their own advantage.

Pedagogical Implications of the Studies

I believe that that the studies offered in this book not only offer insights into the professional lives of Japanese teachers of English in universities, but also it has something important to say to university administrators and policy makers in Japan as well. Considering the impact that university English teachers have over English language education in Japan, there are several pedagogical implications in various areas that could be taken up in further research.

The Need for More Pedagogical Training

University English teachers could benefit from some pre-service pedagogical training that is specifically aimed at teaching English in universities. Although many have acquired a secondary school teaching license as undergraduates, holding such a license is not a requirement for tertiary language teaching (Nagasawa, 2004). Even if teachers have obtained a teaching license, the focus would have been on secondary education, which is inappropriate and inadequate for the tertiary context.

Therefore, it would be useful for graduate schools in Japan with English departments to offer courses in second language pedagogy and *encourage* the students majoring in English literature and linguistics to take such classes in order to prepare for the likelihood that they will be teaching English language at university. The second quote that opened this book, a comment from a participant in a questionnaire survey from a different study I had conducted, is highly illustrative of the necessity for this. This teacher is baffled by the gap between her life as a student and the reality of the life she now leads as a teacher. She said she was encouraged to study literature by her professors, but not to improve her teaching skills. Such an attitude by professors in universities seems misguided, considering that most graduate students will ultimately teach English. The confusion that Miwa felt when she first entered the classroom as an English language teacher with the required textbook to teach from might have been lessened had she had a greater theoretical understanding of language pedagogy.

I do not mean to suggest that Japanese English language teachers must adapt their teaching to the model of Western applied linguistics. Instead, I believe it is important to introduce to prospective university teachers alternative ways of viewing language teaching. Although previous beliefs toward language teaching are said to remain unchanged through teacher-training classes (Peacock, 2001), it has been extensively argued that teacher-training programs should provide opportunity for trainees to explore their beliefs in relation to linguistic and pedagogical theories (e.g. Burns, 1992, 1996; Clarke, 2008; Phan Le Ha, 2008; Tsui, 2007; Woods, 1997). Such programs may be essential because, as Peacock (2001) cautions, incorrect beliefs toward second language learning and the subsequent teaching that develops from such beliefs could actually be detrimental to learners since ineffective teaching may lead to loss of motivation. These programs also could provide prospective teachers with practical and useful information that would enable teachers to develop and understand aspects of teacher knowledge that go beyond content knowledge (Shulman, 1986).

Furthermore, creating a professional discourse that embraces the practices and beliefs of those teaching English in Japanese universities could help raise the status of English language teaching, which is often viewed as a 'necessary evil' for those who see themselves as academics. If new teachers are better equipped to teach English language, they may experience greater satisfaction in their work and have a stronger sense of identity as an English language teacher.

Merits of an 'Apprenticeship' (Lave & Wenger, 1991) System

Not only should prospective university English teachers be provided with more practical and theoretical pedagogical training, a system where these teachers are eased into the profession would be beneficial for prospective students and for universities. Universities should provide more opportunities for their Japanese doctoral students to teach English language to Japanese students in conjunction with the pedagogical training discussed above. Such a system is in place in universities all over the world, where doctoral students are initiated into the academic teaching community by teaching introductory subjects to lower-division students. As Lave and Wenger (1991) argue in their apprenticeship model of learning, developing skills and competencies under the guidance of an experienced expert in the field enables efficient learning to take place. Instead of sending unprepared teachers into the classroom, such an apprenticeship system could be implemented in Japanese universities as well to ensure that all prospective teachers were prepared for their teaching roles. Not only would such a program provide valuable teaching experience for upcoming researchers and teachers, it would also take away from senior professors some of their burden of teaching.

Although it is fairly common for graduate students in Japan to teach part-time at other universities, teaching in a sheltered situation under the mentorship of specialists in language pedagogy could be an important way for the teachers to develop their teaching skills as well as to explore their beliefs toward teaching, which will have an influence over the rest of their professional lives.

Concluding Remarks

The theme of tertiary ELT identity in this book was motivated by my desire to better understand the context in which I have been working for nearly 30 years by exploring the professional identity of Japanese teachers.

Conclusion

As mentioned in the first chapter, the idea for this study was sparked by a conversation that I happened to have with a former student who was struggling with the demands of teaching English even though she was proficient in English and was an up-and-coming scholar in her own right. During the course of the research conducted for this book, I travelled throughout Japan and talked with many teachers about their personal and educational backgrounds, the difficulties they face in teaching, their aspirations for their futures and what they hope their students can accomplish inside and outside of their classes. I believe that the greatest value of my study lies in exposing the clear and frank self-reflection the participants provided during the interviews.

This book, though a small-scale study, contributes to the area of teacher research and development in an extremely important yet under-researched category of teachers. It contributes to the body of knowledge that focuses on teacher identity, which is now recognized to influence numerous aspects of classroom teaching and of student learning. This book has argued that in order to gain a more complete picture of English language education in Japan, it is essential to examine the teaching practices of those who ultimately, hold the most power in shaping English language education policies and practices in Japan.

References

Almarza, G. (1996) Student foreign language teachers' growth. In D. Freeman and J.C. Richards (eds) *Teacher Learning in Language Teaching* (pp. 50–78). Cambridge: Cambridge University Press.

Amano, I. (1989) The dilemma of Japanese education today. In J.J. Shields (ed.) *Japanese Schooling: Patterns of Socialization, Equality, and Political Control* (pp. 111–123). University Park, PA: Pennsylvania State University Press.

Amano, I. and Poole, G.S. (2005) The Japanese university in crisis. *Higher Education* 50 (4), 685–711.

Amano, M. (1997) Women in higher education. *Higher Education* 34 (2), 215–235.

Amin, N. (1997) Race and the identity of the nonnative ESL teacher. *TESOL Quarterly* 31 (3), 580–583.

Arksey, H. and Knight, P. (1999) *Interviewing for Social Scientists*. London: Sage Publications.

Aspinall, R.W. (2006) Using the paradigm of 'small cultures' to explain policy failure in the case of foreign language education in Japan. *Japan Forum* 18 (2), 255–274.

Atkinson, R. (1998) *The Life Story Interview*. Thousand Oaks, CA: Sage Publications.

Atkinson, R. (2001) The life story interview. In J.F. Gubrium and J.A. Holstein (eds) *Handbook of Interview Research: Context and Method* (pp. 121–140). Thousand Oaks, CA: Sage Publications.

Bailey, K. (2006) Marketing the *eikaiwa* wonderland: ideology, *akogare,* and gender alterity in English conversation school advertising in Japan. *Environment and Planning D: Society and Space* 24 (1), 105–130.

Basturkmen, H., Loewen, S. and Ellis, R. (2004) Teachers' stated beliefs about Incidental focus on form and their classroom practices. *Applied Linguistics* 25 (2), 243–272.

Bax, S. (2003). The end of CLT: A context approach to language teaching. *ELT Journal* 57 (3), 278–287.

Bazeley, P. (2007) *Qualitative Data Analysis with NVivo*. London: Sage Publications.

Beauchamp, E.R. (1987) The development of Japanese educational policy, 1945–85. *History of Education Quarterly* 27 (3), 299–324.

Becker, C.B. (1990) Higher education in Japan: Facts and implications. *International Journal of Intercultural Relations* 14 (4), 425–447.

Beijaard, D. (1995) Teachers' prior experiences and actual perceptions of professional identity. *Teachers and Teaching: Theory and Practice* 1 (2), 281–294.

Beijaard, D., Verloop, N. and Vermut, N. (2000) Teachers' perceptions of professional identity: An exploratory study from a personal knowledge perspective. *Teaching and Teacher Education* 16 (7), 749–764.

Beijaard, D., Meijer, P.C. and Verloop, N. (2004) Reconsidering research on teachers' professional identity. *Teaching and Teacher Education* 20 (2), 107–128.

Bell, J.S. (2002) Narrative inquiry: more than just telling stories. *TESOL Quarterly* 36 (2), 207–213.

Benjamin, G.R. and James, E. (1989) Public and private schools and educational opportunity in Japan. In J.J. Shields (ed.) *Japanese Schooling: Patterns of Socialization, Equality and Political Control* (pp. 152–162). University Park, PA: Pennsylvania State University Press.

References

Blank, M.A. (2008) J-Lo's story: Can the diva and the genius co-exist? *Networks* 10 (2), 1–10.

Bonney, N., Stockman, N. and Xuewen, S. (1994) Shifting spheres: The work and family life of Japanese female graduates. *Work, Employment and Society* 8 (3), 387–406.

Borg, S. (2003) Teacher cognition in language teaching: A review of research on what language teachers think, know, believe, and do. *Language Teaching Research* 36, 81–109.

Bourdieu, P. (1991) *Language and Symbolic Power*. Malden, MA: Polity Press.

Bourdieu, P. and Wacquant, L. (1992) *An Invitation to Reflexive Sociology*. Chicago: University of Chicago Press.

Braine, G. (ed.). (1999a) *Non-Native Educators in English Language Teaching*. Mahwah, NJ: Lawrence Erlbaum Associates.

Braine, G. (1999b) Introduction. In G. Brain (ed.) *Non-native Educators in English Language Teaching* (pp. xiii–xx). Mahwah, NJ: Lawrence Erlbaum Associates.

Bramald, R., Hardman, F. and Lear, D. (1995) Initial teacher trainees and their views of teaching and learning. *Teacher and Teacher Education* 11 (1), 23–31.

Breen, M. (ed.) (1991) *Learner Contributions to Language Learning: New Directions in Research*. Harlow, Essex: Pearson Education Limited.

Breen, M., Hird, B., Milton, M., Oliver, R., and Thwaite, A. (2001) Making sense of language teaching: Teachers' principles and classroom practices. *Applied Linguistics* 22 (4), 470–501.

Briggs, C.L. (2002) Interviewing, power/knowledge, and social inequality. In J.F. Gubrium and J. A. Holstein (eds) *Handbook of Interview Research* (pp. 911–922). Thousand Oaks, CA: Sage Publications.

Briggs, J.B., and Moore, P.J. (1993) *The Process of Learning* (3rd edn). Sydney: Prentice-Hall.

Brinton, M. (1988) The social-institutional bases of gender stratification: Japan as an illustrative case. *AJS* 94 (2), 300–334.

Brown, B.A., Reveles, J.M. and Kelly, G.J. (2005) Scientific literacy and discursive identity: A theoretical framework for understanding science learning. *Sci Ed* 89 (5), 779–802.

Brown, J.D., Robson, G., and Rosenkjar, P. (2001) Personality, motivation, anxiety, strategies, and language proficiency of Japanese students. In Z. Domyei and R. Schmidt (eds) *Motivation and Second Language Acquisition* (pp. 361–398). Honolulu: University of Hawaii Press.

Brown J.D. and Yamashita, S. (1995) English language entrance examinations at Japanese universities: 1993–1994. In J.D. Brown and S. Yamashita (eds) *Language Testing in Japan* (pp. 5–11). Tokyo: Japan Association for Language Teachers.

Brown, J. and McGannon, J. (1988) What do I know about language learning? The story of the beginning teacher. Paper presented at the 23rd ALAA (Australian Linguistics Association of Australia) Congress, Griffith University, Brisbane.

Browne, C.M., and Wada, M. (1998) Current issues in high school English teaching in Japan: An exploratory survey. *Language, Culture and Curriculum* 11 (1), 97–112.

Brutt-Griffler, J. and Samimy, K.K. (2001) Transcending the nativeness paradigm. *World Englishes* 20 (1), 99–106.

Bueno, E.P. and Caesar, T. (eds) (2003) *I Wouldn't Want Anybody to Know: Native English Teaching in Japan*. Tokyo: JPGS Press.

Bullough, R.J. (2005) Being and becoming a mentor: School-based teacher educators and teacher educator identity. *Teaching and Teacher Education* 21 (2), 143–155.

Burns, A. (1992) Teacher beliefs and their influence on classroom practice. *Prospect* 7 (3), 56–56.

Burns, A. (1996) Starting all over again: From teaching adults to teaching beginners. In D. Freeman and J.C. Richards (eds) *Teacher Learning in Language Teaching*. 154–177.

Burton, S.K. (2004) Interviews with female Japanese study abroad students in England. *NUCB JLCC* 6 (1), 1–11.

Butler, Y.G. and Iino, M. (2005) Current Japanese reforms in English language education: The 2003 'action plans'. *Language Policy* 4 (1), 25–45.

Caesar, T. and Bueno, E.P. (2003) Introduction. In E.P. Bueno and T. Caesar (eds) *I Wouldn't Want Anybody to Know: Native English Teaching in Japan* (pp. 14–27). Tokyo: JPGS Press.

Canagarajah, A.S. (1993) Critical ethnography of a Sri Lankan classroom: Ambiguities in student opposition to reproduction through ESOL. *TESOL Quarterly* 27 (4), 601–626.

Canagarajah, A.S. (1999) *Resisting Linguistic Imperialism in English Teaching*. Oxford: Oxford University Press.

Casey, K. (1995–1996) The new narrative research in education. *Review of Research in Education* 21, 221–253.

Chase, S. (2002) Learning to listen: Narrative principles in a qualitative research methods course. In R. Josselson, A. Lieblich and D. McAdams (eds) *Up Close and Personal: The Teaching and Learning of Narrative Research*. Washington, DC: American Psychological Association.

Chase, S. (2005) Narrative inquiry: Multiple lenses, approaches, voices. In N.K. Denzin and Y.S. Lincoln (eds) *Handbook of Qualitative Research* (3rd edn, pp. 651–679). Thousand Oaks: CA: Sage Publications.

Clandinin, D.J. (1985) Personal practical knowledge: A study of teachers' classroom images. *Curriculum Inquiry* 15 (4), 361–385.

Clandinin, D.J. (1986) *Classroom Practice: Teacher Images in Action*. London: The Falmer Press.

Clandinin, D.J. and Connelly, E.M. (1987) Teachers' personal knowledge: What counts as personal in studies of the personal. *Journal of Curriculum Studies* 19 (6), 487–500.

Clandinin, D.J. and Connelly, E.M. (1996) *Teachers' Professional Knowledge Landscapes*. Teachers College Press, New York.

Clandinin, D.J. and Connelly, E.M. (2000) *Narrative Inquiry: Experience and Story in Qualitative Research*. San Francisco: Jossey-Bass.

Clark, C.M. and Peterson, P.L. (1986) Teachers' thought processes. In M.C. Wittrock (ed.) *Handbook of Research on Teaching* (Vol. 255–296). New York: Simon and Schuster Macmillan.

Clark, G. (1998) Overcoming Japan's English allergy. *Japan Quarterly*, April–June.

Clarke, M. (2008) *Language Teacher Identities: Co-constructing Discourse and Community*. Clevedon: Multilingual Matters.

Coldron, J. and Smith, R. (1999) Active location in teachers' construction of their professional identities. *Journal of Curriculum Studies* 31 (6), 711–726.

Connelly, F.M. and Clandinin, D.J. (1985) Personal practical knowledge and the modes for knowledge: Relevance for teaching and learning. In E. Eisner (ed.) *Learning and Teaching the Ways of Knowing* (Vol. 84th yearbook of the national Society for the Study of Education, Part II, pp. 174–198). Chicago: University of Chicago Press.

Connelly, E.M. and Clandinin, D.J. (1990) Stories of experience and narrative inquiry. *Educational Researcher* 19 (5), 2–14.

References

Connelly, F.M. and Clandinin, D.J. (1995) Narrative and education. *Teachers and Teaching: Theory and Practice* 1 (1), 73–85.

Connelly, E.M. and Clandinin, D.J. (1999) *Shaping a Professional Identity: Stories of Educational Practice*. New York: Teachers College Press.

Cook, M. (2010) Offshore outsourcing teacher in-service education: The long-term effects of a four-month pedagogical program on Japanese teachers of English. *TESL Canada Journal* 28 (1), 60–76.

Corder, P. (1967) The signficance of learners' errors. *International Review of Applied Linguistics* 4, 161–169.

Creswell, J.W. (2007) *Qualitative Inquiry and Research Design: Choosing among Five Approaches*. Thousand Oaks, CA: Sage Publications.

Cummings, W.K. and Amano, I. (1979) The changing role of the Japanese professor. In W. K. Cummings, I. Amano and K. Kitamura (eds) *Changes in the Japanese University: A Comparative Perspective*. (pp. 127–148). New York: Praeger.

Cutts, R. (1997) *An Empire of Schools: Japan's Universities and the Molding of a National Power Elite*. London: M.E. Sharpe.

Daizen, T. and Yamanoi, A. (2008) The changing academic profession in the era of university reforms in Japan. The Changing Academic Profession in International Comparative and Quantitative Perspectives: RIHI International Seminar Reports, 12. Hiroshima: Research Institute for Higher Education.

Davies, A. (1991) *The Native Speaker in Applied Linguistics*. Edinburgh: Edinburg University Press.

Davies, B. and Harre, R. (1990) Positioning: The discursive production of selves. *Journal for the Theory of Social Behaviour* 20 (1), 43–63.

Davies, B. and Harre, R. (1999) Positioning and personhood. In R. Harre and L.v. Langenhove (eds) *Positioning Theory*. Oxford: Blackwell Publishers Ltd.

Dilatush, L. (1976) Women in the professions. In J. Lebra, J. Paulson and E. Powers (eds) *Women in Changing Japan* (pp. 191–208). Stanford, CA: Stanford University Press.

Doi, T. (1971) *The Anatomy of Dependence*. Tokyo: Kodansha.

Duff, P.A. and Uchida, Y. (1997) The negotiation of teachers' sociocultural identities and practices in postsecondary EFL classrooms. *TESOL Quarterly* 31 (3), 451–486.

Duff, P.A. (2002) The discursive co-construction of knowledge, identity and difference: an ethnography of communication in the high school mainstream. *Applied Linguistics* 23 (3), 289–322.

Eades, J.S. (2005) The Japanese 21st center of excellence program. In J.S. Eades, R. Goodman and Y. Hada (eds) *The 'Big Bang' in Japanese Higher Education: The 2004 Reforms and the Dynamics of Change*. Melbourne: Trans Pacific Press.

Eades, J.S., Goodman, R. and Hada, Y. (eds) (2005) *The 'Big Bang' in Japanese Higher Education: The 2004 Reforms and the Dynamics of Change*. Melbourne: Trans Pacific Press.

Edge, J. (1996) Cross-cultural paradoxes in a profession of values. *TESOL Quarterly* 30 (1), 9–28.

Edge, J. and Richards, J. (1998) 'May I see your warrant please?' Justifying outcomes in qualitative research. *Applied Linguistics* 19 (3), 334–356.

Elbaz, F. (1983) The teacher's 'practical knowledge': Report of a case study. *Curriculum Inquiry* 11 (1), 43–71.

Ellis, R. (1994) *The Study of Second Language Acquisition*. Oxford: Oxford University Press.

Elliot, J. (2005) *Using Narrative in Social Research: Qualitative and Quantitative Approaches*. London: Sage Publications.

Enders, J. and Teichler, U. (1997) A victim of their own success? Employment and working conditions of academic staff in comparative perspective. *Higher Education* 34 (3), 347–372.

Erikson, E.H. (1968) *Identity, Youth and Crisis*. New York: W.W. Norton & Company.

Ehrlich, S. (1997) Gender as social practice. Implications for second language acquisition. *Studies in Second Language Acquisition* 19 (4), 421–446.

Evanoff, R. (1993) Making a career of university teaching in Japan. In P. Wadden (ed.) *A Handbook for Teaching English at Japanese Colleges and Universities* (pp. 15–26). New York: Oxford University Press.

Fairclough, N. (2003) *Analysing Discourse: Textual Analysis for Social Research*. London: Routledge.

Farrell, T.S.C. (2003) Learning to teach English language during the first year: Personal influences and challenges. *Teaching and Teacher Education* 19 (1), 95–111.

Farrell, T.S.C. (2005) The first year of language teaching: Imposing order. *System* 34 (2), 211–221.

Freeman, D. (1993) Renaming experience/reconstructing practice: Developing new understandings of teaching. *Teaching and Teacher Education* 9 (5/6), 485–497.

Freeman, D. (1996a) Redefining the relationship between research and what teachers know. In K. Bailey and D. Nunan (eds) *Voices From the Language Classroom*. Cambridge: Cambridge University Press.

Freeman, D. (1996b) The 'unstudied problem': Research on teacher learning in language teaching. In D. Freeman and J.C. Richards (eds) *Teacher Learning in Language Teaching* (pp. 351–378). Cambridge: Cambridge University Press.

Freeman, D. (2002) The hidden side of the work: Teacher knowledge and learning to teach: A perspective from North American research on teacher education in English language teaching. *Language Teaching* 35 (1), 1–13.

Freeman, D. and Johnson, K. (1998) Reconceptualizing the knowledge base of language teacher education. *TESOL Quarterly* 32 (3) 397–417.

Freeman, D. and Richards, J. (1996) *Teacher Learning in Language Teaching*. New York: Cambridge University Press.

Freire, P. (2000, 1972) *Pedagogy of the Oppressed*. New York: The Continuum Publishing Company.

Fries, C. (1947) *Teaching and Learning English as a Foreign Language*. Ann Arbor, MI: The University of Michigan Press.

Fromm, M. (2005) *New Words for a New Century*. Tokyo: Thomson Learning.

Fujimoto, K. (2004) Feminine capital: forms of capital in the Japanese labor market. *The Sociological Quarterly* 45 (1), 91–111.

Fujimoto, K. (2005) From women's college to work: Inter-organizational networks in the Japanese female labor market. *Social Science Research,* 34 (4), 651–681.

Fujimura-Fanselow, K. (1989) Women's participation in higher education in Japan. In James J. Shields (ed.) *Japanese Schooling: Patterns of Socialization, Equality, and Political Control*. University Park, PA: Pennsylvania State University Press.

Fujimura-Fanselow, K. (1995) College women today: options and dilemmas. In K. Fujimura-Fanselow and A. Kameda (eds) *Japanese Women: New Feminist Perspectives on the Past, Present and Future* (pp. 125–154). New York: The Feminist Press.

Fujita, F. (2006) The status of women faculty: A view from Japan. *Journal of Women's History,* 18 (1), 177–180.

Fukuzawa, R. (1994) The path to adulthood according to Japanese middle schools. *Journal of Japanese Studies* 20 (1), 61–86.

Gatbonton, E. (1999) Investigating experienced ESL teachers' pedagogical knowledge. *The Modern Language Journal* 83 (1), 33–50.

Gee, J.P. (1996) *Social Linguistics and Literacies: Ideology in Discourses* (2nd edn). London: Taylor & Frances.

Gee, J.P. (2000) Identity as an analytic lens for research in education. In W.G. Secada (ed.) *Review of Research in Education* (Vol. 25). Washington, DC: American Educational Research Association.

Gee, J.P. (2005) *An Introduction to Discourse Analysis: Theory and Method.* New York: Routledge.

Gibbs, G.H. (2002) *Qualitative Data Analysis: Explorations with NVivo.* Maidenhead, UK: Open University Press.

Glaser, B.G. and Strauss, A.L. (1967) *The Discovery of Grounded Theory: Strategies for Qualitative Research.* Chicago: Aldine.

Goffman, E. (1959) *The Presentation of Self in Everyday Life.* London: Penguin.

Golembek, P.R. (1998) A study of language teachers' personal practical knowledge. *TESOL Quarterly* 23 (3), 447–464.

Goodman, R. (2005) Whither the Japanese university? An introduction to the 2004 higher education reforms in Japan. In J.S. Eades, R. Goodman and Y. Hada (eds) *The 'Big Bang' in Japanese Higher Education: The 2004 Reforms and the Dynamics of Change* (pp. 1–31). Victoria, Australia: Trans Pacific Press.

Goodman, R. (2009) The Japanese professoriate. In G. Poole and Y. Chen (eds) *Higher Education in East Asia: Neoliberalism and the Professoriate* (pp. 15–32). Rotterdam: Sense Publishers.

Gordon, J. (2005) Inequities in Japanese urban schools. *The Urban Review* 37 (1), 49–62.

Gorsuch, G. (1999) Mombusho approved textbooks in Japanese high school EFL classes: An aid or hindrance to educational policy innovations? *The Language Teacher* 23 (10), 5–15.

Gorsuch, G. (2000) EFL educational policies and educational cultures: Influences on teachers' approval of communicative activities. *TESOL Quarterly* 34 (4), 675–709.

Gorsuch, G. (2001) Japanese EFL teachers: perceptions of communicative, audiolingual and yakudoku activities: The plan versus the reality. *Education Policy Analysis Archives* 9 (10). http://epaa.asu.edu/epaa/v9n10.html. Accessed 20 May 2007.

Guest, M. (2000) 'But I have to teach grammar!': An analysis of the role 'grammar' plays in Japanese university English entrance examinations. *The Language Teacher* 24 (11), 23–29.

Habu, T. (2000) The irony of globalization: The experience of Japanese women in British higher education. *Higher Education* 39 (1), 43–66.

Hada, Y. (2005) Postgraduate and professional training in Japanese higher education: Causes and directions for change. In J.S. Eades, R. Goodman and Y. Hada (eds) *The 'Big Bang' in Japanese Higher Education: The 2004 Reforms and the Dynamics of Change* (pp. 219–241). Melbourne: Trans Pacific Press.

Hall, I.P. (1997) *Cartels of the Mind: Japan's Intellectual Shop Closed.* New York: W.W. Norton & Company.

Hall, J.K. (1995) '(Re)creating our worlds with words: A sociohistorical perspective on face-to-face interaction'. *Applied Linguistics* 16 (2), 206–232.

Harre, R. and Langenhove, L.v. (1999) *Positioning Theory.* Oxford: Blackwell Publishers, Ltd.

Hashimoto, K. (2000) 'Internationalisation' is 'Japanisation': Japan's foreign language education and national identity. *Journal of Intercultural Studies* 21 (1), 39–51.

Hausman, R., Tyson, L. and Zahidi, S. (2010) *The Global Gender Gap Report 2010.* Geneva: World Economic Forum.

Hayes, B.E. (2011) Hiring criteria for Japanese university English-teaching faculty. In T. Skutnabb-Kangas (ed.) *The Native Speaker English Teacher: From Exclusion to Inclusion.* Linguistic Diversity and Language Rights Series. Abingdon, Oxon, UK: Multilingual Matters.

Hayes, C. (1979) Language contact in Japan. In W. Mackey and J. Ornstein (eds.) *Sociolinguistic Studies in Language Contact: Methods and Cases* (pp. 363–376). The Hague: Mouton.

Hinchman, L. and Hinchman, S. (eds). (2001) *Memory, Identity, Community. The Idea of Narrativity in the Human Sciences.* New York: New York University Press.

Hino, N. (1988) *Yakudoku*: Japan's dominant tradition in foreign language learning. *JALT Journal* 10 (1), 4–5.

Hogg, M.A. and Abrams, D. (1988) *Social Identifications: A Social Psychology of Intergroup Relations and Group Processes.* New York: Routledge.

Holliday, A. (1994) *Appropriate Methodology and Social Context.* Cambridge: Cambridge University Press.

Holliday, A. (1999) Small cultures. *Applied Linguistics* 20 (2), 237–264.

Holliday, A. (2005) *The Struggle to Teach English as an International Language.* Oxford: Oxford University Press.

Holt-Reynolds, D. (1992) Personal history-based beliefs as relevant prior knowledge in course work. *American Educational Research Journal* 29 (2), 325–349.

Honda, Y. (2004) The formation and transformation of the Japanese system of transition from school to work. *Social Science Japan Journal* 7 (1), 103–115.

Horwitz, E. (1985) Using student beliefs about language learning and teaching in the foreign language methods course. *Foreign Language Annals* 18 (4), 333–340.

Horwitz. (1988) The beliefs about language learning of beginning university foreign language students. *The Modern Language Journal* 72 (3), 283–294.

Hughes, H. (1999) Cultivating the walled garden: English in Japan. *English Studies* 80 (6), 556–568.

Ike, M. (1995) A historical review of English in Japan (1600–1880). *World Englishes* 14 (1), 3–11.

Ishida, H. (1993) *Social Mobility in Contemporary Japan: Educational Credentials, Class and the Labour Market in a Cross-national Perspective.* Stanford, CA: Stanford University Press.

Ishikawa, T. (2008) Education: Women-only universities swimming against the tide. *The Asahi Shinbun.*

Ishikida, M.Y. (2005) *Japanese Education in the 21st Century.* Lincoln, NE: Universe.

Japan Society for the Promotion of Science (2006) JSPS's new restart postdoctoral fellowship. *JSPS Quarterly* 18, 2. www.jsps.go.jp/english/e-quart/19/jsps19.pdf. Accessed 24 June 2011.

Johnson, C.G., and Watson, G. (2004) Constructing identities in informal study groups: An account of socialisation into an affinity group of learners. In B. Bartlett, F. Bryer and D. Roebuck (eds) *Weaving Research into Practice* Vol. 2 (pp. 187–194). Nathan, QLD: Griffith University, School of Cognition, Language and Special Education.

Johnston, B. (1997) Do EFL teachers have careers? *TESOL Quarterly* 31 (4), 681–712.

Johnston, B. (1999) The expatriate teacher as postmodern paladin. *Research in the Teaching of English* 34 (2), 255–280.

Josselson, R. (ed.) (1996) *Ethics and Process in the Narrative Study of Lives*. Newbury Park, CA: Sage Publications.
Josselson, R. (2007) The ethical attitude in narrative research. In D.J. Clandinin (ed.) *Handbook of Narrative Inquiry: Mapping a Methodology*. Thousand Oaks, CA: Sage Publications.
Kachru, B.B. (1989) Teaching world Englishes. *Indian Journal of Applied Linguistics* 15, 85–95.
Kachru, B.B. (1992) Teaching world Englishes. In B.B. Kachru (ed.) *The Other Tongue: English Across Cultures* (pp. 355–366). Chicago: University of Illinois Press.
Kamhi-Stein, L.D. (ed.) (2004) *Learning and Teaching from Experience: Perspectives on Nonnative English-speaking Professionals*. Ann Arbor, MI: The University of Michigan Press.
Kan, S. (28 April 2009) English offers mothers control over careers. *The Daily Yomiuri*.
Kariya, T. and Rosenbaum, J. (1987) Self-selection in Japanese junior high schools: A longitudinal study of students' educational plans. *Sociology of Education* 60 (3), 168–180.
Keio University (n.d.) Student enrollment. On WWW at http://www.keio.ac.jp/en/about_keio/data_info/students.html. Accessed 27 June 2009.
Kelly, C. and Adachi, N. (1992) A chrysanthemum maze. In P. Wadden (ed.) *A Handbook for Teaching English at Japanese Colleges and Universities* (pp. 156–171). Oxford: Oxford University Press.
Kelskey, K. (2001) *Women on the Verge: Japanese Women, Western Dreams*. Durham, NC: Duke University Press.
Kemper, K., and Makino, M. (1993) Cultural influences on the construction of knowledge in Japanese higher education. *Comparative Education* 29 (2), 185–199.
Kern, R.G. (1995) Students' and teachers' beliefs about language learning. *Foreign Language Annals* 28 (1), 71–92.
Kiernan, P. (2010) *Deconstructing Narrative Identity in English Language Teaching: Exploring Teacher Interviews in Japanese and English*. Basingstoke: Palgrave MacMillan.
Kimble, C., Hildreth, P. and Bourdin, I. (2008) *Communities of Practice: Creating Learning Environments for Educators* (Vol. 2). Charlotte, NC: Information Age Publishing.
Kimura, S., and Visgatis, B. (1996) High school English textbooks and college entrance examinations: A comparison of reading passage difficulty. *JALT Journal* 18 (1), 81–95.
Kinmouth, E. (2005) From selection to seduction: the impact of demographic change on private higher education in Japan. In J.S. Eades, R. Goodman and Y. Hada (eds) *The 'Big Bang' in Japanese Higher Education: The 2004 Reforms and the Dynamics of Change* (pp. 106–135). Melbourne: Trans Pacific Press.
Kitao, K. and Kitao, S.K. (1995) *English Teaching: Theory, Research and Practice*. Tokyo: Eichosha.
Kobayashi, Y. (2002) The role of gender in foreign language learning attitudes: Japanese female students' attitudes toward English learning. *Gender and Education* 14 (2), 181–197.
Kobayashi, Y. (2007a) Japanese working women and English study abroad. *World Englishes* 26 (1), 62–71.
Kobayashi, Y. (2007b) TEFL policy as a part of stratified Japan and beyond. *TESOL Quarterly* 41 (3), 566–571.
Koike, M. (2000) American studies and the liberation of a Japanese woman: A personal narrative. *American Studies Journal* 38 (3), 72–78.

Koike, I. and Tanaka, H. (1995) English in foreign language education policy in Japan: Toward the twenty-first century. *World Englishes* 14 (1), 13–25.

Krashen, S. (1981) *Second Language Acquisition and Second Language Learning.* Oxford: Pergamon.

Krashen, S., and Terrell, T. (1983) *The Natural Approach: Language Acquisition in the Classroom.* Hayward, CA: Alemany.

Kubo, M. (2006) Support for Female Researchers in Japan: Current actions of Japanese funding agencies to assist female researchers *JSPS Quarterly* 18 Winter On WWW at http://www.jsps.go.jp/english/e-quart/18/index_01.html. Accessed 1 June 2011.

Kubota, R. (1999) Japanese Culture Constructed by Discourses: Implications for Applied Linguistics Research and ELT. *TESOL Quarterly* 33 (1), 9–35.

Kvale, S. (2006) Dominance through interviews and dialogues. *Qualitative Inquiry* 12 (3), 480–500.

Kwan, C.H. (2002) Why the Japanese are poor English speakers - A proposal to reform English language instruction in Japan [electronic version]. *The Research Institute of Economy, Trade and Industry.* http://www.rieti.go.jp/en/columns/a01_0053.html Accessed 20 December 2008.

Lamie, J. (1998) Teacher education and training in Japan. *Journal of In-Service Education* 24 (3), 515–534.

Laimie, J.M. (2000) Teachers of English in Japan: Professional development and training at a crossroads. *JALT Journal* 22 (1), 27–45.

Lamie, J. (2002) An investigation into the process of change: The impact of in-service training on Japanese teachers of English. *Journal of In-Service Education* 28 (1), 135–162.

Lave, J. and Wenger, E. (1991) *Situated Learning: Legitimate Peripheral Participation.* Cambridge: Press Syndicate of the University of Cambridge.

Law, G. (1995) Ideologies of English language teaching in Japan. *JALT Journal* 17 (2), 213–23.

Lebra, T.S. (1984) *Japanese Women: Constraint and Fulfillment.* Honolulu: University of Hawaii Press.

LeTendre, G. (1994) Guiding them on: Teaching, hierarchy and social organization in Japanese middle schools. *Journal of Japanese Studies* 20 (1), 37–59.

LeTendre, G., Rohlen, T.P. and Zeng, K. (1998) Merit or family background? Problems in research policy initiatives in Japan. *Education Evaluation and Policy Analysis* 20 (4), 285–297.

Liddle, J. and Nakajima, S. (2000) *Rising Suns, Rising Daughters: Gender, Class and Power in Japan.* New York: Zed Books Ltd.

Li, M. (2004) Culture and classroom communication: A case study of Asian students in New Zealand language schools. *Asian EFL Journal* 6 (1), Article 7. http://www.asian-efl-journal.com/04_ml.php. Accessed 15 May 2011.

Lincoln, Y.S. and Denzin, N. (1994) *Handbook of Qualitative Research.* Thousand Oaks, CA: Sage Publications.

Liu, D. (1998) Ethnocentrism in TESOL: Teacher education and the neglected needs of international TESOL students. *ELT Journal* 52 (1), 3–9.

Liu, J. (1999) Nonnative-English speaking professionals in TESOL. *TESOL Quarterly* 33 (1), 85–102.

Lo Castro, V. (1996) English language education in Japan. In H. Coleman (ed.) *Society and the Language Classroom.* London: Cambridge University Press.

Lortie, D.C. (1975) *Schoolteacher.* Chicago: Chicago University Press.

Lyons, N. and LaBoskey, V.K. (2002) Why narrative inquiry or exemplars for scholarship of teaching? In N. Lyons and V.K. LaBoskey (eds) *Narrative Inquiry in Practice: Advancing the Knowledge of Teaching* (pp. 11–30). New York: Teachers College Press.

MacDonald, M., Badger, R. and White, G. (2001) Changing values: What use are theories of language learning and teaching? *Teaching and Teacher Education* 17 (8), 949–963.

Mahboob, A. (2004) Native or nonnative: What do students enrolled in an intensive English program think? In L.D. Kamhi-Stein (ed.) *Learning and Teaching from Experience: Perspectives on Nonnative English-speaking Professionals* (pp. 121–148). Ann Arbor, MI: University of Michigan Press.

Mahboob, A., Uhrig, K., Newman, K. and Hardford, B. (2004) Children of a lesser English: Status of nonnative English speakers as college-level English as a second language teachers in the United States. In L.D. Kamhi-Stein (ed.) *Learning and Teaching from Experience: Perspectives on Nonnative English-speaking Professionals* (pp. 100–120). Ann Arbor, MI: University of Michigan Press.

Matsuda, P.K. (2002) Negotiation of identity and power in a Japanese online discourse community. *Computers and Composition* 19 (1), 39–55.

Matsui, M. (1995) Gender role perceptions of Japanese and Chinese female students in American universities. *Comparative Education Review* 39 (3) 356–378.

Matsumoto, K. (1994) English instruction problems in Japanese schools and higher education. *Journal of Asian Pacific Communication,* 5 (4), 209–214.

Matsuura, H., Chiba, R. and Hilderbrant, P. (2001) Beliefs about learning and teaching communicative English in Japan. *JALT Journal* 23 (1), 69–89.

McConnell, D. (1996) Education for global integration in Japan: A case study of the JET program. *Human Organization* 55 (4), 446–457.

McConnell, D. (2000) *Importing Diversity: Inside Japan's JET Program.* Berkeley: University of California Press.

McMahill, C. (2001) Self-expression, gender, and community: A Japanese feminist English class. In A. Pavlenko, A. Blackledge, I. Piller and M. Teutsch-Dwyer (eds) *Multilingualism, Second Language Learning and Gender.* Berlin: Mouton de Gruyter.

McNeill, D. (2007) Few women reach the top in Japanese universities [electronic version]. *The Chronicle of Higher Education 54,* NA. http://chronicle.com/article/Few-Women-Reach-the-Top-in/29651. Accessed 22 April 2009.

McVeigh, B.J. (2002) *Japanese Higher Education as Myth.* Armonk, NY: M.E. Sharp, Inc.

McVeigh, B.J. (2004) Foreign language instruction in Japanese higher instruction. *Arts & Humanities in Higher Education* 3 (2), 211–227.

Mead, G.J. (1934) *Mind, Self and Society.* Chicago: University of Chicago Press.

Medgyes, P. (1992) Native or non-native: Who's worth more? *English Language Teaching Journal* 46 (4), 340–349.

MEXT (2003) Regarding the establishment of an action plan to cultivate 'Japanese with English abilities'. http://www.mext.go.jp/b_menu/shingi/chousa/shotou/020/sesaku/020702.htm. Accessed 1 September 2006.

MEXT (n.d.) Japan's education at a glance. http://www.mext.go.jp/english/statistics/. Accessed 15 October 2007.

MEXT (2006) OECD Thematic review of tertiary education - Country background report of Japan. http://www.oecd.org/document/16/0,3746,en_2649_33723_35580240_1_1_1_1,00.html. Accessed 15 October 2007.

Miles, M.B. and Huberman, M. (1994) *Qualitative Data Analysis: An Expanded Source Book* (2nd edn). Thousand Oaks, CA: Sage Publications.

Ministry of Labor, Japan (1989) White Paper on Labor (Rodo Hakusho).

Ministry of Labor, Japan (1998) *White Paper on Working Women.*
Mishler, E. (1986) *Research Interviewing: Context and Narrative.* Cambridge, MA: Harvard University Press.
Morita, N. (2004) Negotiating participation and identity in second language academic communities. *TESOL Quarterly* 38 (4), 573–603.
Nagasawa, K. (2004) Teacher training and development. In V. Makarova and T. Rodgers (eds) *English Language Teaching: The Case of Japan.* (pp. 280–295). Mnchen: Lincom Europa.
Nakane, C. (1970) *Japanese Society.* Berkeley, CA: University of California Press.
Neustupny, J.V. and Tanaka, S. (2004) Language use in Japan and English language teaching. In V. Makarova and T. Rodgers (eds) *English Language Teaching: The Case of Japan* (pp. 11–28). Mnchen: Lincolm.Europa.
Newby, H., Weko, T., Breneman, D., Johanneson, T. and Maassen, P. (2009) OECD reviews of tertiary education: Japan. http://www.oecdbookshop.org/oecd/display.asp?K=5KS NS07TDQHL&lang=EN&sort=sort_date%2Fd&stem=true&sf1=Title&st1=OECD+ Reviews+of+tertiary+education&sf3=SubjectCode&st4=not+E4+or+E5+or+P5& sf4=SubVersionCode&ds=OECD+Reviews+of+tertiary+education%3B+All+Subjec ts%3B+&m=8&dc=26&plang=en. Accessed 23 June 2011.
Nguyen, C. (n.d.) Australian higher education's identities: International students' perspectives. http://www.tasa.org.au/conferences/conferencepapers07/papers/342.pdf. Accessed 24 November 2009.
Nishino, T. (2008) Japanese secondary school teachers' beliefs and practices regarding communicative language teaching: an exploratory survey. *JALT Journal* 30 (1), 51–69.
Normile, D. (2001) Women faculty battle Japan's *Koza* system [electronic version]. *Science 291.5505*, 817. http://www.sciencemag.org/content/291/5505/817.summary. Accessed 22 April 2009.
Norton, B. and Pavlenko, A. (2004) Addressing gender in the EFL/ESL classroom. *TESOL Quarterly* 38 (3), 50–514.
Nunan, D. (1988) *The Learner-centered Curriculum: A Study in Second Language Teaching.* Cambridge: Cambridge University Press.
NVivo (2002) QSR International Pty. Melbourne, Australia.
Ochs, E. and Capps, L. (2001) *Living Narrative: Creating Lives in Everyday Storytelling.* Cambridge, MA: Harvard University Press.
Okada, A. (2005) A history of the Japanese university. In J.S. Eades, R. Goodman and Y. Hada (eds) *The 'Big Bang' in Japanese Higher Education: The 2004 Reforms and the Dynamics of Change.* Melbourne: Trans Pacific Press.
Okano, K. (1995) Justice principles in job distribution to Japanese youth. *Asian Studies Research Papers* 6, La Trobe University.
Okano, K. (2000) Social justice and job distribution in Japan: Class, minority and gender. International Review of Education/*Internationale Zeitschrift fr Erziehungswissenschaft/ Revue Internationale de l'Education* 46 (6), 545–563.
Okano, K. and Tsuchiya, M. (1999) *Education in Contemporary Japan: Inequality and Diversity.* Cambridge: Cambridge University Press.
O'Leary, V.E. and Mitchell, J.M. (1990) Women connecting with women: Networks and mentors in the United States. In S. Stiver Lie and V.E. O'Leary (eds) *Storming the Tower: Women in the Academic World.* New York: Nichols Pub Co.
Ono, H. (2001) Who goes to college? Features of institutional tracking in Japanese higher education. *American Journal of Education* 109 (2), 161–195.

Ono, H. (2004) Are sons and daughters substitutable? A study of intra-household allocation of resources in contemporary Japan. *Journal of the Japanese and International Economics* 18, 143–160.
Ono, H. and Piper, N. (2004) Japanese women studying abroad, the case of the United States. *Women's Studies International Forum* 27 (2), 101–118.
Ota, Y. (1994) The 'decline' of English language competence in modern Japan. *Journal of Asian Pacific Communication* 5 (4), 201–206.
Otsu, T. (n.d.) The unified test by the NCUEE - its role in Japanese university admissions. Tokyo: The National Center for University Entrance Examinations.
Pajares, M.F. (1992) Teachers' beliefs and educational research: Clearing up a messy construct. *Review of Educational Research* 62 (3), 307–332.
Pavlenko, A. (2002) Narrative study: Whose story is it, anyway? *TESOL Quarterly* 36 (2), 213–218.
Peacock, M. (1999) Beliefs about language learning and their relationship to proficiency. *International Journal of Applied Linguistics* 9 (2), 247–265.
Peacock, M. (2001) Pre-service ESL teachers' beliefs about second language learning: A longitudinal study. *System* 29 (2), 177–195.
Pennycook, A. (1989) The concept of method, interested knowledge and the politics of language teaching. *TESOL Quarterly* 23 (4), 589–618.
Pennycook, A. (1994) *The Cultural Politics of English as an International Language*. London: Longman.
Pennycook, A. (1998) *English and the Discourses of Colonialism*. London and New York: Routledge.
Pham, H.H. (2005) Imported communicative Language teaching: Implications for local teachers. *English Teaching Forum* 43 (4), 2–9.
Phan Le Ha (2008) *Teaching English as an International Language: Identity, Resistance and Negotiation*. Clevedon: Multilingual Matters.
Phillipson, R. (1992) *Linguistic Imperialism*. Oxford: Oxford University Press.
Piller, I. and Takahashi, K. (2006) A passion for English: Desire and the language market. In A. Pavlenko (ed.) *Languages and Emotions of Multilingual Speakers* (pp. 59–83). Clevedon, UK: Multilingual Matters.
Poole, G.S. (2003) Higher education reform in Japan: Amano Ikuo on 'the university in crisis'. *International Education Journal* 4 (3), 149–176.
Poole, G.S. (2010) *The Japanese Professor: An Ethnography of a University Faculty*. Rotterdam, the Netherlands: Sense Publishers.
Poole, M., Bornholt, L. and Summers, F. (1997) An international study of the gendered nature of academic work: Some cross-cultural explorations. *Higher Education* 34 (3), 373–396.
Prabhu, N.S. (1990) There is no best method - why? *TESOL Quarterly* 24 (2), 161–176.
Rampton, M.B.H. (1990) Displacing the 'native speaker': Expertise, affiliation, and inheritance. *English Language Teaching Journal* 44 (2), 97–101.
Raymo, J. (2003) Educational attainment and the transition to first marriage among Japanese women. *Demography* 40 (1), 83–103.
Reesor, M. (2003) Japanese attitudes to English: Toward an explanation of poor performance. *NUCB JLCC* 5 (2), 57–65.
Reischauer, E.O. (1974) *Japan: The Story of a Nation*. Revised edition. New York: Alfred A. Knopf.
Reischauer, E.O. and Jansen, M.B. (1988) *The Japanese Society Today: Change and Continuity*. Cambridge, MA: Belknap Press.

Reves, T. and Medgyes, P. (1994) The non-native English speaking ESL/EFL teacher's self-image: An international survey. *System* 22 (3), 353–367.
Richards, J.C. (1990) *The Language Leaching Matrix*. Cambridge: Cambridge University Press.
Richards, J.C. (1998) *Beyond Training*. Cambridge: Cambridge University Press.
Richards, J.C. and Rodgers, T. (2001) *Approaches and Methods in Language Teaching*. Cambridge: Cambridge University Press.
Riessman, C.K. (1993) *Narrative Analysis* (Vol. 30). Newbury Park, CA: Sage Publications.
Riessman, C.K. (2002) Analysis of personal narrative. In J.F. Gubrium (ed.) *Handbook of Interview Research*. Thousand Oaks, CA: Sage Publications.
Riessman, C.K. (2008) *Narrative Methods for the Human Sciences*. Thousand Oaks, CA: Sage Publications.
Rohlen, T.P. (1977) Is Japanese education becoming less egalitarian? Notes on high school stratification and reform. *Journal of Japanese Studies* 3 (1), 37–70.
Roesgaard, M.H. (2006) Japanese Education and the Cram School Business. Copenhagen: NIAS Press.
Rosenbaum, J.E. (1978) The structure of opportunity in school. *Social Forces* 57 (1), 236–256.
Sakui, K. and Gaies, S.J. (2003) A case study: Beliefs and metaphors of a Japanese teacher of English. In P. Kalaja and A.M.F. Barcelos (eds) *Beliefs About SLA: New Research Approaches* (pp. 153–170). The Netherlands: Kluwer Academic Publishers.
Sakui, K. (2004) Wearing two pairs of shoes: Language teaching in Japan. *ELT Journal* 58 (2), 155–163.
Samimy, K. and Brutt-Griffler, J. (1999) To be a native or a nonnative speaker: Perceptions of 'non-native' students in a graduate TESOL program. In G. Braine (ed.) *Non-native Educators in English Language Teaching*. Mahwah, NJ: Erlbaum.
Sampson, G.P. (1984) Exporting language teaching methods from Canada to China. *TESL Journal* 1 (1), 19–32.
Sato, K. (2002) Practical understandings of CLT and teacher development. In S. Savignon (ed.) *Interpreting Communicative Language Teaching* (pp. 41–81). New Haven, CT: Yale University Press.
Sato, K. and Kleinsasser, R. (2004) Beliefs, practices, and interactions of teachers in a Japanese high school English department. *Teaching and Teacher Education* 20 (8), 797–816.
Schmenk, B. (2004) Language learning: a feminine domain? The role of stereotyping in constructing gendered learner identities. *TESOL Quarterly* 38 (3), 514–524.
Seargeant, P. (2008) Ideologies of English in Japan: The perspectives of policy and pedagogy. *Language Policy* 7 (2), 121–142.
Seidman, I. (2006) *Interviewing as Qualitative Research: A Guide for Researchers in Education and the Social Sciences* (3rd edn). New York: Teachers College Press.
Shavelson, R.J., and Stern, P. (1981) Research on teachers' pedagogical thoughts, judgments, decisions and behavior. *Review of Educational Research* 51 (4), 455–498.
Shimbori, M. (1981) The Japanese academic profession. *Higher Education* 10 (1), 75–87.
Shulman, L.S. (1986) Those who understand: knowledge growth in teaching. *Educational Researcher* 15 (2), 4–14.
Shulman, L.S. (1987) Knowledge and teaching: Foundations of the new reform. *Harvard Educational Review* 57 (2), 1–22.
Silverman, D. (1993) *Interpreting Qualitative Data: Methods for Analyzing Talk, Text and Interaction*. London: Sage Publications.

Simon-Maeda, A. (2004a) The complex construction of professional identities: Female EFL educators in Japan speak out. *TESOL Quarterly* 38 (3), 405–436.
Simon-Maeda, A. (2004b) Transforming emerging feminist identities: A course on gender and language issues. In B. Norton and A. Pavlenko (eds) *Gender and English Language Learners* (pp. 127–142). Alexandria, VA: TESOL.
Simon-Maeda, A., Churchill, E. and Cornwell, S. (2006) Negotiating academic practices, identities and relationships in a doctoral program: a case from an overseas institution in Japan. *TESL-EJ* 10 (2), 1–25.
Sinclair, J.M. and Coulthard, M. (1975) *Toward an Analysis of Discourse: The Language of Pupils and Teachers*. Oxford: Oxford University Press.
Singh, G. and Richards, J.C. (2006) Teaching and learning in the language teacher education course room: A critical sociocultural perspective. *RELC* 37 (2), 149–175.
Smith, R.C. and Imura, M. (2004) Lessons from the past: Traditions and reforms. In T.R. Veronika Makarova (ed.) *English Language Teaching: The Case of Japan* (pp. 29–48). Mnchen: Lincom GmbH.
Sodei, T. (2005) A comparative study of the research conditions of women scientists and the present states of women's/gender studies in Asian countries toward the sustainable development. Paper presented at the Fifth Conference of the Science Council of Asia (SCA).
Strauss, A.L. and Corbin, J. (1990) *Basics of Qualitative Research. Grounded Theory Procedures and Techniques*. London: Sage Publications.
Stewart, A. (2005) Teaching positions: A study of identity in English language teachers in Japanese higher education. PhD thesis, University of London.
Stewart, A. (2006) An inquiry into the social aspects of language teacher expertise. In A. Yoshitomi, T. Umino and M. Negishi (eds) *Readings in Second Language Pedagogy and Second Language Acquisition: In Japanese Context*. Amsterdam: John Benjamins Publishing.
Stevenson, D.L., and Baker, D.P. (1992) Shadow education and allocation in formal schooling: Transition to university in Japan. *AJS* 97 (6), 1639–1657.
Strober, M.H., and Chan, A.M.K. (2001) *The Road Winds Uphill All the Way: Gender, Work and Family in the United States and Japan*. Boston, MA: Massachusetts Institute of Technology.
Sunderland, J. (2000) Issues of language and gender in second and foreign language education. *Language Teaching* 33 (4), 203–233.
Tajfel, H. (ed.) (1978) *Differentiation Between Social Groups. Studies in Social Psychology*. London: Academic press.
Takahashi, K. (2006) Language desire: A critical ethnography of Japanese women learning English in Australia. PhD thesis, the University of Sydney, Sydney.
Tang, C. (1997) On the power and status of nonnative ESL teachers. *TESOL Quarterly* 31 (3), 577–580.
Teichler, U. (1997) Higher education in Japan: A view from the outside. *Higher Education* 34 (2), 275–298.
Terauchi, H. (1995) Issues in English language teaching in Japanese universities. http://www.brookes.ac.uk/schools/education/eal/jl-archive/jl-bestof/11.pdf. Accessed 26 September 2008.
Thornbury, S. (2002) Unbearable lightness. *ELT Journal* 55 (4), 397–402.
Tsang, W.K. (2004) Teachers' personal practical knowledge and interactive decisions. *Language Teaching Research* 8 (2), 163–198.

Tsui, A.B.M. (2007) Complexities of identity formation: a narrative inquiry of an EFL teacher. *TESOL Quarterly* 41 (4), 657–680.

University of Tokyo Admission Information (n.d.) http://www.u-tokyo.ac.jp/index/e00_e.html. Accessed 8 October 2009.

University of Tokyo. (n.d.) Gender-equal participation basic plan for the University of Tokyo. http://72.14.234.132/search?q=cache:n9DQmgp5qy4:kyodo-sankaku.u-tokyo.ac.jp/en/UT/History/documents/GenderEqualityBasicPlan.pdf. Accessed 17 May 2009.

Varghese, M., Morgan, B., Johnston, B. and Johnson, K.A. (2005) Theorizing language teacher identity: Three perspectives and beyond. *Journal of Language Identity and Education* 4 (1), 21–44.

Warrington, S. (2006) The time in between: Socialization training as a learning priority for Japanese university students. *Asian TEFL Journal, Professional Teaching Articles* 12, 1–14.

Walker, Patricia (2006) Teachers and tea-fetchers—what the future holds for Japan's junior college graduates: Female student perceptions of the status, purpose, and value of a junior college education. *Electronic Journal of Contemporary Japanese Studies*, Article 3 in 2006, First Posted on 7 December 2006. On WWW at http://www.japanesestudies.org.uk/articles/2006/Walker.html Accessed 1 December 2009.

Watson, C. (2006) Narratives of practice and the construction of identity in teaching. *Teachers and Teaching: Theory and Practice* 12 (5), 509–526.

Watson, G., Johnson, C.G. and Walker, T. (2005) Building a better understanding of the learning community of postgraduate coursework students. Paper presented at the HERDSA. http://www98.griffith.edu.au/dspace/handle/10072/2464. Accessed 6 November 2009.

Webster, L. and Mertova, P. (2007) *Using Narrative Inquiry as a Research Method: An Introduction to Using Critical Event Analysis in Research on Learning and Teaching*. Oxford: Routledge.

Wells, C. (1993) Re-evaluating the value of the IRF sequence: A proposal for the articulation of theories of activity and discourse for the analysis of teaching and learning in the classroom. *Linguistics and Education* 5, 1–37.

Wenger, E. (1998) *Communities of Practice: Learning, Meaning and Identity*. Cambridge: Cambridge University Press.

Williams, K. and Andrade, M. (2008) Foreign language learning anxiety in Japanese EFL university classes: causes, coping and locus of control. *Electronic Journal of Foreign Language Teaching* 5 (2), 181–191.

Wolcott, H. (2001) *Writing up Qualitative Research* (2nd edn). Thousand Oaks, CA: Sage Publications.

Woods, D. (1996) *Teacher Cognition in Language Teaching: Beliefs, Decision-making, and Classroom Practice*. Cambridge: Cambridge University Press.

World Economic Forum (2010) The Global Gender Gap Report 2010. http://www.weforum.org/reports/global-gender-gap-report-2010?fo=1. Accessed 13 June 2011.

World Education News and Reviews (2006) Japan. http://www.wes.org/ewenr/PF/06aug/pfjapan.htm. Accessed 31 May 2007.

Wordell, C. (1992) Politics and human relations in the Japanese university. In P. Wadden (ed.) *A Handbook for Teaching English at Japanese Colleges and Universities* (pp. 145–155). Oxford: Oxford University Press.

Wright, T. (2005) *Classroom Management in Language Education*. Hampshire, UK: Palgrave Macmillan.

Yamashiro, A. and McLaughlin, J. (2001) Relationships among attitudes, motivation, anxiety and English language proficiency in Japanese college students. In S. Cornwell and P. Robinson (eds) *Individual Differences in Foreign Language Learning: Proceedings of the Symposium on Intelligence, Aptitude and Motivation.* Aoyama Gakuin University: Tokyo.

Name Index

A

Abrams, D. 81
Adachi, N. 181 (also in epitaph)
Almarza, G. 52
Amano, I. 21, 39, 79
Amano, M. 10, 21, 25, 26, 27, 28, 29, 31, 126, 143
Amin, N. 56
Andrade, M. 17
Arksey, H. 73
Aspinall, R. 1, 2, 4, 5, 14, 181
Atkinson, R. 70

B

Bailey, K. 10, 32, 33
Baker, D.P. 21
Basturkmen, H. 53
Bax, S. 58
Bazeley, P. 76
Beauchamp, E.R. 4, 16, 17, 21, 96
Becker, C.B. 17, 21
Beijaard, D. 54, 55
Bell, J.S. 68, 69, 78
Benjamin, G.R. 21
Blank, M.A. 118
Bonney, N. 26
Borg, S. 54, 55, 163
Bourdieu, P. 21, 81
Braine, G. 56
Bramald, R. 52
Breen, M. 52
Briggs, C.I. 73
Briggs, J.B. 163
Brinton, M. 10, 25, 26, 27, 28, 29, 127
Brown, B.A. 118
Brown, J. 52
Brown, J.D. 4, 16, 17
Browne, C.M. 3, 4, 15, 16, 62
Brutt-Griffler, J. 56, 61
Bueno, E.P. 5, 63, 65
Bullough, R.J. 119
Burns, A. 52, 55, 187
Burton, S.K. 26, 32, 33, 131, 132
Butler, Y.G. 4, 16

C

Caesar, T. 5, 63, 65
Canagarajah, A.S. 55, 61, 65
Capps, L. 63
Casey, K. 68
Chase, S. 68, 73
Clandinin, D.J. 49, 50, 55, 68
Clark, C.M. 49
Clark, G. 16
Clarke, M. 82, 187
Coldron, J. 55
Connelly, E.M. 50, 55, 68
Cook, M. 15
Corbin, J. 76
Corder, P. 51
Coulthard, M. 157, 162
Creswell, J.W. 68, 69
Cummings, W.K. 39
Cutts, R. 22

D

Daizen, T. 18, 36, 37, 38, 39, 40
Davies, A. 67
Davies, B. 81
Denzin, N. 68
Dilatush, L. 26, 29
Doi, T. 14
Duff, P.A. 62, 63, 64, 81, 117, 157

E

Eades, J.S. 17, 21
Edge, J. 164
Elbaz, F. 49, 50, 68, 109
Ellis, R. 31
Elliot, J. 74
Enders, J. 39
Erikson, E.H. 81
Ehrlich, S. 32
Evanoff, R. 34, 142

F

Fairclough, N. 63
Farrell, T.S.C. 53

Freeman, D. 51
Freire, P. 163
Fries, C. 51
Fromm, M. 155
Fujimoto, K. 26, 27, 28, 29
Fujimura-Fanselow 10, 21, 25, 26, 27, 29
Fujita, F. 26, 43, 116
Fukuzawa, R. 21, 24

G

Gaies, S.J. 63
Gatbonton, E. 51, 109
Gee, J.P. 8, 74, 108, 110, 118, 119, 120, 121, 122, 126, 132, 133, 140, 146, 182
Gibbs, G.H. 76
Glaser, B.G. 76
Goffman, E. 81
Golembek, P.R. 51, 109
Goodman, R. 11, 17, 18, 79, 80
Gordon, J. 21
Gorsuch, G. 3, 4, 16, 62
Goto, M. 45
Guest, M. 4, 16

H

Habu, T. 26, 33
Hada, Y. 17, 37, 80, 114, 127, 131
Hall, I.P. 5
Hall, J.K. 63
Harre, R. 63, 81
Hashimoto, K. 61
Hausman, R. 25
Hayes, B.E. 65, 67
Hayes, C. 14
Hinchman, L. 68
Hinchman, S. 68
Hino, N. 3, 15, 165
Hogg, M.A. 81
Holliday, A. 4, 49, 56, 58, 60, 67, 78, 157, 164, 165, 166, 176, 181
Holt-Reynolds, D. 52
Honda, Y. 24
Horwitz, E. 52
Huberman, M. 154
Hughes, H. 16

I

Iino, M. 4, 16
Ike, M. 9, 12, 13, 61
Imura, M. 4, 16
Ishida, H. 4, 16, 17, 21, 96
Ishikawa, T. 28
Ishikida, M.Y. 20

J

James, E. 21
Japan Society for the Promotion of Science 119
Johnson, C.G.
Johnson, K. 51
Johnson, K.A. 65
Johnston, B. 65
Josselson, R. 73, 78

K

Kachru, B. B. 55, 65
Kamhi-Stein, L.D. 56
Kan, S. 32
Kariya, T. 21
Kelly, C. 181 (also in epitaph on first page)
Kelskey, K. 33
Kemper, K. 18
Kern, R.G. 52
Kiernan, P. 63
Kimble, C. 82
Kimura, S. 4, 16
Kinmouth, E. 5, 34, 175
Kitao, K. 13, 61
Kitao, S.K. 13, 61
Kleinsasser, R. 18, 62
Knight, P. 73
Kobayashi, Y. 10, 26, 32, 33, 127, 131, 132, 143
Koike, I. 11, 13, 14, 15
Koike, M. 10, 33
Krashen, S. 51
Kubo, M. 44
Kubota, R. 55
Kvale, S. 73
Kwan, C.H. 17

L

LaBoskey, V.K. 69
Lamie, J. 3
Langenhove, L.v. 63, 81
Lave, J. 57, 60, 81, 82, 100, 106, 177, 188
Law, G. 17
Lebra, T.S. 26, 29
LeTendre, G. 21
Li, M. 165
Liddle, J. 25, 29, 30, 32, 116
Lincoln, Y.S. 68
Liu, D. 55, 56, 61
Lo Castro, V. 15, 16, 32
Lortie, D.C. 87
Lyons, N. 69

M

MacDonald, M. 52
Mahboob, A. 56
Makino, M.. 18, 103
Matsuda, P.K. 80, 131
Matsui, M. 26, 32, 33, 131
Matsumoto, K. 17
Matsuura, H. 63
McConnell, D. 16
McGannon, J. 52
McLaughlin, J. 17
McMahill 34
McNeill, D. 44
McVeigh, B.J. 1, 5, 17, 65, 181
Mead, G.J. 81
Medgyes, P. 56, 65, 133
Mertova, P. 63
Miles, M.B. 154
Mishler, E. 73
Mitchell, J.M. 46
Moore, P.J. 163
Morita, N. 82

N

Nagasawa, K. 2, 3, 16, 17, 80, 152, 187
Nakajima, S. 25, 29, 30, 32, 116
Nakane, C. 14, 74, 135
Neustupny, J.V. 1, 2, 3, 16
Newby, H. 17

Nguyen, C. 119
Nishino, T. 4, 16, 62
Normile, D. 33, 38, 116
Norton, B. 33
Nunan, D. 55

O

O'Leary, V.E. 46
Ochs, E. 63
Okano, K. 21, 22, 25, 28
Ono, H. 4, 5, 10, 16, 17, 21, 22, 26, 27, 29, 32, 33, 96
Ota, Y. 9, 11, 12, 13, 48, 62
Otsu, T. 21

P

Pajares, M.F. 51, 52, 53, 54
Pavlenko, A. 33, 68, 69
Peacock, M. 52, 53, 60, 187
Pennycook, A. 55, 58, 78
Peterson, P.L. 49
Pham, H.H. 61
Phan, Le Ha 53, 56, 58, 59, 61, 164, 165, 187
Phillipson, R. 58, 65, 67, 78
Piller, I. 33
Piper, N. 27, 29, 32, 33
Poole, G.S. 5, 10, 20, 34, 39, 40, 41, 42, 46, 48, 79, 100, 141, 144, 145
Prabhu, N.S. 61

R

Rampton, M.B.H. 56, 67
Raymo, J. 33
Reesor, M. 16
Reischauer, E.O. 10, 14
Reves, T. 56
Richards, J. 51, 55, 60, 82, 164, 165
Riessman, C.K. 68
Rodgers, T. 60
Roesgaard, M. H. 23
Rohlen, T.P. 17, 21, 24, 25
Rosenbaum, J.E. 21

S

Sakui, K. 4, 15, 16, 62, 63
Samimy, K. 56, 61

Sampson, G.P. 58
Sato, K. 16, 62
Schmenk, B. 31
Seargeant, P. 15, 16
Seidman, I. 70, 73, 76, 84, 153
Shavelson, R.J. 49
Shimbori, M. 35, 36
Shulman, L.S. 49, 50, 68, 171, 188
Silverman, D. 76
Simon-Maeda, A. 5, 17, 33, 62, 64, 66, 82, 115, 116, 117, 157
Sinclair, J.M. 162
Singh, G. 82
Smith, R. 55
Smith, R.C. 4, 16
Sodei, T. 44, 142
Stern, P. 49
Stevenson, D.L. 21
Stewart, A. 5, 6, 17, 45, 62, 63, 64, 65, 66, 115, 117, 164
Stockman, N. 26
Strauss, A.L. 76
Strober, M.H. 29
Sunderland, J. 31

T

Tajfel, H. 81
Takahashi, K. 33
Tanaka, H. 11, 13, 14, 15
Tanaka, S 1, 2, 3, 16
Tang, C. 56
Teichler, U. 39
Terauchi, H. 96
Terrell, T. 51
Thornbury, S. 78
Tsang, W.K. 51
Tsuchiya, M. 21, 25, 28
Tsui, A.B.M. 56, 57, 61, 68, 82, 112, 165, 187
Tyson, L. 25

U

Uchida, Y. 62, 63, 64, 117, 157

V

Varghese, M. 55, 67
Visgatis, B. 4, 16

W

Wada, M. 3, 4, 15, 16, 62
Walker, P. 25
Warrington, S. 17
Watson, C. 25
Watson, G. 68, 119
Webster, L. 69, 121
Wells, C. 162
Wenger, E. 7, 57, 60, 81, 82, 83, 84, 85, 86, 100, 102, 103, 106, 107, 108, 111, 117, 118, 119, 140, 151, 152, 176, 177, 180, 181, 182, 186, 188
Williams, K. 17
Wolcott, H. 9
Woods, D. 54, 55, 187
Wordell, C. 5
Wright, T. 162, 163, 164, 180

X

Xuewen, S. 26

Y

Yamanoi, A. 18, 36, 37, 38, 39, 40
Yamashiro, A. 17
Yamashita, S. 4, 16

Z

Zahidi, S. 25
Zeng, K. 21

Subject Index

A

A-identity (affinity-identity) 118–120, 122, 140–147
academia 10, 26, 42, 45, 46, 80, 107, 108, 109, 116, 132, 149
academics 36, 37, 42, 44, 46, 106, 107, 110, 114, 115, 138, 142, 145, 150, 151, 188
Action Plan 1, 2, 13, 15, 62
administration 37, 38, 95
administrators 40, 85, 186
akahara (academic harassment) 44
akogare 33
alignment 66, 82, 83, 84, 85, 86, 100, 102, 104, 107, 108, 111, 112, 182
apprenticeship 3, 87, 106, 107, 188
attitudes 42, 47, 54, 56, 61, 64, 76, 81, 88, 89, 90, 91, 93, 114, 122, 135, 127, 134, 135, 136, 137, 141, 142, 143, 145, 150, 151, 153, 166, 167, 176, 178, 184, 185
authentic readings 169

B

BANA (Britain, Australia and North America) 49, 60, 78, 158, 164, 165, 176
beliefs 1, 4, 5, 6, 7, 8, 9, 26, 32, 43, 47-69, 76, 81, 86, 88, 96, 111, 124, 138, 141, 153, 157, 158, 163, 166, 167, 174, 177, 178, 179, 180, 181, 187, 188
bottom up 4, 164, 165, 168, 179, 185

C

children (childcare) 26
children (educating) 14, 22, 23, 24, 25,27, 31
children (raising) 45, 125, 126, 127, 128, 129, 144, 149
Chinese 15, 56, 58, 155
classroom 14, 15, 47, 49, 50, 51, 52, 53, 55, 58, 62, 64, 66, 70, 71, 77, 78, 85, 86, 92, 98, 100, 107, 110, 112, 114, 117, 143, 147, 152, 153, 154, 157, 158, 162, 163, 164, 165, 166, 168, 170, 173, 174, 177, 178, 179, 180, 183, 184, 185, 187, 188, 189
classroom discourse 157, 158, 162
classroom observations 77, 78, 152, 153, 157, 174, 177, 180
commercial high schools 23, 90, 123
communication 1, 3, 4, 13, 14, 16, 17, 47, 74, 97, 99, 105, 109, 135, 142
communicative language teaching 3, 16, 56, 60, 67
contract/contracted positions (see also ninkisei) 35, 41, 42, 65, 77, 100, 105, 106, 109, 112, 113, 115, 127, 130, 153, 172
CoP (communities of practice) 60, 81, 84, 85, 110, 111
cultural capital 21, 30, 31, 34, 126, 130
culture 127, 157, 164, 166, 167, 176, 177, 178, 179, 180, 181

D

D-identity (discourse-identity) 118, 119, 122, 133, 139
data collection 84–86
daughters 24, 27, 28, 29, 31, 45, 64, 121, 122, 147, 148, 151
degrees (bachelors) 37, 128
degrees (masters) 3eika
degrees (PhD) 6, 30, 36, 37, 41, 42, 64, 71, 72, 80, 101, 107, 108, 114, 126, 127, 131, 136, 149, 150, 172, 179
discrimination 44, 98, 135
discursive practices 108, 110, 119, 132, 135, 139, 146, 148, 150
divorce (ending marriage) 129
doctorate (also see PhD) 36, 37, 72, 79, 127, 128

E

educational reforms 61
eikaiwa (English conversation) 33
ekiben daigaku 18, 19, 48
employment 22, 24, 25, 26, 31, 32, 36, 41, 42, 80, 96, 106, 112, 116, 121, 122, 125, 126, 127, 131, 141, 148, 149
employment (opportunities) 26, 148
empower/ empowerment 25, 28, 32, 33, 57, 99, 185, 186

engagement 57, 82, 83, 85, 86, 100, 104, 106, 107, 108, 109, 111, 112, 113, 114, 120, 151, 152, 178, 181
engagement in teaching 85, 86, 111, 112
engagement in the wider social context 85, 86, 107, 111, 113, 114
engagement in the workplace 85, 86, 100, 104, 106, 111, 112, 113
English department 56, 102, 124, 142, 145, 176, 187
English education 1, 2, 3, 6, 12, 13, 32, 34, 61, 71, 72, 129, 134, 181
English-speaking 7, 15, 48, 55, 56, 58, 61, 65, 67, 90, 164, 167, 177, 178, 185
entrance exams 2, 4, 16, 88
escalator schools 24, 48
ethnography 10, 39, 48
examination hell 17, 24, 27, 31, 77
expertise 64, 65, 107, 117, 164, 170

F

family 25, 26, 27, 31, 32, 35, 41, 44, 45, 47, 48, 90, 103, 116, 122, 123, 124, 131, 132, 134, 140, 143, 144, 145
family background 21
fathers 29
female researchers 30, 44, 43
feminism 34
feminist 64, 98, 108, 114, 134, 135, 139, 146, 151
financial resources 23, 24, 32
foreign teachers 5, 64, 65, 66, 167

G

gatekeeping 21, 25, 46, 61
gender 6, 7, 8, 10, 21, 25, 27, 28, 30, 31, 32, 34, 42, 45, 46, 47, 48, 63, 64, 67, 72, 89, 97, 98, 102, 113, 116, 117, 118, 119, 121, 122, 123, 124, 125, 126, 128, 130, 131, 132, 134, 137, 138, 139, 140, 141, 142, 144, 145, 146, 147, 148, 149, 150, 151, 182, 186
gender equality 44
gender isolation 46
gender stratification 27
generational encounters 108
Global Gender Gap 25, 116
graduate school 35, 45, 57, 78, 80, 88, 117, 125, 126, 127, 128, 129, 130, 132, 138, 139, 149, 187
grammar-translation 3, 14, 15, 60

H

habatsu (univeristy political faction) 101, 141
Headquarters for the Promotion of Gender Equality 116
high schools 18, 19, 20, 21, 22, 23, 24, 48, 50, 53, 75, 89, 90, 96, 103, 108, 112, 123, 124, 127, 128, 134
history of English language education in Japan
housewife/ housewives 25, 129, 130, 133, 140, 143, 146, 147, 151
housework 44

I

I-identity (institutional-identity)
identification 48, 50, 65, 82, 83, 86, 95, 111, 114, 119, 140, 166, 177, 183, 184, 186
identity
ideologies 40, 116, 121
images 33, 54, 87, 88, 89, 94, 111, 112
imagination 82, 83, 84, 85, 86, 87, 89, 95, 100, 102, 107, 108, 111, 182
Inazo Nitobe 11
inbound trajectory 100, 101, 106, 115, 176
income 20, 24, 27, 32, 33, 35, 44, 122, 127, 132, 148, 150
industry 7, 9, 10, 14, 17, 18, 22, 28, 32, 33, 34, 47, 62, 114
interviewees (see participants)
interviews 7, 45, 62, 63, 68, 70, 71, 72, 73, 74, 75, 76, 77, 78, 84, 86, 106, 107, 111, 114, 117, 118, 122, 125, 132, 147, 151, 152, 153, 157, 163, 174, 175, 177, 178, 184, 186, 189

J

jobs 7, 17, 22, 25, 26, 27, 32, 45, 64, 100, 108, 131, 146, 164, 182
juku (cram schools) 23
junior colleges (see also two-year colleges) 18, 19, 20, 22, 24, 28, 44, 116, 128, 142

Subject Index

K

Kato Hiroyuki 11

L

keigo 105
kyojukai (professors' council) 100
linguistic imperialism 57, 67, 78
linguistics 60, 72, 118, 152, 166, 175, 187
listening 93, 154, 158, 159, 160, 165, 168, 174, 178
literature 2, 6, 16, 60, 65, 71, 72, 90, 91, 98, 107, 109, 110, 117, 122, 122, 123, 124, 126, 128, 129, 131, 137, 138, 139, 140, 143, 152, 153, 166, 172, 173, 174, 175, 176, 177, 178, 179, 180, 181, 182, 187
literature nerd 138, 152, 166, 175, 177

M

male colleagues 101, 105, 128, 146, 147, 150
marginalization 55, 58, 67, 83, 101, 106, 186
marriage 25, 26, 28, 29, 31, 33, 34, 42, 98, 121, 134, 143, 147, 148
materials (for EFL teaching/learning) 15, 34, 52, 54, 60, 77, 82, 89, 91, 95, 98, 99, 130, 133, 163, 166, 168, 169, 170, 174, 178, 179
membership 40, 41, 81, 83, 84, 85, 100, 107, 108, 114, 119, 122, 140
MEXT (see Ministry of Education, Health, Science and Welfare) 1, 3, 4, 5, 13, 15, 15, 16, 19, 20, 23, 34, 35, 36, 37, 42, 43, 44, 61, 66, 80
Ministry of Education 1, 11, 12, 35
Ministry of Education, Health, Science and Welfare (MEXT)
modest 93, 102, 132, 138, 140
mothers 25, 29, 48, 121, 145, 147

N

N-identity (nature-identity) 118, 119, 121, 122, 126, 131, 139, 146
narrative 68–70
narrative inquiry 69, 153
narrative study 56, 64, 69, 78, 117
nationalism 12
native speakers 56, 60, 65
negotiability 81, 82, 83, 84
negotiation of meaning 82
ninkisei 35, 42
NNEST (non-native English speaking teachers) 59
Number One Higher School 12

O

office lady (secretary) 28, 114
open-campus 79
ownership of meaning 82, 83

P

parental attitudes 27, 29
parents 4, 16, 22, 23, 24, 27, 28, 29, 31, 45, 75, 88, 90, 92, 122, 123, 124, 125, 126, 130, 134, 148, 149, 151
Participant Miwa ix, 8, 70, 71, 75, 77, 84, 88, 89, 90, 91, 92, 95, 96, 98, 100, 106, 107, 109, 112, 113, 114, 120, 123, 125, 126, 127, 130, 131, 132, 136, 137, 138, 139, 146, 150, 152–180, 182, 184, 185, 187
Participant Kana 71, 84, 88, 90, 92, 94, 96, 99, 100, 105, 106, 110, 112, 113, 114, 120, 123, 125, 126, 127, 130, 131, 132, 135, 137, 139, 146, 149, 184
Participant Keiko 72, 120, 124, 128, 130, 131, 142, 143, 145, 149
Participant Kumiko 71, 75, 84, 88, 91, 92, 93, 94, 95, 96, 97, 98, 100, 101, 102, 104, 107, 108, 109, 112, 113, 114, 120, 122, 123, 124, 126, 127, 128, 131, 132, 134, 135, 136, 137, 139, 140, 141, 146, 148, 149, 150, 151, 183, 184
Participant Naomi 72, 120, 130, 131, 132, 141, 149, 150
Participant Shizuko 71, 120, 129, 130, 131, 143, 144, 145, 147, 148, 150, 151, 183
Participant Taeko 72, 120, 121, 124, 129, 130, 131, 133, 139, 146, 148, 149, 150, 185
Participant Taka 70, 71, 84, 87, 88, 91, 92, 93, 94, 96, 99, 100, 102, 103, 104, 108, 111, 112, 113, 114, 183, 184, 185
patronizing attitudes 136
pedagogical training 172, 187, 188
personal identity 107
personal knowledge 50, 52, 66

personal practical knowledge 50, 51, 53, 57
policy 2, 5, 14, 25, 101, 186
poor English skills 16, 35
postwar 13, 18, 26, 30, 35, 47, 120
process of analysis 76–77
productivity 39
professional identity 6, 7, 8, 54, 55, 56, 62, 64, 66, 69, 78, 79, 81, 85, 86, 89, 95, 101, 107, 108, 109, 110, 111, 113, 114, 116, 117, 118, 119, 121, 126, 140, 145, 146, 147, 148, 150, 158, 166, 167, 177, 178, 179, 180, 182, 186, 188
professionalism 64, 117, 164
promoting self 30, 43, 44
publications 36, 172

R

reading 4, 12, 14, 89, 91, 93, 98, 110, 138, 154, 156, 157, 158, 159, 160, 162, 163, 164, 165, 166, 167, 168, 169, 170, 174, 176, 178, 179, 185, 186
research questions 7–8, 81, 118, 147, 177–178
research/ researchers 1, 3, 5, 7, 9, 18, 21, 30, 31, 36, 37, 38, 39, 40, 41, 42, 43, 44, 45, 46, 49, 50, 51, 55, 59, 60, 62, 65, 66, 67, 68, 69, 70, 71, 72, 73, 74, 76, 77, 78, 78, 80, 81, 93, 102, 107, 108, 110, 111, 113, 114, 118, 130, 131, 133, 141, 143, 147, 148, 150, 151, 165, 175, 176, 177, 178, 179, 183, 186, 187, 188, 189
reverse tournament method of entrance exams 22
Rinshiro Ishikawa 12

S

secondary schools 1, 2, 3,4, 6, 15, 16, 17, 18, 24, 27, 32, 34, 43, 47, 49, 60, 62, 67, 78, 90, 118, 120, 181, 187
secretary (office lady) 91, 168
sekuhara (sexual harassment) 44
sexist 105, 135, 141, 150
sexual harassment 30, 44, 128
Shega Shigetaka 12
situated learning 57
social context 59–61
sociopolitical attitudes 7, 10, 47, 90, 114, 122, 125, 127

Soichi Oya 18
sons 27, 31, 45, 151
sotomuki (facing outward) 40–42, 48, 100, 101, 145
speaking 16, 74, 91, 105, 115, 118, 120, 134, 135, 164, 168
study abroad 10, 22, 32, 33, 44, 79, 130, 149
supplementary income 132

T

teacher beliefs 51–54
teacher cognition 49–54
teacher education 2, 3, 6, 51, 52, 53, 54, 59, 60, 66, 88
teacher identity 54–56
teacher knowledge 50–51
teachers' stories 68–70
teaching license 3, 88, 123, 149, 172, 176, 187
tenure 34, 35, 36, 37, 43, 45, 77, 80, 85, 92, 100, 101, 105, 113, 115, 116, 127
TESEP (tertiary, secondary, primary) 49, 58, 60, 61, 78, 157, 164, 165, 166
TESOL 183
top-down 2, 4, 62, 164
tournament method of entrance exams 21, 22
transcription method 74–76
transmitting knowledge 163
tuition 20, 22, 27, 28, 90

U

uchimuki (facing inward) 40, 41, 48, 100, 104, 144
university (national) 41, 126, 128, 129, 142, 149, 153, 175
university (private) 20, 39, 48, 101, 123, 129
University of Tokyo 10, 11, 12, 21, 29, 30, 35, 44, 48
university reforms 17, 79, 130
university student 12, 17, 20, 34, 103, 111, 118, 125, 166
university teachers (assistant professors) 34, 35, 36, 42, 43, 71, 116, 129, 141
university teachers (associate professors) 34, 35, 36, 72, 77, 100, 105, 116, 127, 128, 181, 142
university teachers (ninkisei) 35, 42

university teachers (part time) 6, 17, 34, 35, 40, 43, 44, 45, 46, 71, 72, 77, 90, 92, 106, 107, 125, 127, 128, 129, 131, 132, 133, 136, 144, 150, 153, 161, 175, 188
university teachers (professors) 2, 7, 10, 11, 12, 21, 30, 34, 35, 36,37, 39, 40, 41, 42, 44, 45, 46, 48, 70, 79, 80, 91, 103, 104, 105, 106, 108, 113, 116, 128, 135, 140, 141, 142, 143, 144, 145, 148, 149, 165, 166, 167, 177, 178, 187, 188

V

Vietnamese 54, 56, 58, 59
vocational school 21, 22, 24

W

wives/wife 25, 44, 48, 121, 145, 147
women's universities 28, 48, 102, 123
workforce 2, 9, 10, 17, 18, 21, 22, 23, 25, 26, 27, 28, 29, 31, 32, 42, 45, 62, 92, 109, 115, 123, 127, 130, 131, 133, 146, 148
World War II 13
writing 3, 9, 59, 94, 97, 106, 120, 165, 167

Y

yakudoku (grammar-translation) 3, 15, 16, 165
yobiko (preparatory school) 23